A Treatise
Concerning
the Principles
of Human Knowledge
with Critical
Essays

A Treatise Concerning the Principles of Human Knowledge / George Berkeley

with Critical Essays

Edited by

Colin Murray Turbayne

THE BOBBS-MERRILL COMPANY, INC.
INDIANAPOLIS   NEW YORK

The Bobbs-Merrill
Text and Commentary
Series / Harold Weisberg,
General Editor

FIRST PRINTING
Copyright © 1970 by The Bobbs-Merrill Company, Inc.
PRINTED IN THE UNITED STATES OF AMERICA
Library of Congress Catalog Card Number 69–16531

Contents

Critical Essays

v

A Treatise Concerning the Principles of Human Knowledge

Introduction

What is generally considered to be Berkeley's main philosophical work, *A Treatise Concerning the Principles of Human
Knowledge*, is presented here preceded by a collection of
essays, some of which are already classics, which form an
extended critical commentary upon the text.

The revival of interest in Berkeley's philosophy is reflected
in the enormous increase in demand for editions of his two
best-known works, the *Principles* and the *Three Dialogues Between Hylas and Philonous*. Since the time of Berkeley's final
editions of these works, interest in his philosophy has grown
steadily. During the two centuries from 1734 to 1933 there
appeared at least twenty-four editions of the former and
twenty-three of the latter. Since that time there have been

at least twenty-five of the *Principles* and twenty of the *Dialogues*.[1]

Berkeley would have been astonished and pleased at the present sales of these books, for in his lifetime they were failures. Hardly anybody read them. He was, indeed, lucky to have his first works published. Writing at the end of the scientific revolution, he was antagonistic to the intellectual tone of his age. He opposed all the scientists of his day not on their "happy discoveries" of the laws of nature but on their conceptions of the nature of science. He opposed Newton's authoritative accounts of absolute space, time, and motion, of force, gravity, and attraction, and said that many of Newton's views were "so directly opposite" to his own. He even disputed Newton's mathematics. He disagreed with Locke's distinction and, indeed, that of all scientists, between primary and secondary qualities—the view that there are two worlds, one real, existing outside our minds, which physics investigates, the other a picture and an effect of the former, existing only in our minds. He took issue with Locke and all philosophers on the traditional doctrines of abstract ideas and the picture theory of meaning of general terms. He opposed all earlier optical theorists on the question of the nature of vision, rejecting their causal and picture theories of how we see.

Nowadays it is doubtful whether such opposition to established doctrines and established authorities by a clergyman who had just turned twenty-five would get into print. It is a credit to the discernment of Berkeley's publisher in Dublin, Jeremy Pepyat, that he saw fit to publish in 1709 Berkeley's perhaps

[1] See T. E. Jessop, *A Bibliography of George Berkeley* (Oxford: Oxford University Press, 1934), and Colin M. Turbayne and Robert Ware, "A Bibliography of George Berkeley, 1933–1962," reprinted (New York, 1963) by and from the *Journal of Philosophy*, LX, No. 4 (February 14, 1963), 93–112.

most important, but neglected, work, *An Essay Towards a New Theory of Vision*, and, in the following year, its sequel, the *Principles*. The latter work produced in England the expected reaction. It was immediately received, as Berkeley says, with "raillery and scorn" and with "ridicule and contempt." In England during his lifetime his works, if they were noticed, were treated with hostility. By the time of his death, however, in 1753, some of the seeds of his later eminence had been sown, especially in Scotland and France. Hume, who took Berkeley seriously, had recognized his greatness. So had Voltaire and Condillac, who were captivated by his theory of vision.

Berkeley would have been astonished and chagrined to discover why his *Principles* and *Dialogues* are so widely read today. In our contemporary philosophy, in which all emphasis is placed upon argument, his works are generally recognized as paradigms of argumentative discourse in philosophical literature. In the words of George Saintsbury, "he is unquestionably the best model in English, if not in any language, for philosophical, and indeed for argumentative, writing generally."[2] In addition, Berkeley's arguments, like those of Zeno, have another pedagogical value. His paradoxes offer a challenge to the introductory student to detect the submerged fallacy. Finally, his central contribution is still commonly understood as an argument for skepticism, the very position he tried to refute. In the words of Hume,[3] "all his arguments, though otherwise intended, are in reality merely skeptical." Indeed they "form the best lessons of skepticism," better even than Bayle's. Even in this he is a successful failure, for his central contribution is

---

[2] *A Short History of English Literature* (London: Macmillan, 1929; first published 1898), p. 546.
[3] *An Inquiry Concerning Human Understanding* (Indianapolis and New York: Bobbs-Merrill Co., 1955), p. 163n.

commonly understood as merely an *ad interim* stage in the *reductio ad absurdum* argument of British empiricism. Berkeley is an inconsistent Hume who, given Locke's original premise, failed to deduce the whole of the absurd conclusion, the deepest skepticism.

This narrow view of Berkeley is still the dominant one. It has diverted critical attention from richer areas in his thought, such as his account of language, his theory of universals, his theories of meaning and reference, his philosophy of science including his accounts of theoretical terms, of causation and of the nature of explanation in science, his treatments of the problem of illusion and of error in general, of self-knowledge and of our knowledge of other minds. Now, at long last, as some of the essays that follow indicate, these other regions are being increasingly explored.

The extraordinary range of Berkeley's achievements is often forgotten. For a non-professional philosopher engaged in more pressing practical affairs, such as founding a university and practicing medicine, his productivity was amazing. In 1710, having prepared his audience for the reception of his new way of looking at the world with the publication in the previous year of the *Essay*, he published the *Principles*. This was Part I of a projected series. Part II was to deal with the philosophy of mind including ethics, Part III with the philosophy of physics, and Part IV with the philosophy of mathematics. The immediate failure of Part I prompted him to delay the continuation of his project and to re-present the contents of the *Principles* in a more easily digestible form as the *Three Dialogues*. Any one of these three masterpieces would have brought Berkeley enduring fame. Full recognition of these parts of his contribution came a century and a half later. In 1864, T. K. Abbott wrote of the *Essay:* "If we were challenged to point out a single discovery in mental science which is universally admitted, we should at once name the theory of vision of Bishop Berkeley."[4] In 1871, J. S. Mill referred to Berkeley's "three first-rate philosophical discoveries [the theory of vision; reasoning is about only particulars; and physical objects are bundles of sensations] . . . which by their combination have determined the whole course of subsequent philosophical speculation."[5]

It is commonly held that Berkeley did not complete the remaining sections of his ambitious project. This, I think, is a mistake. The design for Part II was fulfilled in *Alciphron*, written in Rhode Island, and published in 1732. Part III was represented by *De Motu*, written in Lyons, and published in 1721. Part IV was represented by the *Analyst*, written in London, and published in 1734. In addition to these works, Berkeley published *The Theory of Vision* (1733) in which he presented the contents of his earlier *Essay* systematically. The *Querist* (1735–37), like the *Analyst*, is an instance of Berkeley's brilliant "meddling out of my profession," this time in economics. *Siris* (1744) is a loosely linked concatenation of reflections on various subjects beginning with tar water and ending with God. It contains, however, some of Berkeley's most penetrating remarks upon the nature of science. Of these works, the *Analyst* and the *Querist* were most influential. The former, by exposing the weak foundations of the calculus, marked, in the words of Florian Cajori, "a turning point in the history of mathematical thought in Great Britain."[6] Referring to the latter, J. M. Keynes wrote, "Bishop Berkeley wrote some

---

[4] *Sight and Touch: An Attempt to Disprove the Received (or Berkeleian) Theory of Vision* (London: Longman, Green, Longman, Roberts and Green, 1864), p. 1.

[5] In *Fortnightly Review*, reprinted in *Dissertations and Discussions*, IV (London: J. W. Parker, 1875), 155.

[6] *A History of Mathematics* (New York: Macmillan, 1919), p. 218.

of the shrewdest essays on these subjects available in his time."[7]

The significance and contemporary relevance of Berkeley's "secondary" publications are slowly being recognized. Karl Popper has exhibited the "strikingly new look" of Berkeley's contribution to the philosophy of physics presented in the "highly original and in many ways unique essay," *De Motu,* and in *Siris.*[8] The great importance of *Alciphron,* its contribution in the fields of the philosophy of mind and the philosophy of language (its theory of signs), has not yet been fully recognized. After a century of neglect, Berkeley's very great very small works, the *Essay Towards a New Theory of Vision* and *The Theory of Vision, or Visual Language,* which illuminate his whole philosophy and reveal his grasp of scientific method, are now, at long last, being carefully studied and their ideas applied.[9]

Berkeley's *Principles* is often misunderstood because its critics fail to discern the underlying structure of the argument. The subtitle reveals much of this structure and part of the content. It is a book "wherein the chief causes of error and difficulty in the sciences, with the grounds of skepticism, atheism, and irreligion, are inquired into." This Berkeley enlarges upon at *Introduction* 4 where he says he will try to "discover what

[7] Quoted in F. A. Iremonger, *William Temple* (London: Oxford University Press, 1948), p. 439.

[8] "A Note on Berkeley as Precursor of Mach and Einstein." See below, pp. 129–144.

[9] In my *The Myth of Metaphor* (New Haven: Yale University Press, 1962. Revised ed., Columbia: University of South Carolina Press, 1970), I adopt much of Berkeley's theory while making modifications to suit my needs. Nelson Goodman's *The Structure of Appearance* (Indianapolis and New York: Bobbs-Merrill Co., 1966) is also not a study of Berkeley, but the student will discern the influence of Berkeley's theory. A. D. Ritchie, in *George Berkeley: A Reappraisal* (Manchester: Manchester University Press, and New York: Barnes and Noble, 1967), subordinates immaterialism to the theory of vision.

those principles are which have introduced all that doubtfulness and uncertainty, those absurdities and contradictions." So far, it looks as though the book is purely destructive, an inquiry into, and a revelation of, error. This is how many, including his wife, understood him: "Had he built as he has pulled down, he had been then a master builder indeed. But unto every man his work. Some must remove rubbish. . . ."[10] But in the First Draft of *Introduction* 4 Berkeley continues: "And at the same time, to substitute such principles in their stead, as shall be free from the like consequences."[11] This suggests that Berkeley is employing the ancient method of analysis, described by Plato in the *Phaedo*, "the way of hypothesis," otherwise called "the hypothetico-deductive method." This involves the setting up of rival hypotheses and the testing of them by their consequences.

Throughout the *Principles*, Berkeley presents rival hypotheses or rival principles, his own, and those of the philosophers, at several different levels. In the *Introduction* he sets up the ultimate rivals. "The source," he says, "seems to me to be language." By *Principles* 85 he can "take a view of our tenets [and those of our opponents] in their consequences." Here is a skeleton of the argument:

The Traditional Doctrine	*Berkeley's Rival Theory*
Introduction 1–25	
I The *Unum Nomen Unum Nominatum* Doctrine	I The *Definiendum-Definiens* Theory
The only use of language is descriptive	There are many uses, including raising passion and directing action

---

10 *The Works of George Berkeley, Bishop of Cloyne,* ed. A. A. Luce and T. E. Jessop (9 vols.; Edinburgh: Thomas Nelson and Sons, 1948–1957), VII (ed. A. A. Luce, 1955), 388.
11 *Works,* II (ed. T. E. Jessop, 1949), 122.

The Traditional Doctrine	*Berkeley's Rival Theory*

Introduction 1–25

II The Doctrine of Abstract Ideas	II The Theory of Concrete Ideas
General terms are proper names of abstract entities in which particulars partake	General terms have definitions which particulars satisfy

Principles 1–33

III Materialism	III Immaterialism
i) Physical objects are substances supporting primary qualities	i) Physical objects are combinations of sensible qualities
ii) Physical objects exist independently of being perceived	ii) The *esse* of physical objects is *percipi*
iii) Physical objects are archetypes of our ideas	iii) The archetypes of our ideas are ideas
iv) Explanation in terms of physical causes	iv) Explanation in terms of laws of nature

Principles 34–84

IV Sixteen Objections to Immaterialism anticipated and answered

Principles 85–156

CONSEQUENCES[12]

V "Skepticism, atheism, and irreligion"	V "The reality and perfection of human knowledge, the incorporeal nature of the human soul, and the immediate providence of a deity"

[12] The statements of the consequences of the traditional doctrine are taken from the subtitle of the *Principles*, those of Berkeley's rival theory from the subtitle of the *Dialogues*.

The Traditional Doctrine	*Berkeley's Rival Theory*

Principles 85–156

VI "Error and difficulty in the sciences"	VI "A method for rendering the sciences more easy, useful, and compendious

    (i)   *Physics* (97–117)
    (ii) *Mathematics* (119–134)
    (iii) *Psychology* and *Morality* (135–145)
    (iv) *Theology* (146–156)

Berkeley's original ideas have made him a figure of controversy from his day to ours. The key words of the titles of many of the essays that follow reflect those issues which have been at the center of debate upon his philosophy: "Nominalism," "Solipsism," "Pyrrhonism," "Idealism," "Realism," "Mind," "Notions," and "God." The sequence of the topics of the essays roughly parallels the sequence of Berkeley's argument in his *Principles*: the central importance of language, the rejection of the doctrine of abstract ideas, the assertion of *esse* is *percipi*, skepticism, the philosophy of science, the philosophy of mind, ethics, and theology. Wherever possible I have coupled essays which present rival views.

Berkeley is peculiarly contemporary in his attitude toward language. In his linguistic awareness he was an anachronism, possessing something that Hume and Kant lacked. This feature of his thought has never been adequately examined. In the opening essay I bring to the surface the details of his language model submerged in the *Principles*. This model illuminates his "entire scheme."

In the *Introduction*, Berkeley rejects the traditional doctrine of abstract ideas. Posterity, accordingly, has treated Berkeley as holding a nominalistic view in regard to the ancient problem of universals. In the next two papers, Hay and Van Iten present opposing views on the nature of Berkeley's nominalism.

In the opening sections of the *Principles*, Berkeley presents one of the central paradoxes for which he is notorious, viz., *esse is percipi*. This has been near the center of philosophical debate from his day to ours. Moore's famous refutation of Berkeley's "idealism" is presented together with Stace's refutation of realism.

Berkeley's *Principles* is, in large part, an inquiry into "the grounds of skepticism." Nevertheless, Berkeley often appears "as if [he] were advancing . . . philosophical skepticism."[13] Popkin, in the next essay, examines in detail the peculiar relation that obtains between Berkeley and skepticism.

In *Principles* 97–117, Berkeley inquires into "the chief causes of error and difficulty" in the science of physics. In the next essay, Popper, making use also of Berkeley's other works, including *De Motu*, shows the "modernity" of Berkeley's view "in his protest against essentialist explanations in science."

In *Principles* 135–145, Berkeley presents hints of a theory of mind. It is widely held that his original conception leads to an inconsistency heroically avoided by the *ad hoc* introduction of notions in the second edition (140, 142). In the next two papers Cornman and I present alternative attempts at a consistent Berkeleian theory. While I argue that such terms as "force" and "attraction" in physical science, and "mind" and "spiritual substance" in mental science, are metaphorical, Cornman argues that Berkeley can be an instrumentalist regarding scientific theoretical terms (they are non-denoting), but a realist regarding mind-terms such as "mind" and "God" (they are denoting theoretical terms).

In the same sections, Berkeley makes a few remarks

[13] Hylas' charge in the *Dialogues* III 24.

directly about ethics, but does not develop them. Very little has been published on this subject, probably intended by Berkeley for more extensive treatment in the lost *Principles* Part II. In the next paper Olscamp argues that the ingredients of a systematic moral philosophy can be found in Berkeley's writings, especially in *Alciphron*. He argues that his normative ethics resembles rule-utilitarianism and that his meta-ethics resembles theological definism.

In the last sections of the *Principles,* 146–156, Berkeley gives an account of our knowledge of God and of his nature. In the last essay of this volume Mabbott rejects the orthodox conception of Berkeley as an idealist whose God is based upon "*esse* is *percipi* or *percipere.*" He argues that for Berkeley the *esse* of mind is *velle,* i.e., *agere,* and that "the physical world is thus really a complicated 'good resolution' of God's."

Chronology

1685   George Berkeley born at Kilkenny, March 12

1696   Entered Kilkenny College

1700   Entered Trinity College, Dublin

1704   Received baccalaureate degree

1707   Junior Fellow; M.A.

1709   Ordained deacon; librarian

1710   Ordained priest; Junior Dean

1712   Junior Greek Lecturer

1713   To London; went to Italy, October

1714   Returned to England

1721   To Dublin; took degrees of B.D. and D.D.; appointed Divinity Lecturer

1722   Appointed Senior Proctor; presented by the Crown to the deanery of Dromore, but the Crown's right to appoint challenged by the Bishop; to London

1723   Returned to Dublin; appointed Hebrew Lecturer; executor and legatee of Hester Van Homrigh

1724   Resigned from Trinity College to become Dean of Derry; to London to raise funds for Bermuda project and get Royal Charter

1726   House of Commons voted a grant for St. Paul's College, Bermuda

1728   Married Anne Forster; sailed for America

1729   Arrived Newport

1731   Left for England

1732   Nominated Dean of Down, but not appointed

1734   Bishop of Cloyne

1741   Declined offer of nomination for Vice-Chancellorship of Dublin University

1745   Declined offer of Bishopric of Clogher

1752   To Oxford

1753   Died, January 14; interred in the Chapel of Christ Church, Oxford

Selected bibliography

Principal works by Berkeley

Philosophical Commentaries. Notebooks written 1707–1708.
An Essay Towards a New Theory of Vision. Dublin, 1709.
A Treatise Concerning the Principles of Human Knowledge. Dublin, 1710.
Passive Obedience. Dublin and London, 1712.
Three Dialogues Between Hylas and Philonous. London, 1713.
De Motu. London, 1721.
Alciphron: or the Minute Philosopher. London and Dublin, 1732.
The Theory of Vision, or Visual Language Vindicated and Explained. London, 1733.
The Analyst: or a Discourse Addressed to an Infidel Mathematician. Dublin and London, 1734.
A Defence of Freethinking in Mathematics. Dublin and London, 1735.
The Querist. Dublin and London, 1735–1737.
Siris: A Chain of Philosophical Reflexions and Inquiries Concerning the Virtues of Tar-Water, and Divers Other Subjects. Dublin and London, 1744.

Collected editions

1784 Dublin and London. 2 vols. Edited probably by Joseph Stock (reprinted London, 1820, 3 vols.; and London, 1837, 1 vol.).

1843 London. 2 vols. Edited by G. N. Wright.

1871 Oxford. 4 vols. Edited by A. C. Fraser.

1897–1898 London. 3 vols. Edited by G. Sampson. With a biographical introduction by A. J. Balfour.

1901 Oxford. 4 vols. Edited by A. C. Fraser.

1948–1957 Edinburgh. 9 vols. Edited by A. A. Luce and T. E. Jessop.

Bibliographies

Jessop, T. E. *A Bibliography of George Berkeley*. With an inventory of Berkeley's manuscript remains by A. A. Luce. Oxford: Oxford University Press, 1934.

Turbayne, C. M., and Ware, Robert. "A Bibliography of George Berkeley, 1933–1962," reprinted by and from the *Journal of Philosophy*, LX, No. 4 (February 14, 1963), 93–112. New York, 1963.

Biographies

Adamson, R., and Mitchell, J. M. "Berkeley," in *Encyclopedia Britannica*. Edinburgh, 9th ed., 1875; 11th ed., 1910.

Balfour, A. J. "Biographical Introduction," in *The Works of George Berkeley, Bishop of Cloyne*. Edited by George Sampson. London, 1897.

Fraser, A. C. *Life and Letters of George Berkeley*. Oxford, 1871.

Hone, J. M., and Rossi, M. M. *Bishop Berkeley: His Life, Writings and Philosophy*. With an introduction by W. B. Yeats. London: Faber and Faber, 1931.

Luce, A. A. *The Life of George Berkeley, Bishop of Cloyne*. Edinburgh: Thomas Nelson, 1949.

Rand, Benjamin. *Berkeley and Percival*. Cambridge: Cambridge University Press, 1914.

Works on Berkeley

Ardley, G. W. R. *Berkeley's Philosophy of Nature*. Auckland: University of Auckland, Bulletin No. 63, 1962.

Armstrong, David M. *Berkeley's Theory of Vision: A Critical Examination of Bishop Berkeley's Essay Towards a New Theory of Vision*. Melbourne: Melbourne University Press, 1961.

Bracken, Harry M. *The Early Reception of Berkeley's Immaterialism, 1710–1733*. The Hague: Martinus Nijhoff, 1959; revised 1965.

Fraser, A. C. *Berkeley*. Edinburgh, 1881; reprinted 1901.

Gueroult, Martial. *Berkeley, quatre études sur la perception et sur Dieu*. Paris: Aubier, 1956.

Hedenius, Ingemar. *Sensationalism and Theology in Berkeley's Philosophy*. Oxford: Blackwell, 1936.

Hicks, G. Dawes. *Berkeley*. London: Oxford University Press, 1932.

Jessop, T. E. *George Berkeley*. London: Longmans Green, 1959.

Johnston, G. A. *The Development of Berkeley's Philosophy*. London: Methuen, 1923.

Joussain, André. *Exposé critique de la philosophie de Berkeley*. Paris: Boivin, 1921.

Leroy, André-Louis. *George Berkeley*. Paris: Presses Universitaires, 1959.

Levi, A. *La filosofia di Giorgio Berkeley*. Turin: Bocca, 1922.

Luce, A. A. *Berkeley and Malebranche*. Oxford: Oxford University Press, 1934.

————. *Berkeley's Immaterialism*. Edinburgh: Thomas Nelson, 1945.

————. *The Dialectic of Immaterialism*. London: Hodder and Stoughton, 1963.

Metz, R. *George Berkeley, Leben und Lehre*. Stuttgart: H. Kurtz, 1925.

Ritchie, A. D. *George Berkeley: A Reappraisal*. Manchester: Manchester University Press, 1967; New York: Barnes and Noble, 1967.

Sillem, Edward A. *George Berkeley and the Proofs for the Existence of God*. London: Longmans Green, 1957.

Steinkraus, Warren E. (ed.). *New Studies in Berkeley's Philosophy*. New York: Holt, Rinehart and Winston, 1966.

Turbayne, Colin Murray. "Commentary" in George Berkeley, *Works on Vision*. Indianapolis and New York: The Bobbs-Merrill Company, 1963.

Warnock, G. J. *Berkeley*. London: Penguin, 1953.

Wild, John. *George Berkeley: A Study of His Life and Philosophy*. Cambridge: Harvard University Press, 1936.

Wisdom, J. O. *The Unconscious Origins of Berkeley's Philosophy*. London: Hogarth, 1953. New York: Hillary House, 1957.

George Berkeley bicentenary

Bicentaire de la mort de Berkeley. Revue philosophique de la France et de l'étrangère, Paris, Vol. 143, April–June, 1953.
George Berkeley. Berkeley: University of California Press, 1957.
George Berkeley Bicentenary. British Journal for the Philosophy of Science, Edinburgh, Vol. IV, No. 13, 1953.
George Berkeley 1685–1753. Revue internationale de philosophie, Brussels, Vol. VII, Nos. 23–24, 1953.
Homage to George Berkeley. Hermathena, Dublin, Trinity College, No. 82, 1953.

Works with special bearing upon Berkeley's philosophy

Carnap, Rudolf. *Der Logische Aufbau der Welt.* Berlin: Weltkreis Verlag, 1928.
Goodman, Nelson. *The Structure of Appearance.* Cambridge: Harvard University Press, 1951. Second ed., Indianapolis and New York: The Bobbs-Merrill Company, 1965.
Russell, Bertrand. *An Inquiry into Meaning and Truth.* London: Allen and Unwin, 1940.
Turbayne, Colin Murray. *The Myth of Metaphor.* New Haven and London: Yale University Press, 1962. Revised ed., Columbia: University of South Carolina Press, 1970.

Other editions of Berkeley's works published by Bobbs-Merrill

Three Dialogues Between Hylas and Philonous, with an Introduction. Edited by Colin M. Turbayne, Library of Liberal Arts No. 39, 1954.
A Treatise Concerning the Principles of Human Knowledge, with an Introduction. Edited by Colin M. Turbayne, Library of Liberal Arts No. 53, 1957.

Works on Vision: An Essay on Vision, the Theory of Vision or Visual Language, and Selections from Alciphron and Principles, with a Commentary. Edited by Colin M. Turbayne, Library of Liberal Arts No. 83, 1963.

Principles, Dialogues, and Philosophical Correspondence, with an Introduction. Edited by Colin M. Turbayne, Library of Liberal Arts No. 208, 1965.

Textual Note

The commentary consists of articles reprinted from journals, with the exception of the editor's article, BERKELEY'S METAPHYSICAL GRAMMAR, *and the articles by James W. Cornman and Paul J. Olscamp. These three articles were specially written for this volume. Errors were corrected in the reprinted articles, and minor changes made for consistency in footnote styling; other slight editorial additions are in brackets.*

The text of the PRINCIPLES OF HUMAN KNOWLEDGE *is that of Berkeley's final edition published in London in 1734, except that the Preface which Berkeley omitted has been restored. The* PRINCIPLES *was first published in Dublin in 1710. Significant additions in the final version have been bracketed in the text, while significant earlier variants have been given in footnotes. Many of Berkeley's italics which appear to function as quotation marks have been eliminated. Furthermore, spelling, punctuation, and capitalization have been revised to conform to present-day American usage, as they were in my earlier editions of this work published in the Library of Liberal Arts. These editions were LLA 53 (Indianapolis and New York: Bobbs-Merrill, 1957) and LLA 208, with the* THREE DIALOGUES *and* PHILOSOPHICAL CORRESPONDENCE *(Indianapolis and New York: Bobbs-Merrill, 1965).*

Critical

essays

Colin Murray Turbayne / Berkeley's

metaphysical grammar

The problem

Berkeley is peculiarly contemporary in his attitude to language. In recent times only Wittgenstein can be compared with him in the central importance he gives to language in his "entire scheme," and, in his own time, only Vico. In his notebook he wrote: "The chief thing I do or pretend to do is only to remove the mist or veil of words. This has occasioned ignorance and confusion." His major work, *A Treatise Concerning the Principles of Human Knowledge*, is an attempt to implement this program, for in it he tries to show that "innumerable errors" in metaphysics can be traced to their "source" in mistaken

This essay appears for the first time in this volume.

views about language and then eliminated by the adoption of his own views.

In the *Principles* he rejects two main doctrines, one the doctrine of material substance, and the other the doctrine of abstract ideas. It is clear that these two doctrines together constitute the contemporary version of a traditional doctrine of Western philosophy according to which there is a fundamental division of objects into substances and their attributes or particulars and universals. In the contemporary version, universals, being framed by the mind, are called "abstract ideas." There are two main ways of rejecting the traditional doctrine: *first*, by holding that universals are nothing but complexes of particulars, or *second*, by holding that particulars are nothing but complexes of universals. Which is Berkeley's way? The obvious answer ties a knot in the interpretation of Berkeley, for he appears to adopt, not just one of these ways, but both.

In the *Introduction* to the *Principles* Berkeley appears to adopt the first way. This is so because he rejects the established doctrine of abstract ideas to the effect that any general term denotes an abstract, determinate idea, and, instead, adopts the view that a general term denotes any one of many particular ideas. Accordingly, Berkeley is appropriately classified as a nominalist about universals.

In the main part of the *Principles,* however, Berkeley appears to adopt the second way. This is so because he rejects the established doctrine of material substance to the effect that any singular concrete term denotes a substance distinct from the attributes which are predicated of it, and, instead, adopts the view that a singular concrete term denotes a combination of attributes or universals. Accordingly, Berkeley is appropriately classified as an extreme realist about universals.

How does one untie this knot? In the popular tradition descending from Hume through Reid and Mill to the present,

Berkeley is classified as a nominalist about universals, and his rejection of material substance is reconciled with his nominalism: it is the rejection of just another abstract idea and the admission once more only of particular ideas. A difficulty with the popular view is that it makes Berkeley reduce particulars to particulars. Another difficulty is that it ascribes to Berkeley a Humean or a Proper-Name theory of meaning, which Berkeley describes: "Every name has, or ought to have, one only precise and settled signification." But this is the theory that Berkeley rejects, holding that it is the "source" of the doctrine of abstract ideas, and doubtless holding that it is the source of the doctrine of material substance. For if we accept it we are apt to think not only that every *"general name"* or predicate expression names an abstract idea or universal but that every *"noun substantive"* or subject expression names a substance or particular (*Introduction* 18, *Principles* 49, 116).[1]

Now Berkeley's way, as I conceive it, is first to discard the mistaken Proper-Name theory of meaning and its accompanying subject-predicate distinction in grammar: "As to what philosophers say of subject and mode, that seems very groundless and unintelligible" (49); and then to devise a new theory of language much after the same style as he devises a new theory of vision. The key to this interpretation is to be found, so I believe, in Berkeley's sustained use of the language model.

The hypothesis

Accordingly, the hypothesis that I test and appraise in the following pages is that Berkeley uses the same language model, although differently interpreted, throughout his *Principles* that

[1] References to Berkeley's writings are by section numbers. Unless otherwise stated, these are to the *Principles of Human Knowledge*.

he had used in his *Essay Towards a New Theory of Vision* in the previous year. This hypothesis, apparently disconfirmed by the relatively bare use of the vocabulary of the model, is confirmed by the way it works. Once more he uses the model as a pedagogical device. But whereas he had used it in the *Essay* primarily for teaching others, now he uses it almost exclusively for teaching himself. Its role is that of an aid in scientific discovery, for it offers him suggestions on how to extend his theory. If the alternative title for the *Theory of Vision* is *Visual Language*, then the alternative title for the *Principles* ought to be *Phenomenal Language*.

Now an obvious problem for Berkeley, the theorist on language, is the problem of how our language is connected with the world, that is, with what we usually use language to talk about. Berkeley gives his solution in his *Principles of Human Knowledge*. His solution is probably unique. The feature that, more than any other, makes it unique is his attempt to treat the great world itself as constituting a language. Thus the problem may be restated: How is *our* language connected with that *other* language, the language of nature? If this is so, we are given, right at the start, a broad hint of the direction of Berkeley's approach. We use one language to talk about, not a non-linguistic thing, but merely another language. In what follows I shall take this hint.

Ostensibly, Berkeley's book provides "the principles of human knowledge"—of God, of human minds, and of their relation to this world. But if this world is nothing but a language, then this book provides principles dealing with the sayer and the sayees of this language and their relation to the language. Berkeley's *Principles* is, therefore, a grammar book in which he makes "grammatical remarks *on the language*" (109) of nature. Now, a grammar of a language may be expressed in the same language—for example, in English on English—or in a different one—in English on Greek, or in Latin and English on the language of nature, as in Newton's *Principia* and Berkeley's *Principles*, respectively. From Berkeley's remarks we can abstract rules or principles of three related fields:

1) the *pragmatics* of the language of nature dealing with the author of the language and its readers;

2) the *semantics* of our language dealing with the expressions of our language and their designata which, as we now see, dissolves into the attempt to provide rules for translating our language into the language of nature, and conversely; and

3) the *syntax* of the language of nature dealing with the rules of combining the expressions of this language.

But Berkeley's *Principles* is also a book *on the grammar* of the language of nature in which he makes such higher-type remarks as "The best grammar of the kind we are speaking of will be easily acknowledged to be a certain treatise of mechanics" (110), viz., Newton's *Principia*. One can see that while Berkeley regards the *Principia* as the best grammar of its kind, he regards it as limited in scope and fundamentally mistaken. In some respects he offers the *Principles* as a rival grammar to the *Principia*.

The apparatus

In order to elicit the nature of Berkeley's apparatus I shall make use of a model drawn from the way we learn to read and write. When, as children, we learn the written language of our native tongue, our aim is to bridge the gap between two different languages. It is strange that we think them *one* language, for the gap between them is in some respects far wider than that between, for example, spoken English and spoken Italian. This is so because the letters of these two languages, the written and the spoken, belong to two sense realms. There is much more resemblance between the sounds kæt[2] and the sounds **gätto** than between the sounds kæt and the marks c A T. Although these two languages are specifically distinct or heterogeneous, there is a host of words that they have in common, such as "English," "letter," "syllable," and, indeed, all the words listed in the dictionary.

Presented with this new and unknown visual language, which we have to read in order to be admitted as members of our rather exclusive literate society, we are, in fact, confronted with a decoding problem of enormous complexity. We are in much the same posture as a man born blind and made to see. Our eyes, at first, are completely useless for, as Heraclitus said, we have "barbarian souls," that is, souls that do not understand the language. However, we come already equipped with a language that is old and known, namely, our own native but artificial tongue. At once we encounter numerous specimens of this mysterious writing. Or, so it seems. Unfortunately, until we are told, we do not know that these specimens are specimens of a language or that they translate the sounds of our own. Accordingly, our predicament is similar to that of Michael Ventris when he began to try to decipher the written language of the ancient Cretans called by Sir Arthur Evans "Linear B," for, like us, he was not provided with any bilingual clue. He had specimens of only the one language. But we are worse off than was Jean François Champollion when he began to decipher the unknown language of ancient Egypt and thus to open a book that had been closed for two thousand years, for, unlike us, he was given a bilingual clue. He was given specimens of the two languages, one of which he not only knew well but also knew that it was a translation of the other.

Fortunately, we possess the all-important factor which

[2] In order to suggest spoken words I shall often use letters of the International Phonetic Alphabet.

Champollion and Ventris lacked. We have a teacher, usually our mother, who can give us a lamp so that we may tread safely into the unknown. Right at the start she provides us with a Rosetta Stone, a bilingual clue enabling us to translate the characters of this strange new language into the sounds of our mother tongue. This translation link is the alphabet together with its proper names. Alas, only some of these names are acrophonetic! To take some examples, how useless is the alphabet in helping us to translate the marks w h o, for there is so little resemblance between the sounds of the names dɒ·b′l,yū, ēitʃ, and ōu and the sounds hū! Again, when we see the characters A T E, the sound of the proper name of the first letter, ēi, offers a hint for the finished translation into our old language, ēit. But this hint is useless in England where the marks A T E are translated as et. Finally, the name ēitʃ of the letter H offers no link whatsoever between H and its phonetic counterpart in the translation of the marks H E R B either in England (hə̄ɹb) or in New England (əɹb).

The main defects of our ordinary alphabet are as follows:

1) The alphabet has only twenty-six characters, yet the makers of the *Shorter Oxford English Dictionary* utilize a phonetic alphabet of at least eighty letters in order to represent all the different sounds of spoken English.

2) The characters are often ambiguous. One character may represent many different phonemes, e.g., the letter O in GO, DO, DOG, WOMEN.

3) One phoneme may be translated in different ways, e.g., the phoneme common to the sounds commonly translated as TO, WOO, FLEW, CANOE, and RHEUMATISM has more than twenty translations.

4) Some characters do not represent any phonemes, e.g., the E in CAUSE and the B in COMB are not translated into sound.

5) Some phonemes do not have any characters, thus forcing us to use complex combinations such as in WHICH and THAT.

In spite of these defects many of us learn to read. Having learned the letters of the alphabet and their names, we proceed with our teacher's help to establish associations between the letters and the phonemes so that we can translate back and forth in the multitudes of different contexts.

Since the problem of learning the new language is essentially a decoding problem, and since the code of written English is so complex, educators have claimed that the learning process is shortened by letting the pupil first break a simpler code. This is the approach of Sir James Pitman's Initial Teaching Alphabet (I.T.A.).[3] This has many appealing features. Pitman has devised an alphabet of forty-three letters, and has increased the number of vowels to seventeen. Each letter of the resultant new language is used to translate one and only one letter in our old language. Thus, before the pupils start to decipher, all the defects of our present alphabet that I listed above have been eliminated. Another feature, of great importance, so it seems to me, is Pitman's choice of the sound of the shared name of the character and its corresponding phoneme. In every case the sound of the name of the character recurs in the sound of the phoneme itself.

Finally, judging from the reports I have seen, this invention works. In an astonishingly short time, having begun as a cryptanalyst confronted with specimens of this totally new and unknown language with its mysterious writing, and having broken its code, the pupil succeeds in tackling any message like a native decoder, that is, he knows the underlying code. Then, full of confidence, he transfers his cryptanalytical skill to the more complex code of written English.

Now I.T.A. is to written English roughly as the visual language of Berkeley's *Essay on Vision* is to the phenomenal language of the *Principles*. My guess is that Berkeley offered the

[3] See John A. Downing, *The i. t. a. Reading Experiment* (London: University of London Institute of Education, 1964), pp. 5–25.

former work as just such a simple code as a preliminary to offering the more complex code of the latter. This is confirmed in part by his remark to Percival after writing the *Essay*, "I hope to make what is there laid down appear subservient to the ends of morality and religion in a treatise I have now in the press"; by his decision, much later, to insert the *Essay* as an appendix to *Alciphron*; and by his injunction to students to read the *Essay* before reading the *Principles*. He knew that he had a most unusual message to communicate, the presentation of which required the preparation of his audience. The *Essay* was that preparation.

But in only one passage, at sec. 143, does Berkeley describe in any detail his model of the two languages linked, of course, by an alphabet whose names are held in common:

> It is requisite that each [written] word contain in it so many distinct characters as there are variations in the sound it stands for. Thus the single letter A is proper to mark one simple uniform sound; and the word ADULTERY is accommodated to represent the sound[s] [ădɒ · ltĕri] annexed to it—in the formation whereof, there being eight different collisions or modifications of the air by the organs of speech, each of which produces a difference of sound, it was fit the word representing it should consist of as many distinct characters, thereby to mark each particular difference or part of the whole sound. And yet nobody, I presume, will say the single letter A, or the [written] word ADULTERY, are alike unto or of the same species with the respective sounds by them represented.

We notice at once that Berkeley is describing a very simple code sharing the central feature of Pitman's I.T.A. Specifically, unlike the relation between the elements of written and spoken English, there is a one-to-one correspondence between the elements of these two languages. That is to say, each character of the written language translates into one and only one letter of the spoken language.

Berkeley uses this model to work out, but only occasionally to illustrate, how we see. The model he uses in the main to illustrate how we see is that of a word and its referent. Thus, a visual object signifies a tactual object just as the word "cat" signifies any cat. This model works well for most of Berkeley's theorems but it breaks down in his central theorem stated below. In the new model, to cut a long story short, Berkeley interprets the letters of the written language as visual qualities and the letters of the spoken language as tactual qualities. One can readily see how the tame and obvious truth in the language of the model, "The characters of the alphabet are specifically distinct from the corresponding phonemes, called by the same names," becomes, when translated into the language of the theory of vision, a shocking paradox: "The extension, figures, and motions perceived by sight are specifically distinct from the ideas of touch, called by the same names; nor is there any such thing as one idea or kind of idea, common to both senses" (*Essay* 127). This paradox Berkeley calls the "main part and pillar" of his theory of vision (*Theory* 41). One can readily see how he works out the relation between say, the visual square and the tactual square. Just as the written combination ADULTERY and the corresponding spoken combination each contains eight parts, so do the visual square and the tactual square (*Essay* 142), and just as the characters and phonemes of the word "adultery," as well as the combinations of these, are called by the same names, so are the parts of the visual square and the tactual square and their combinations. Berkeley has discovered a model built into which are many features which reappear in his theory of vision. Not the least important of these is the feature in which wholly different things share the same names.

I shall not develop the application of the alphabet model to Berkeley's optics. Let us see how the same model, differently interpreted, is used throughout Berkeley's metaphysics.

The principles

I THE PHENOMENA OF NATURE CONSTITUTE A UNIVERSAL
LANGUAGE OF THE AUTHOR OF NATURE

This, the submerged first principle of Berkeley's metaphysics,
parallels the first principle of his optics:

> The proper objects of vision constitute a universal language
> of the Author of Nature,

which he states as the *"conclusion"* of his *Essay Towards a New
Theory of Vision* (147), and restates as the *"principle"* of his
Theory of Vision, "from thence deducing theorems and solutions" (38). Clearly, Berkeley's optics and metaphysics have
this much in common: the facts of each are representable in the
idioms appropriate to language. They differ, however, in the
interpretation given to the features of the model, for in the latter
this is extended to embrace not only the phenomena of vision
but all the furniture of the earth. In *Principles* 108 Berkeley says
that "the steady consistent methods of nature may not unfitly
be styled the 'language' of its 'Author.' " In sec. 66 he refers to
the phenomena of nature as "this language (if I may so call it)
of the Author of Nature." He gives the fullest single statement
of his principle in *Siris* 254:

> The phenomena of nature, which strike on the senses and are
> understood by the mind, form not only a magnificent spectacle,
> but also a most coherent, entertaining, and instructive . . .
> language or discourse.

In what follows I shall collect some of the main "theorems
and solutions" that Berkeley is able to deduce from this first
principle of his metaphysics. In some cases he presents them in
the vocabulary of the theory, in others in the vocabulary of the
model. The machinery by which he deduces his theorems is not

disclosed. It is probably very simple and works as follows: In his first principle he has already equated the phenomena of nature with a language. From this equation, together with various commonly accepted features of language, he is able to deduce his theorems, for example:

> The phenomena of nature constitute a language;
> A language contains an alphabet; therefore,
> The phenomena of nature contain an alphabet.

II THE AUTHOR OF NATURE COMMUNICATES WITH INTELLIGENT DECODERS SO THAT HE MAY DIRECT THEIR ACTIONS

First, a language exists only if there is a sayer and a sayee. The sayer or author is interpreted as God, the sayee or decoder as any of his intelligent creatures, especially a human mind. The existence of such a decoder is inferred in *Principles* 2: "But besides all that endless variety of ideas or objects of knowledge, there is something which knows or perceives them. . . . This perceiving, active being is what I call 'mind,' 'spirit,' 'soul,' or 'myself.' "

Secondly, the communicating purpose of the Author serves his ulterior purpose, specifically, directing the actions of his audience (*Introduction* 20).

Thirdly, the ultimate purpose of the Author in regard to his creatures, "the general well-being of all men, of all nations, of all ages of the world," is deduced in several steps from the Author's commonly accepted attributes (*Passive Obedience* 7).

III THE PHENOMENA OF NATURE CONSTITUTE A WRITTEN LANGUAGE

A language is traditionally either spoken or written. That the language of nature is conceived as a written language is suggested by the word "author" and confirmed by the opening sentence of the *Principles* from which we learn that ideas are "actually *imprinted* on the senses." The adjective "imprinted" Berkeley uses throughout this book to qualify not only the objects of vision, as in the *Essay* and the *Theory of Vision*, but the objects of all the sense realms. Further confirmation is provided by Berkeley's use of such metaphors as: *"well-read in the language* of nature" (108), *"perusing the volume* of nature" (109), and *"reading other books"* (109).

IV   THE LETTERS OF THE ALPHABET OF NATURE
CONSTITUTE WHAT WE CALL "SENSIBLE QUALITIES"

Only after having mastered the spoken language do we graduate to learning the rudiments of reading and writing, that is, of translating the new and unknown language of, say, written English into our old and known language of spoken English, and the spoken back into the written. The first lesson is on the written alphabet and is conducted in our mother tongue. The proper names of the letters are taught ostensively, that is, the letters are shown "alongside" their proper names. But such names originally belong to the spoken language. The teacher, usually our mother, *shows* a letter and *sounds* its proper name. Exhibiting the letter A, for example, she says: "This is ēi," or "This is called ēi." Mastery of the proper names of the letters is of the utmost importance for the beginner, for these proper names constitute the translation link between the two languages.

This models the way we begin to learn to read and write any foreign language: The spoken language models our mother tongue while the written language models the foreign language. The first lesson of a book introducing ancient Greek, for example, is a lesson on its written alphabet, but the lesson is conducted in English. The letters A, B, Γ, Δ, etc., are listed alongside their proper names "Alpha," "Beta," "Gamma," "Delta," etc.

The proper names are printed in the old and known letters of English, for it is clear that if they were made up of the Greek letters that he still has to learn, the student would be unable to read them.

That the language of nature has an alphabet is an obvious deduction from the nature of language conceived on the Indo-European model. In the first section of the *Principles*, Berkeley describes the alphabet of this language made up of those primitive terms, letters, or elements required for subsequent reading and writing. But he conducts his account in English. Thus the written and spoken languages of his model parallel the language of nature and the language of English of his theory.

What corresponds to the generic name "letters of the alphabet"? In the first sentence, Berkeley gives its obvious counterpart: "ideas actually imprinted on the senses." Leaving the term "ideas" vague, perhaps intentionally, he introduces subsequently the more precise synonyms: "sensations" (3), "sensible qualities" (7), "proper objects" (44), and "natural letters" (*Siris* 252). That these are interchangeable is proved in part by the equation: "Qualities, as has been shown, are nothing else but sensations or ideas" (78).

What corresponds to the specific names, ēi, bī, sī, etc., that is, the proper names of the letters? What corresponds to the inscriptions, imprinted things, or impressions, A, B, C, D, etc., that is, the letters or characters themselves? Now the teacher of written English cannot list the characters in spoken English, but she can exhibit these elements of a different language and refer to them by *using* their proper names. Similarly, Berkeley cannot list the proper objects or natural letters themselves in English, for they are elements of a different language. Nevertheless he can refer to them by name and assume that they are to be learned ostensively. In the next three sentences of section 1 he classifies and specifies the letters of the alphabet of nature:

> By sight I have the ideas of *light* and *colors,* with their several degrees and variations. By touch I perceive, for example, *hard* and *soft, heat* and *cold, motion* and *resistance,* and of all these more and less either as to quantity or degree. Smelling furnishes me with *odors;* the palate with *tastes;* and hearing conveys *sounds* to the mind in all their variety of tone and composition.

A few sections later Berkeley uses only singular abstract nouns as names of qualities: "The sensible qualities are color, figure, motion, smell, taste, and such like" (7). But these have "degrees and variations." Let color be representative. "Variations of color" allows for the different *hues* of redness, blueness, etc., and "degrees of light" allows for different *shades* of redness, etc., such as maroon, scarlet, and pink. But Berkeley's specific examples of qualities extend only to the level of "hues" such as redness, roundness, tartness, bitterness, softness, etc. (*Dialogues* III 19, I 4, I 7). Now, if redness, roundness, etc., are the proper objects, then "redness," "roundness," etc., are their proper names. It is clear that there is no more likeness between the proper object redness and its proper name "redness" than there is between the character A and its proper name ēi.

V   THE LETTERS OF THE ALPHABET OF NATURE ARE
ABSTRACT ENTITIES: THEY NEVER OCCUR EACH OF THEM
APART BY ITSELF AND SEPARATED FROM ALL OTHERS, BUT ARE
MIXED, AS IT WERE, AND BLENDED TOGETHER

This theorem follows from the nature of alphabets which are founded on abstraction from actual language. Its presence in Berkeley's system is confirmed by his statement made in the vocabulary of the theory in *Introduction* 7:

The qualities or modes of things do never really exist each of them apart by itself and separated from all others, but are mixed, as it were, and blended together, several in the same object.

We never perceive, for example, a shade of color by itself, or even imagine it, although we can see and imagine a patch of color. Similarly, although we can experience motion, it is always of an object in motion. Nevertheless, each of the qualities, while never separated, can be distinguished (*Introduction* 16).

VI   THE LETTERS OF THE ALPHABET OF NATURE ARE
UNIVERSALS: THE *same few* ORIGINAL LETTERS RECUR IN
MANY DIFFERENT COMBINATIONS

This theorem follows from the nature of alphabets: The same finite number of letters is used over and over again in the multitude of different combinations. Milton, for example, used the same 26 letters to make 6000 words, whereas Shakespeare used numerically the same letters to make 15,000 different combinations. Berkeley, aware of such "repetition of *a few characters*" (121), draws the parallel between the model and the theory:

> The reason why ideas are formed into . . . regular combinations is the same with that for combining letters into words. That *a few original ideas* may be made to signify a great number of effects and actions, it is necessary they be variously combined together (65).

The same shade of color, for example, or the same size, taste, or smell, may recur at the same time in many different objects or at many different times in qualitatively the same objects. Many men have the same snubnosedness, while every hibiscus partakes of softness.

VII   THE LETTERS OF THE ALPHABET OF NATURE ARE
COMBINED TO MAKE WHAT WE CALL "PARTICULARS"
OR "SENSIBLE THINGS"

Having taught us our letters so that when they are exhibited we
can tell their names, our teacher gives us our second lesson in
reading. This involves translating written letters, when they
occur in a certain order, into spoken words.

$$\begin{array}{ccccc} \text{A} & \text{P} & \text{P} & \text{L} & \text{E} \\ \downarrow & \downarrow & \downarrow & \downarrow & \downarrow \end{array}$$

$$\text{æ p'l} \leftarrow \text{ēi} \quad \text{pī} \quad \text{pī} \quad \text{el} \quad \text{ī}$$

She introduces us to the convention of substituting one complex
term for the many simpler terms or proper names. Exhibiting
some of the letters of the alphabet on a blackboard, and calling
them by their names, she continues:

> As several of these letters are observed to accompany each
> other, they come to be called in our spoken language by one
> name, and so to be reputed as one word. Thus, for example, the
> letters ēi, pī, pī, el, and ī having been observed to go together,
> are accounted one distinct word signified by the name æ p'l.

In the second half of *Principles* 1 Berkeley describes the
second lesson in "the reading of natural letters" which involves
translating these natural letters into the words of English.

$$\begin{array}{ccccc} \text{REDNESS} & \text{SWEETNESS} & \text{SWEETNESS} & \text{ROUNDNESS} & \text{CRISPNESS} \\ \downarrow & \downarrow & \downarrow & \downarrow & \downarrow \end{array}$$

"apple" ← "redness" "sweetness" "sweetness" "roundness" "crispness"

Having listed some of the letters of the alphabet of nature by
telling their names, he continues:

> As several of these are observed to accompany each other, they
> come to be marked by one name, and so to be reputed as one

thing. Thus, for example, a certain color, taste, smell, figure, and consistence having been observed to go together, are accounted one distinct thing signified by the name "apple."

If Berkeley is using the alphabet model, but without saying so, to work out this important theorem in his metaphysics, one expects him to make some inadvertent disclosure of its use, hopefully in some simple but not so obvious parallel. That this expectation is fulfilled in the facts is apparent when it is noticed that the five written letters of the word "apple" are equinumerous with the five qualities he specifies in the *apple*. That this is no coincidence is confirmed by his specification of the three qualities of the visible *sun* in sec. 32, the three qualities of the *die* in sec. 49, and the four qualities of the bar of *iron* in *Dialogues* I 13. It is further confirmed by his use of the eight letters of the written word ADULTERY as a model for the visible square in which he finds eight parts (*Essay* 142, 143). But in this last case he advertently discloses the parallel.

Berkeley describes this basic operation of translation that we perform upon the natural letters on several occasions. In the *Essay*, he anticipates his later doctrine by describing how we translate certain natural letters into our word "coach": "Having been observed constantly to go together, [several qualities] are spoken of as one and the same thing" (46). In the *Dialogues* he tells us how we translate other letters into our word "cherry": "A congeries of sensible impressions . . . are united into one thing (or have one name given them) by the mind because they are observed to attend each other" (III 19). He even tells us the reason for the convention of substituting the more convenient abbreviations. It would be impractical to read, for example, the characters APPLE or the corresponding natural letters always by telling their proper names. "The endless number or confusion of names would render language impracticable. Therefore, to avoid this as well as other inconveniences which are obvious upon a little thought, men combine together several ideas . . . all which they refer to one name and consider as one thing" (III 16).

The claim that in reading natural letters "men combine together" the letters appears to contradict Theorem VI according to which the letters are "variously combined together" by the Author. The apparent contradiction is resolved when one elicits Berkeley's two senses of "combine": (1) to present in regular order; (2) to unite into one thing. The distinction is implicit in *Principles* 1. Certain letters of nature are observed to "accompany each other," having been "combined" by the Author, but they are "reputed as one thing" or "combined" into units by the reader. The language of nature is conceived on the model of the written Greek that Plato read, in which there were no gaps, no periods, and no lower-case letters. There were, therefore, no words in the text until Plato "read them into" it. He translated the *letters* of one language into the *words* of another.

This gives some idea of the enormous contribution made by the reader of the language of nature, of his embellishment of the basic furniture of the earth. "We say 'one book,' 'one page,' 'one line'; all these are equally units, though some contain several of the others. And in each instance it is plain the unit relates to some particular combination of ideas arbitrarily put together by the mind" (12; cf. *Essay* 109). Thus when we see particulars or physical objects we are makers or poets. "Sensible things are rather *considered as one* than truly so" (*Siris* 347).

ARE ANALYZABLE INTO THE LETTERS OF THE
VIII   WHAT WE CALL "PARTICULARS" OR "SENSIBLE THINGS"
ALPHABET OF NATURE

Having taught us the rudiments of reading so that when the letters of written English are exhibited we can translate them into the words of spoken English, our teacher gives us our first lesson in writing. Writing in the primary sense of the word is the use of letters or other conventional characters in order to represent significant sounds. It is, therefore, translating from the spoken into the written language. Writing, apparently, is more difficult to learn than reading. Stanley Sapon[4] of the University of Rochester has taught three-year-old children to read but four-year-olds to write. A concrete symbol for the basic operation that we perform upon the spoken language comes from ancient Egypt. It is the Seated Scribe. The scribe—a follower of Theuth, the inventor of writing—is translating. He is taking dictation, for he can bridge the enormous gap between the two languages in the reverse direction from reading.

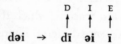

Writing involves transliterating: *Told* the spoken words, we translate them into the written language by *showing* the letters. But once we have completed the spelling of a word by *telling* the proper names of the letters we have effectually bridged the gap between the two languages. Told dəi, for example, our major task of translation is finished once we can spell out the proper names dī, əi, ī. This done, the exhibition of the letters D, I, E, presents little difficulty, for we have long since mastered the ostensive definitions of the proper names of the letters. Accordingly, how the finished translation is exhibited, by *inscribing, scrawling,* or *scribbling* the letters on paper with a pen, by pressing the *keys* to the letters as in *typewriting,* by displaying them on a board as in *scrabble,* or merely by *telling* their names as in *spelling,* is accidental to the operation.

---

[4] Stanley M. Sapon, "Operant Studies in the Refinement and Expansion of Verbal Behavior in Disadvantaged Children" (Washington, D.C.: Office of Economic Opportunity, 1966).

Thus, in writing as in reading, the proper names of the letters constitute the translation link, the Rosetta Stone as it were, between the two languages. Spelling is a scaffolding erected to help us in bridging the gap from one side or the other. When we have done the bridging on numerous occasions we take down the scaffolding. It is clear, however, that while it constitutes only the beginning of the task of reading, spelling constitutes practically the end of the task of writing. This is so because it is only accidental that the sounds of the proper names of the letters are acrophonetic.

Now giving the spelling of the spoken words shows our ability to indicate or to pick out certain combinations of letters wherever they recur in the once unfamiliar or foreign language. Once we can translate **dəi**, for example, we are able to indicate any combinations of letters that satisfy the spelling **dī, əi, ī.**

Translation from the spoken into the written language models Berkeley's accounts of definition and denotation.

HARDNESS	EXTENSION	SQUARENESS
↑	↑	↑

"die" → "hard" "extended" "square"

Definition and denotation are two main ways of connecting our language with the world. Since Berkeley construes the world as a language he must be giving an account of how we translate into the language of nature. Definition parallels transliteration, the spelling out or unplaiting of our words into the letters of another language. It merely reverses the operation of the previous theorem, that of substituting one complex term for the many simpler terms or proper names. Here we begin with a complex and spell out its simples. We analyze a whole into parts. In *Principles* 49 Berkeley gives an example of this basic operation that we perform upon the complex terms of our language:

> To say a die is hard, extended, and square is . . . only an explication of the meaning of the word "die."

The words "complex" and "explication" have the same root in the Greek "plekein" = "to weave" or "to plait." Just as to transliterate or to spell a spoken word is to translate it into the letters of the corresponding written language by telling their proper names, so, to give "an explication of the meaning of" (49), to "attend to what is meant by" (3), or to give a definition of (*Introduction* 18) a complex term is to analyze it into the elements or letters of the alphabet of nature by giving their proper names. In this way we "see what ideas are included in any compound idea" (*Introduction* 22). As previously noted in the example of the apple, the three specified qualities of the die are equinumerous with the letters of the word "die." It is clear that this operation of spelling or explicating is the reverse of the operation of composing or combining, and that both are present in Berkeley's account.

The proper names of the proper objects or sensible qualities constitute the translation link between our artificial language and the language of nature. If we know the definition of a complex term we are able to pick out particulars or sensible things that satisfy the definition. These, we say, are denoted or signified by the term. Thus a general name, such as "die," which, "considered in itself, is particular [i.e., is itself a complex], becomes general by being made to represent or stand for all other particular [dies] of the same sort" (*Introduction* 12). They are "of the same sort" because they satisfy the same definition. The definientes "hard," "extended," and "square" that name the determinables hardness, extension, and squareness, "hold equally true" of any particular die whatsoever even though all the qualities of the latter are determinate (*Introduction* 11).

IX   THE RULES OF SYNTAX OF THE LANGUAGE OF NATURE
ARE CALLED "THE LAWS OF NATURE"

The rules of composition and syntax (= a putting together in order) of a language describe the ways in which the letters and their combinations are combined. Rules of this kind can be formulated by the grammarian because the letters recur "not anyhow and at random" but in a certain "order and concatenation" to make "regular combinations," combinations that "must be made by rule and with wise contrivance" by the writer (109, 64, 57, 65).

At *Principles* 30–32, 60–66, 102–110, Berkeley makes remarks on the laws of physics. These laws can be framed because the phenomena of nature have "a steadiness, order, and coherence, and are not excited at random . . . but in a regular train or series . . . [by the] Author." "The best grammar of the kind we are speaking of [i.e., syntax] will be easily acknowledged to be a treatise of mechanics," viz., Newton's *Principia* (30, 108).

X   RULES OF SYNTAX PROVIDE EXPLANATIONS

Having formulated the rules, the grammarian can show how specimens of the language conform to them. He is "able to *say by what rule* a thing is so or so." He explains, for example, such occurrences as a vowel in a word, a verb in a sentence, a verb in the plural, and a noun in the accusative case by "reducing" them to their respective rules or by showing how statements of the former "follow from" statements of the latter (108, 109).

"Those men who frame general rules from the phenomena,

and afterwards *derive the phenomena from* those rules seem to be grammarians, and their art the grammar of nature." Once the laws of nature have been found out, it is the physicist's task "to show that each phenomenon is in *constant conformity with* those laws, that is, *necessarily follows from* those principles." From the general laws, he proceeds to "deduce the other phenomena." A law being general applies to instances. For example, the law-statement, "the change of motion is proportional to the impressed force," is to be understood of motion in general. By this "it is only implied that whatever motion I consider . . . the axiom concerning it *holds equally true.*" Thus if I know the law, then, on encountering any particular instance of a change of motion, I can infer that it is proportional to the impressed force (107, 108; *De Motu* 37; *Introduction* 11).

XI RULES OF SYNTAX PROVIDE PREDICTIONS AND RETRODICTIONS

It is in virtue of the previous feature that knowing the rules helps us to *read* the language. The rules of syntax are a grammar for the understanding of a language enabling us to make predictions and retrodictions in ordinary discourse. Confronted, for example, with an occurrence of the letter Aitch at the start of a word, and knowing the rule, the reader can *predict* the imminent occurrence of a vowel. Seeing a plural verb, the reader who knows the rule can *retrodict* the earlier occurrence of a plural noun or pronoun.

This enables me to elicit a second sense of the verb "to read." The *Shorter Oxford English Dictionary* distinguishes four main senses of the word, of which two are present in my account. The first, which has dominated our previous theorems, is: "to peruse and utter in speech," i.e., "to translate from the written into the spoken language." This sense is present in the

Roman citizen's injunction to Mark Antony: "Read the will; we'll hear it Antony." Being illiterate, these plebeians had to have the Latin document translated into the Latin tongue. The second is: "to interpret, discern, etc.," or as Berkeley puts it, "to interpret [a sign] or tell what it signifies." This includes: "to guess what," and "to foresee, foretell, predict." It is present in Lady Macbeth's discerning remark: "Your face, my thane, is as a book whereon men may read strange matters." She might have said: "Your intentions are written all over your face." It is present also in: "He reads hands and the skies." Prediction or foretelling, and, correspondingly, retrodiction, involve saying or telling, i.e., uttering in speech, but they also involve saying or telling what will happen and what has happened, respectively.

The second sense of the verb "to read" dominates Berkeley's account of natural syntax or mechanics. The laws of nature enable us to make retrodictions and predictions, for they "enable us to make very probable conjectures touching *things that may have happened* at very great distances of time, as well as to predict *things to come*." Berkeley stresses the connection between laws and predictive power: The laws of nature "are a grammar for the understanding of nature . . . whereby we are enabled to foresee what will come to pass in the natural course of things." We can do this because "the art of presaging is in some sort *the reading of natural letters* denoting order." For example, "You and the cook may judge of a dish on the table equally well, but while the dish is making, the cook can better foretell what will ensue from this or that manner of composing it," and, "He that foretells the motions of the planets, or the effects of medicines or mechanical experiments, may be said to do it by natural vaticination."

What are the mechanics of such prediction and, correspondingly, of retrodiction, when these are grounded upon laws? Now, the logic of these procedures is exactly the same as the logic of explanation. This is so because a law, although expressed in the present tense, is understood to apply not only now but always. Accordingly, if I know that the change of motion is proportional to the impressed force, then, no matter what motion I consider, I can retrodict or predict with *certainty* that it was or will be proportional to the impressed force. But Berkeley, as we have just seen, says that we make not certain predictions but only "very *probable conjectures*" about the past and the future. He realizes correctly that it is not our logic that is deficient but our knowledge. He realizes the hypothetical character of the rules of natural syntax, the so-called "laws of nature": "All deductions of that kind *depend on a supposition* that the Author of Nature always operates uniformly and in a constant observance of those rules we take for principles, which we cannot evidently know" (105; *Siris* 252, 253).

XII RULES OF SYNTAX ARE EXPRESSED IN TERMS OF "SIGN" AND "THING SIGNIFIED"

In conformity with their role in helping us to *read* the language, the rules of syntax are expressed more appropriately in terms of sign and thing signified than in terms that suggest a causal connection. Although grammar tells us, for example, that *ab* "takes" the ablative, that a transitive verb "takes" the accusative, that one word "governs" another, and that another is "dependent upon" its antecedent, these words do not imply the relation of cause and effect. They merely tell the reader that one word "forewarns" him of a certain state of affairs and that another is a "sign of" its antecedent.

Although the laws of nature are frequently stated in causal terms, Berkeley holds that "the connection of ideas does not imply the relation of *cause* and *effect*, but only of a mark or *sign* with the thing *signified*." The words "cause" and "effect" are each appropriately translated as "sign." If the former, prediction is involved: "The fire which I see is not the cause of the pain I suffer upon my approaching it, but the mark that forewarns me of it." If the latter, retrodiction: "In like manner, the noise that I hear is not the effect of this or that motion or collision of the ambient bodies, but the sign thereof" (65).

XIII   RULES OF SYNTAX HELP US TO WRITE

Because the rules of syntax provide explanations, they help us to *write* in the language. Although the rules, as we say, "govern" our entire writing, although we write "in obedience to" them, and although they "forbid" certain combinations of letters, nevertheless we have the power to manipulate the communal letters to make a great variety of combinations.

Consideration of such control that we have over a language enables me to elicit a second well-known sense of the verb "to write." The first sense, which has dominated our previous theorems, is: "to use letters or other conventional characters in order to represent significant sounds," i.e., "to translate from the spoken into the written language." The second sense is: "to produce as an author or composer," which is present, for example, in: "to write a sonnet" or "to write a symphony."

This sense of the verb "to write" dominates Berkeley's account of natural syntax or mechanics. Having been told that nature constitutes a language, we expect Berkeley to tell us how, equipped with a knowledge of the rules of its grammar, we are helped to become authors or composers, albeit limited ones, of this language—limited, because in all that we write, we are "governed" by rules which we cannot alter. This he does, using the vocabulary of his theory. He tells us that the laws of nature are applied by us not only to explaining the various phenomena and to making conjectures about the past and the future, but "as well to the framing artificial things for the use and ornament of life." The laws help us to find "what methods are proper to be taken for the exciting such and such ideas." They direct us how to act (62, 65).

What is the mechanics of this process of harnessing nature to our purposes, of making some things happen and preventing others from happening? Berkeley tells us that knowledge of the laws of nature "gives us a sort of foresight which enables us to regulate our actions for the benefit of life." This is so because if we know the laws, then "we *know . . . that* to obtain such or such ends, such or such means are conducive." If we *know that* "food nourishes, sleep refreshes, and fire warms us; that to sow in the seedtime is the way to reap in the harvest," then we know the means whereby we can obtain these ends. While Berkeley does not claim that knowing the relevant laws is a sufficient condition for knowing how to regulate our actions, he does claim that it is necessary: "Without this [knowledge] we should be eternally at a loss; we could not *know how* to act . . ." (30, 31).

XIV   RULES OF SYNTAX ARE PRESCRIPTIONS

In so far as they help us to *write* in the language, the rules of syntax are treated more appropriately as prescriptions than as descriptions. For us as passive *spectators*, grammar *describes*. It tells us that certain things actually occur in the language. The rules are expressed in the indicative mood, for example: "Prepositions, in keeping with their name, *are* placed before the word they govern." But in so far as we are *actors*, i.e., *writers* in the language, who "observe" and "follow" its rules, then grammar directs us how to act. It prescribes or tells us what we should do. In keeping with their name, rules are appropriately expressed in the *imperative* mood: "Prepositions *must* be placed before the word they govern."

Consonant with their role in helping us to control nature for our benefit and against damage to ourselves, the laws of nature are treated more appropriately as prescriptions than as descriptions. Berkeley describes and illustrates the main step in the metamorphosis of a law-statement into a rule-directive, of an indicative into an imperative, in the passage just quoted. The law-statement, "Sleep refreshes," is transformed first into "In order to obtain refreshment, sleep is conducive" in accordance with the formula, "To obtain such or such ends such or such means are conducive." By this rendering, Berkeley indicates that the law is to be construed as a recipe for action, a prescription that we can fill or not as we choose, or an "admonition" of what end we can secure "in consequence of such and such actions." It is appropriately expressed hypothetically and in the imperative mood, for example, "In order to obtain refreshment, let one try sleep" (31, 44).

The alphabet model and immaterialism

My hypothesis that Berkeley, having adopted the alphabet model in order to work out his new theory of vision, never dropped it when he came to work out his new theory of reality, I shall now take to be established. Many corollaries that clarify features in his "entire scheme" can now be drawn. This whole task I shall postpone, contenting myself here with showing how the model illuminates the central thesis of his immaterialism.

There is no doubt that Berkeley offers his new theory of immaterialism as a rival theory to the traditional doctrine of materialism which is commonly summarized as follows:

Particular things are substances supporting their qualities or attributes.

Berkeley's rival theory, on the other hand, has as its central thesis:

Particular things are nothing but collections of qualities.

There remains, however, after all this time, considerable doubt about the precise nature of this rivalry.

Now theorems VIII and VII show that within Berkeley's central thesis there are two theses:

Particular things are *analyzed* into qualities.
Qualities are *combined* into particular things.

As we have seen, these are modelled upon the two basic operations that we perform with the help of the alphabet, viz., writing and reading. But these operations are paradigms also of the equally basic procedures of scientific method, viz., analysis and synthesis, or resolution and composition. There is little doubt that the Greeks had the alphabet in mind when they devised them.

First, analysis: Just as, in writing, when told a word, the main problem of translation is to spell out the letters by telling their proper names, so, in analysis, given a definiendum, such as "point" or "line" (to use Euclid's examples), the problem is to find the definientes or irreducible terms such as "part," "length," and "breadth" that name ultimate entities.

Second, synthesis: Just as, in reading, when shown certain letters, the main problem of translation is to substitute for the proper names a new and shorter term, so, in synthesis or composition, given certain primitive terms, such as "part," "length," and "breadth," the system builder substitutes for them derived terms, such as "point" and "line."

It is clear that definitions have no place in a system or synthesis, although they are central in analysis. Euclid's "definitions," so translated, are properly translated as "combinations" or "compositions." What were definienda, the beginnings of analysis, have become derived terms in the synthesis, which, although superfluous, are introduced by the system builder for ease and expedition. I need not describe the functional analogy between terms and propositions, derived terms and demonstrated theorems, etc.

These procedures, used by Berkeley in the *Essay* and the *Theory of Vision*, enable me to elicit the nature of the rivalry between materialism and immaterialism. The relevant passages are those concerning the *analysis* of "the die" at *Principles* 49:

A die is hard, extended, and square,

and the *synthesis* of the "the apple" at *Principles* 1:

A certain color, taste, smell, figure, and consistence, having been observed to go together, . . . come to be marked by one name. . . .

Berkeley first tells how the materialists interpret these propositions. "They will have it that the word 'die' denotes a *subject* or *substance* distinct from the hardness, extension, and figure which are *predicated* of it. . . ." Berkeley ascribes to the materialist Hylas a similar analysis of "the cherry" at *Dialogues* III 19: "By the word 'cherry' you mean an unknown nature distinct from all those sensible *qualities* [of softness, moisture, redness, tartness]." Clearly the word "is" in the first proposition is understood to be the copula or the "is" of predication. To the second proposition, the materialists make a significant addition. They add "and so to be reputed as one thing," or "accounted one distinct thing" (1). Berkeley is describing the traditional doctrine according to which the subject-predicate distinction in grammar parallels the substance-attribute, or particular-universal distinction in ontology. Subscribers to this doctrine admit into their ontology both particulars and universals.

Berkeley now tells how *he* interprets these propositions. "To me a die seems to be nothing distinct from those things which are termed its modes or accidents. And to say a die is hard, extended, and square is not to *attribute* those *qualities* to a *subject* distinct from and supporting them, but only an explication of the meaning of the word 'die.' " In this passage Berkeley shows that he drops both sides of the traditional parallel. He dispenses with the "is" of predication and replaces it with the "is" of identity, thus interpreting the first proposition not as a subject-predicate proposition but as a definiendum-definientes expression. He interprets the second proposition not as one in which predicates are ascribed to a subject but as one in which primitive terms are replaced by a derived term. He is aware that there is no copula either in a definition (analysis) or in a composition or combination (synthesis), and that a definiendum or a derived term names no new entity distinct from those entities named by the definientes of analysis or the primitive terms of the synthesis. But Berkeley also drops, as one expects, the parallel substance-attribute ontology, and adopts an immaterialist or no-substance theory. He does this by claiming that a die is the same as its qualities and that those qualities (which, we commonly say, are *of* the apple) compose the apple. Thus while subscribers to the traditional doctrine admit both particulars and universals, Berkeley admits only universals, and dispenses altogether with particulars.

This interpretation of Berkeley's immaterialism is not the usual one.[5] In the received view, Berkeley subscribes, in the words of Bertrand Russell, to "the theory which admits only

---

[5] A similar interpretation is given by Richard J. Van Iten, "Berkeley's Alleged Solipsism," *Revue internationale de philosophie*, XVI, No. 61–62 (1962), 447–452, who argues for the conclusion that Berkeley is a realist about universals. This article is reprinted in the present volume on pp. 47–56.

particulars and dispenses altogether with universals."[6] Alternatively, Berkeley holds that the qualities of which particular things are composed are themselves particulars. This view appears to be supported by Berkeley's "nominalistic" maxim, "Everything which exists is particular" (*Dialogues* I 8), and by his rejection of the doctrine of abstract ideas.

Such apparent difficulties, however, are readily accommodated by my interpretation. Berkeley's "nominalistic" maxim, which appears to exclude universals, merely excludes complex universals and denies their abstract or separate existence. Theorem V shows that qualities never exist each of them apart by itself and separated, but are always "observed to accompany each other," and then are combined by us to make what we call "particular objects." His rejection of the doctrine of abstract ideas, which appears to be a rejection of universals, is properly interpreted as a rejection of the proper-name theory of the meaning of complex terms. Theorem VIII and the subsequent account of the method of analysis show how complex terms, which have the grammatical appearance of proper names, are defined into simple terms capable of being ostensively defined. The pseudo-proper names are defined in terms of Berkeley's new proper names which name the proper objects of each of the sense realms. These are the definientes or ends of analysis which will become primitive terms in his synthesis. They are the "Alpha," "Beta," etc., the *names* of the letters of the alphabet of the language of nature.

Clearly, these considerations do not affect the issue between the received view and my own. There is, however, a very simple but overlooked factor that gives additional support to my view. This is present in *Principles* 49 where Berkeley exhibits the

---

[6] "On the Relations of Universals and Particulars" (1911), in *Logic and Knowledge* (London: George Allen and Unwin, 1956), p. 111.

rivalry between his own theory and the traditional doctrine. According to the latter, any particular thing is "a *subject* or substance distinct from [its qualities or attributes] which are *predicated* of it, and *in which they exist*." Now it is certain that in this doctrine, which derives from Aristotle, the qualities or attributes are conceived as universals. This is because they are predicated of a subject. Indeed, Berkeley's statement of the doctrine strikingly echoes Aristotle's original: "Some things are universal, others particular. By the term 'universal' I mean that which is of such a nature as to be predicated of many subjects; by 'particular' that which is not thus predicated" (*De Interpretatione* 7). Moreover, Berkeley's phrase "in which [subject] they exist" parallels Aristotle's "to exist in *(eneinai)* a subject" (*Categoriae* 2). Finally, it is certain that in the traditional doctrine, the universals, being "predicated of many subjects," are recurrent entities (cf. Theorem VI).

Against this traditional doctrine Berkeley sets up his own theory. When he does so, he presents it in the same terms. He refers to "those things" and "those qualities" which are nothing but the universals "predicated" of a "subject" in the rejected traditional doctrine. These universals define or compose concrete things. He does not transform universals into particulars. If he were to do so, he would not be setting up a rival theory. Accordingly, Berkeley's immaterialism is the theory which admits only universals and dispenses altogether with particulars.

W. H. Hay / Berkeley's

argument from nominalism

I

The philosophical tenets of George Berkeley have both startled and enraged many generations. It is my purpose in this paper to show that the first or solipsistic stage of his idealism follows from the combination of certain other views. If my contention is sound, we do not have to be content with the explanation of Berkeley's views as the imaginative vision of a religious man. I believe they follow validly from a certain commonly entertained account of language taken together with a commonly entertained account of perception. In this discussion I shall draw

From REVUE INTERNATIONALE DE PHILOSOPHIE, VII, No. 23–24 (1953), fasc. 1–2, pp. 19–27. Reprinted by permission of the author and the REVUE INTERNATIONALE DE PHILOSOPHIE, Brussels.

largely on his *Principles of Human Knowledge,* since it contains the first and fullest statement of the views and reasonings of his early period.[1]

First we shall consider what Berkeley thought it "proper to premise, by way of introduction, concerning the nature and abuse of language."[2] It is through an abuse of language that "men impose upon themselves by imagining they believe those propositions they have often heard, tho' at bottom they have no meaning in them."[3] Men commit such errors because they are blinded by the "receiv'd opinions, that language has no other end but the communicating our ideas."[4] Berkeley reminds us that in the use of language "there are other ends, as the raising of some passion, the exciting to, or deterring from an action, the putting the mind in some particular disposition."[5] Such effects of words "arise in his mind upon the perception of certain words, without any ideas coming between."[6] That explains how "general names are often used in the propriety of language without the speaker's designing them for marks of ideas in his own, which he would have 'em raise in the mind of the hearer."[7] If language does produce effects without ideas coming between, we can see how any one would make mistakes who were to insist on finding ideas in every use of language.

This account of the abuses to which the varied ends of language expose us gives, however, only more evidence that Berkeley believes that where words *are* significant it is because

---

[1] Unless otherwise noted all references will be to the number of a paragraph in the *Principles of Human Knowledge.* I quote the text printed in the edition of T. E. Jessop (Edinburgh: Thomas Nelson and Sons, 1945).
[2] Introduction 6.
[3] Intro. 54.
[4] Intro. 19.
[5] Intro. 20.
[6] Intro. 20.
[7] Intro. 20.

of "the ideas they are made to stand for."[8] Therefore he recommends that in philosophy we attend to what is "signified and draw off our attention from the words which signifie."[9] Berkeley resolved to "use his utmost endeavors, to obtain a clear view of the ideas he'd consider, separating from them all that dress and incumbrance of words which so much contribute to blind the judgment and divide the attention."[10]

In summary we may state that Berkeley holds (1) that language is sometimes significant and sometimes not; (2) that where language is significant, it is significant of ideas that have entered the mind; and (3) that significant language may be laid aside in favor of considering the ideas signified.

Berkeley's account of *what* is signified has been recognized as nominalistic by such previous commentators as Professor Fraser and Professor Dawes Hicks.[11] Berkeley reports that he does not find the word, triangle, to stand for "a triangle, which *is neither oblique nor rectangle, equilateral equicrural nor scalenon, but all and none of these at once.*"[12] Such a denial is quite compatible with admitting that there are general *words*. General words, however, do not signify a different *kind* of idea, but signify particulars in a different *manner*.[13] "A word becomes general by being made the sign, not of an abstract general idea, but, of several particular ideas, any one of which it indifferently suggests to the mind."[14] Berkeley gives as an example a geometer drawing a figure for a demonstration. "He draws a black

8 Intro. 19.
9 Intro. 23.
10 Intro. 24.
11 Cf. A. C. Fraser, *Berkeley* (Edinburgh: Blackwood, 1881), p. 189, and G. Dawes Hicks, *Berkeley* (London: Benn, 1932), p. 92.
12 Intro. 13.
13 Cf. G. Berkeley, "Rough Draft of the Introduction to the Principles of Human Knowledge" in *Works*, ed. A. C. Fraser (Oxford, 1871), I, 418.
14 Intro. 11.

line of an inch in length, this which in itself is a particular line is nevertheless with regard to its signification general, since as it is there used, it represents all particular lines whatsoever."[15]

We have evidence from the early notebooks that Berkeley held to nominalism in the earliest period of his philosophical thought. One entry reads: "Locke says all our knowledge is about Particulars, if so, pray what is the following ratiocination but a jumble of words Omnis Homo est animal, omne animal vivit, ergo omnis Homo vivit. It amounts (if you annex particular ideas to the words animal & vivit) to no more than this. Omnis Homo est Homo, omnis Homo est Homo, ergo omnis Homo est Homo."[16] That is, it is one and the same particulars for which stand "homo," "animal," and "vivit." This same view appears quite clearly in an earlier and discarded version of the Introduction to the *Principles*. In discussing the significance of statements Berkeley remarks: "On laying aside all thought of the words 'Melampus is an animal,' I have remaining in my mind one only naked and bare idea, viz. that particular one to which I gave the name Melampus."[17] "All that I intend to signify thereby being only this—that the particular thing I call Melampus has a right to be called by the name animal."[18] We may take it then as established that Berkeley held that *all* that is signified by language is certain particular ideas.

II

Berkeley has confessed in his Introduction that by giving an account of language he will be led "in some measure to antici-

[15] Intro. 12.
[16] G. Berkeley, *Philosophical Commentaries*, ed. A. A. Luce (Edinburgh: Nelson, 1944).
[17] *Works*, ed. A. C. Fraser, I, 427.
[18] *Ibid.*, I, 427.

pate" his design. He has indeed. For there is nothing in the Introduction which would establish that the signification of language
is ideas, if by "ideas" we mean any more than a collective term
for what we can notice. Nothing has been said which will serve
as evidence that the objects signified may not exist at times
when we do not perceive them. After all, mediaeval nominalism
did not arrive at solipsism. In the *Principles* proper, we find
Berkeley arguing this point. There he briefly states what he believes we encounter when we "lay words aside." "The objects
of human knowledge . . . are either ideas actually imprinted on
the senses, or else such as are perceiv'd by attending to the passions and operations of the mind, or lastly ideas form'd by help
of memory."[19] Among the objects perceived by the senses he
mentions an "apple, a stone, a tree, a book."[20] Yet "what are
the foremention'd objects but the things we perceive by sense,
and what do we perceive besides our own ideas or sensations?"[21]
What has happened when we speak of an apple is that "a certain
colour, taste, smell, figure, and consistence having been observ'd
to go together, are accounted one distinct thing, signified by
the name *apple*."[22]

This part of Berkeley's argument consists of maintaining
that if, in our search for the particulars for which words stand,
we look at the particular objects perceived, we find that each of
these is *in fact* perceived and so in the mind in fact at the time
they are perceived. It is at the time of perception "impossible
that any colour or extension at all, or other sensible quality
whatsoever, should exist in an unthinking subject without the
mind."[23] This point is still further obscured because Berkeley
uses the language of Aristotelian tradition as modified by

[19] 1.
[20] 1.
[21] 4.
[22] 1.
[23] 15.

Descartes and Locke in which perception is viewed as the reception of certain forms in the mind. Already in Descartes we are puzzled whether ideas are in the soul as *shadows* are in a well or as *buckets* are in a well.

Berkeley grants that the prevailing opinion is "that houses, mountains, rivers, and in a word all sensible objects have an existence natural or real, distinct from their being perceiv'd by the understanding."[24] Indeed when Berkeley's view is pronounced one is inclined to ask how the fact that *this* is perceived can prove there is nothing that is *not* perceived. It is here that the nominalistic account of language enters the argument. The first point is that what we perceive *is* in fact in the mind. Then he can use his account of language to infer that it is *impossible* (because self-contradictory) to speak of or consider anything existing outside of my mind. It is self-contradictory because if the statement is significant it signifies certain particulars which are in the mind. To say that these particulars are *not* in the mind is to contradict oneself, or to utter a meaningless sentence which awakens passions in the mind without any ideas coming in between. The following list of phrases taken from the first twenty sections of the *Principles* shows how Berkeley's argument depends on the charge of self-contradiction or meaninglessness in his opponents. We find him label other proposals as "perfectly unintelligible," "manifest contradiction," "plainly repugnant," "impossible for us to conceive," "cannot have any meaning at all," "no distinct meaning," "not in my power to form an idea," and his own view as "sufficiently demonstrated *a priori*."

We shall now summarize the premises from which Berkeley's celebrated mentalism can be deduced. From his account of language we find that

1) All that is signified by any significant sentence is some particulars I have met.

24 4.

From his discussion of perception and imagination we find that

2) All the particulars I have met are perceived by me

and

3) All that is perceived by me is dependent at that time for existence on my mind.

From these we can infer validly that

4) All that is signified by any significant sentence is particulars perceived by me, at that time dependent for existence on my mind.

I believe that my reconstruction of his line of argument makes it easier to understand the challenge he offers in both the *Principles* and the *Three Dialogues*. Of this challenge he says, "I am content to put the whole upon this issue."[25] "If you can but *conceive* it possible for one extended moveable substance, or in general, for any one idea, or any thing like an idea, to exist otherwise than in a mind perceiving it, I will readily give up the issue."[26] Berkeley recognizes that you might think it easy to meet his challenge by saying that you "imagine trees, for instance, in a park, or books existing in a closet, and nobody by to perceive them."[27] This he rejects on the ground that "you yourself perceive or think of them all the while."[28] He is delighted if some one will try to "show that you can conceive it possible the objects of your thought may exist without the mind."[29] He can then argue that to do so "it is necessary that you conceive them existing unconceiv'd or unthought of."[30]

[25] 22 and *Three Dialogues between Hylas and Philonous* in *Works*, ed. A. C. Fraser, I, 291.

[26] 22.

[27] 23.

[28] 23.

[29] 23.

[30] 23.

Berkeley claims that this last statement, "you conceive them existing unconceiv'd or unthought of" is a manifest contradiction.

Why does Berkeley suppose that this is a contradiction? Some who have discussed Berkeley's argument have thought this contradiction is forced on us by an ambiguity; that when that ambiguity is pointed out the contradiction disappears and Berkeley's argument collapses. For example, the late Professor Dawes Hicks grants that "material things cannot be *thought of* as existing, apart from a thinking mind."[31] He holds, on the other hand, that it is quite another affair to maintain that material things cannot be thought of as existing-apart-from-a-thinking-mind."[32] He agrees that to deny the former would be a contradiction. He maintains, however, that it is the knowledge of the truth of the latter on which Berkeley's argument depends, and that to deny the latter statement is by no means to assert a contradiction. Professor Dawes Hicks did not see that on Berkeley's account of language the words, "existing-apart-from-a-thinking-mind" will not have any meaning at all. For when we lay the words aside we find no particular ideas corresponding to them. If our purpose were to refute Berkeley, which is beyond the scope of this paper, we should have to revise his account of language, and not merely ignore it.

III

So far we have constructed from Berkeley a proof for solipsism. This is not a solipsism of scepticism, which might be formulated as saying that I can have no evidence that anything exists besides myself and what I see or imagine. It takes the stronger

[31] *Op. cit.*, p. 117.
[32] *Ibid.*, p. 118.

form of a proof that to *say* anything exists except myself and what I see or imagine is self-contradictory. His argument does prove that all I can speak of is what is in a mind, because only of what is in *my* mind. Yet how can Berkeley account for any difference between "in *my* mind" and "in *a* mind?" On nominalistic ground "in *my* mind" would simply be a way of identifying a group of present particulars. The phrase "in *a* mind" can mean no more than that either, unless it is admitted that there is a property, mental or spiritual, which is possessed by me, and might be possessed by something else. If we admit that, nominalism goes out the window. For we would no longer be interpreting all words which are apparently general as merely "signifying indifferently certain particulars." Berkeley does, however, abandon his nominalism and states that "we know other spirits by means of our soul which, in that sense, is the image or idea of them."[33] Indeed, he seems to surrender altogether at this point and admit not only the property (or as he would say the general idea) mental (or as he says, spiritual), but also properties of the objects of sense. For he goes on to say that our soul has "a like respect to other spirits that blueness or heat by me perceiv'd has to those ideas perceived by another."[34] Unfortunately a nominalist cannot consistently talk about blueness or heat as ideas perceived by another. Berkeley is aware of his inconsistency in admitting other souls and tries somewhat lamely to patch up the admission of spiritual as a general idea by denying that it is an idea at all. This distinction is attempted in detail in the second edition of the *Principles* by saying that we "have some knowledge or notion of our own minds, of spirits, and active beings, whereof in a strict sense we have not ideas."[35] As he grew older Berkeley appears to have seen the conflict more

[33] 140.
[34] 140.
[35] 89 (second edition only according to Jessop).

and more clearly and rests his immaterialism wholly on Platonic considerations. A. C. Fraser reports that the third edition of *Alciphron*, which was published in the last year of Berkeley's life, omits "the sections in the seventh dialogue which contain a defence of the early phenomenalistic Nominalism."[36]

At this point I conclude. I have cited passages to show that in the *Principles* Berkeley argues from a nominalistic account of language that limits the significance of statements to particulars present at that time to my mind. I have claimed that his inclusion of significant statements about other minds is inconsistent with this nominalism. Thus his system stands in an odd and embarrassing position. In order to prove that it is contradictory to suppose that there exists anything not in my mind, he maintains his version of nominalism is true. Then since there are true statements not about any particulars in my mind, he offers to explain them by particulars in some other mind. If, however, this device of other minds is admitted, nominalism has been abandoned and the previous proof is destroyed. Berkeley himself chose to resolve this inconsistency by abandoning nominalism. Solipsists and phenomenalists have chosen to abandon the significance of statements about some one else's thoughts and feelings. I think we would reach a more satisfactory result if we were to revise Berkeley's nominalism. I believe it can be done without embracing Platonic universals, but that is another story.

[36] A. C. Fraser, *Berkeley*, pp. 188–189.

Richard J. Van Iten / Berkeley's

alleged solipsism

Berkeley's nominalism is sometimes mistaken for what it is not. When it is, Berkeley is mistaken for what he is not. For example, Hay, by misinterpreting Berkeley's nominalism, claims, mistakenly, that Berkeley is a solipsist.[1] In this paper I hope to show what Berkeley's nominalism is and what it is not, thus clarifying the connection between it and his alleged solipsism. More specifically, I shall show that Berkeley's nominalism does not entail solipsism.

From REVUE INTERNATIONALE DE PHILOSOPHIE, XVI, No. 61–62 (1962), fasc. 3–4, pp. 447–452. Reprinted by permission of the author and the REVUE INTERNATIONALE DE PHILOSOPHIE, Brussels.
[1] Hay, W. H., "Berkeley's Argument from Nominalism," Revue internationale de philosophie, VII (1953), 19–28 [pp. 37–46, above].

In the original Introduction to the *Principles*[2] Berkeley asserts: "On laying aside all thoughts of the words 'Melampus is an animal,' I have remaining in my mind one naked bare idea, viz. that particular one to which I give the name Melampus. . . . I intend to signify thereby . . . that the particular thing I call Melampus has a right to be called by the name Melampus."

Although the referent of 'Melampus' is a "particular thing," it is not unanalyzable. Indeed, one of Berkeley's most striking ontological innovations is to argue that (C) *Particular things are collections of qualities* and not, as those before him argued, substances together with their qualities.[3] In Sec. 49 Berkeley himself states this innovation simply though forcibly: " . . . to say that a die is hard, extended and square is not to attribute those qualities to a subject distinct from and supporting them, but only an explication of the word *die*."

Berkeley's claim may be explicated as follows. 'This is green,' truly asserted of a colored spot, is so analyzed that 'This' refers to a collection of qualities, 'green' to a member or part of it.

(C) is one cornerstone of Berkeley's ontology. Another is: (P) *Only particular things exist*.[4] This one is the core of his nominalism. Concerning it, two things must be said. First, by 'particular' Berkeley means the sort of thing referred to by 'Melampus,' i.e., a collection of qualities. This explication of Berkeley's use of 'particular' is not the usual one. In fact, I know of no one who so explicates it in analyzing (P). Unfortunately, those, e.g., Hay, who do not so explicate 'particular' are in danger of arguing that Berkeley is a solipsist. Second, by 'exist'

[2] *The Works of George Berkeley*, ed. T. E. Jessop and A. A. Luce (9 vols.; Edinburgh: Thomas Nelson and Sons, 1948–1957), II, 136. All references to Berkeley are from this edition and volume.

[3] Berkeley, p. 41. Note that Berkeley begins the *Principles* with this analysis. Arguments for it are made in the *Dialogues* (cf. p. 175).

[4] Berkeley, p. 192.

Berkeley means perceived, i.e., what exists is what is perceived. In other words, in claiming that 'only particular things exist,' he is claiming that we never perceive *a* quality but only qualities which "are mixed, as it were, and blended together in the same object."[5] Expressed somewhat differently, Berkeley's claim is that we perceive apples, not apple; red things, not red; and so on. Explicated in this way, (P) is at one with Berkeley's attack on abstract general ideas. Indeed, that attack seems designed to prove (P), even though he uses (P) to refute the doctrine of abstract general ideas. Let me explain. On the one hand, Berkeley seems to argue that since we cannot imagine an abstract general idea, only particular things exist. On the other hand, he sometimes argues that since only particular things exist, we cannot imagine abstract general ideas. Be that as it may, granting Berkeley's identification of possible with imaginable, (P) amounts to the denial of abstract general ideas.[6]

By embracing (P), Berkeley embraces nominalism: What exists is what is perceived, namely particular things (i.e., collections of qualities). However, this nominalism only applies to bundles of qualities. It does not apply to the qualities themselves. Thus, we may ask Berkeley: Are the constituents of a particular collection particulars or universals? To express the question differently: Can a simple quality be a constituent of two collections? If Berkeley answers affirmatively, he is a realist in the sense that (R) the constituents are universals; if negatively, he is a nominalist in the sense that (N) the constituents are particulars.

Now for two comments. First, (N) must be carefully dis-

---

[5] Berkeley, p. 27.
[6] In Sec. 10 of the Introduction of the *Principles* (P) is implicit in Berkeley's argument for the impossibility of imagining anything other than a particular thing. In that same section he seems to shift to the view that because we cannot imagine anything that is not particular (P) must be the case.

tinguished from (P). Second, (P) does not entail (N), nor does (N) entail (P). As we shall see, Hay's mistake stems from either not distinguishing them or from believing that (P) entails (N).

Though the distinction between (P) and (N) is clear, Berkeley's attitude towards (N) is not. He does not explicitly answer the question as to whether the constituents are particulars or universals. Moreover, there is little evidence to enable one to decide whether he believed the constituents to be particulars or universals. Consequently, it is extremely difficult to determine whether Berkeley accepted (N) or (R). To overcome that difficulty I shall approach the problem in the following way. I shall show that if one assumes that Berkeley accepts (N) one must also argue, as Hay does, that he is a solipsist, notwithstanding his rejection of it, i.e., solipsism. I shall also show that if one assumes that Berkeley is not a solipsist, then one must argue that he is forced to accept (R).

Let us assume that other minds exist. This assumption together with (N) entails solipsism, i.e., that no two minds could ever be aware of the same thing. Again, assume that simple ideas are perceived. Consider, then, the case of two different minds "seeing" the same simple idea. If simples are construed as particulars, then the idea perceived by, say, my mind is different from that perceived by yours. For, if they were not, they would not be, as we have assumed, particular. That is, simple ideas are particular in the sense that two minds cannot "see" one and the same simple ideas. Stated within the context of Berkeley's analysis of a thing as merely a collection of simple ideas, the assumption of (N) means that two minds could never perceive the same particular thing. That is, since a particular thing is nothing but a collection of simples, no two minds could perceive the same particular thing without perceiving the same simple ideas. The point is that, given (C), *sameness* at the level of particular things must be accounted for by *sameness* at the level of their constituents.

Let us now assume that Berkeley is not a solipsist; i.e., that he affirms that two minds can perceive the (literally) same particular thing. It follows that he must accept (R). For, as we have just seen, (N) entails solipsism.[7]

To approach the same problem from a somewhat different direction, consider the question: Are the ideas of which a mind is aware the *exclusive* property of that mind? Or, are the ideas of which I am aware my ideas—in the sense that they cannot be the ideas of another? There are places at which Berkeley seems to speak that way.[8] They are relatively few. At many other places he emphatically denies the "privacy" of ideas.[9]

". . . it will be objected that from the foregoing principle it follows, things are every moment annihilated and created anew . . . though we hold indeed the object of sense to be noth-

[7] It might be objected that the move to (R) is made too quickly. That is, one might argue that Berkeley can accept (N) and still avoid solipsism. For example, though the ideas we have, "caused" by God, are *private*, i.e., no two minds can perceive the same simple (and hence, complex) ideas, they are *that by which* we are acquainted with a common object or objects. Though this is a view held by the "later Berkeley," (cf. *Alciphron* and *Siris*), in Sections 89 and 90 of the *Principles* he argues (1) ideas are objects of knowledge and (2) they are *public* in the sense that the same particular things, i.e., complex ideas, may be perceived by two minds. In this discussion I shall follow Hay's lead, considering the issue in the context of Berkeley's position as expressed in the *Principles* and *Dialogues*. I point out this later development of Berkeley's philosophy in order to avoid the criticism of Berkelian scholars as well as to indicate the extent to which Berkeley took seriously the problem of solipsism.

[8] Berkeley, p. 248. Here Berkeley allows Hylas to press the problem of solipsism: his answer, "Your difficulty . . . that no two see the same thing, makes equally against the materialists and me," may simply mean that he, too, did not see the distinction between (P) and (N). Notice, too, that this position assumed in the *Dialogues* seems to contradict Berkeley's claims in the *Principles*.

[9] Berkeley, p. 61; p. 80; cf. p. 212.

ing else but ideas which cannot exist unperceived; yet we may not hence conclude that they have no existence except only while they are perceived by us, since there may be some other spirit that perceives them, though we do not.

"Sensible objects may likewise be said to be without the mind in another sense, namely when they exist in some other mind. . . . the things I saw may still exist, but it must be in another mind."

Berkeley's denial of solipsism is clear and emphatic. This I take to be evidence for his realism. We have seen that if Berkeley accepts (N), solipsism follows. Therefore, his rejection of solipsism can be made good only if he also rejects (N) and accepts (R). Since there is no direct evidence for Berkeley's holding (N), or for that matter (R), whereas there is abundant evidence for his rejecting solipsism, it appears wrongheaded to do what Hay does: viz. to impute (N) to Berkeley and argue that he is thereby committed to solipsism. The far more reasonable course is to argue that since Berkeley rejects solipsism, he rejects, if only implicitly, (N). Hay, of course, sees that nominalism and solipsism hang together. However, he fails to see the difference between and independence of (P) and (N).[10] That is why he argues as he does. Hay's failure is a common one; many Berkeley interpreters are guilty of it.

In the Introduction to the *Principles* Berkeley launches an attack on Locke's doctrine of abstract general ideas. Its purpose is to refute the "Platonism" implicit in Locke's theory. Crudely stated, Berkeley construes Locke to be holding the view that qualities (can) *exist* independently of collections, i.e., apart from particular things. The attack is thus motivated by an opposition

---

[10] If Hay does construe Berkeley as a nominalist in the sense of (N), then it is clear that he misconstrues Berkeley's attack on abstract general ideas. As a matter of fact, all of the evidence he offers to show that Berkeley is a nominalist is taken from within the context of that attack. Cf. Hay, pp. 20–21 [pp. 39–40, above].

to the *independent* existence of universals and not, I submit, to universals *per se*. In this respect Berkeley is like Aristotle who criticizes Plato for granting the Forms an *independent* (substance-like) existence. That comparison aside, some have assumed that Berkeley's denial of abstract general ideas is a denial of (R) and thus an admission of (N). Those who do so interpret Berkeley construe ". . . an idea, which considered in itself is particular, becomes general, by being made to represent or stand for all other particular ideas of the same sort . . ."[11] to apply to *all* ideas, simple as well as complex. However, they overlook the fact that Berkeley is concerned with the problem of showing how a particular thing, or an idea of a particular thing, e.g., *a* triangle, is made to represent triangles without construing it as an abstract general idea. Nowhere in the Introduction does he concern himself with simple ideas. Hay himself, rather than offer any new arguments for Berkeley's holding (N), allows this traditional interpretation of Berkeley to speak for him.[12] More-over, he does not explicitly discuss (N). For that reason it is difficult to be certain that Hay confuses (P) with (N). His reference to a "group of present particulars"[13] is certainly pro-vocative: it is my guess that Hay does have (N) in mind at this point. Of course, Berkeley does speak of the constituents of a particular thing as particulars. Consider his assertion that: "I find I have a faculty of imagining, conceiving or representing to myself the ideas of those particular things I have perceiv'd, and of variously compounding and dividing them. . . . But then what-ever eye or nose I imagine they must have some *particular* shape

11 Berkeley, p. 32.
12 Hay, p. 20 [p. 39, above]. Here Hay relies upon Fraser and Hicks in stating his case for Berkeley's nominalism. They, too, fail to distinguish between (P) and (N). Cf. F. Copleston, *A History of Philosophy* (London: Burns and Oates, 1960), IV, 218.
13 Hay, p. 25 [p. 45, above]. This is the sole indication that Hay saw the distinction between (P) and (N). Paradoxically, all of the arguments he gives to establish Berkeley's nominalism support the former, *not* the latter.

and colour. The idea of man that I frame to my self must be either *a* white or *a* black, *a* tawny, *a* straight or *a* crooked, *a* tall or *a* low or *a* middling sized man. *I cannot by any effort of imagination frame to my self an idea of man prescinding from all particulars that shall have nothing particular in it.*"[14]

It is difficult to say whether or not Hay is misled by Berkeley's use of 'particular' in this argument. Be that as it may, the point is that one might well be, especially if one began with the conviction that Berkeley is a nominalist in the sense of (N). But it is clear in the quoted passage that Berkeley is merely contending that a thing must have *a* color, not color; *a* shape, not shape. Used in this way, 'particular' is neutral with regard to the question of whether Berkeley accepts (N) or (R). It would not be had Berkeley argued that a thing must have a unique color in the sense that no other thing could have it. But this is not what he says. At this point it may perhaps be useful to repeat a comment made above: Berkeley's attack on abstract general ideas involves (P). It does not involve either (N) or (R). Nor is it in any way hindered by not involving them. Nor would it be helped if it did. That is, even if Berkeley were to argue for (N), he would still have to argue independently for (P). It does not follow from the particularity of the constituents of bundles that those constituents cannot occur independently of the bundles. That is why I said above that (N) does not entail (P). My own guess is that Berkeley's concern with securing (P) (i.e., rejecting Platonism) was so great that he overlooked the issue concerning the particularity or universality of the constituents.

Thus far I have argued that there is no evidence for imputing (N) to Berkeley. Indeed, I have argued that one ought to impute (R) to him, since he emphatically denies solipsism which is incompatible with (N). Moreover, I have suggested that his antisolipsism is the only evidence relevant to the issue. Never-

[14] Berkeley, p. 125. (The italics are mine.)

theless, there is another kind of evidence for (N) which must be examined.

Recall that in arguing for Berkeley's realism it was shown that his divorce from solipsism is final if and only if he also holds that two minds can "see" the (literally) same simple idea. To solve that problem, i.e., of *sameness*, the constituents of a particular collection must be construed as universals. This solution begets an embarrassment. If Berkeley takes a particular thing to be nothing more than a collection of universals, how can he individuate between, say, *this* yellow square and *that* yellow square? This embarrassment may be made more telling by considering the following situation. Suppose one mind is acquainted with *two* particular things which are alike in all non-relational respects, a possibility insured by (R). Since (R) and (C), i.e., the claim that a particular thing is merely a collection of qualities, preclude solving the problem of individuation,[15] one might argue that Berkeley ought therefore to accept (N). That would be unexceptionable if it were not for the fact that (N) entails solipsism to which Berkeley is emphatically opposed. This embarrassment, *not* the one Hay suggests, is the genuine one for Berkeley. On the one hand, if he solves the problem of individuation, he is forced to solipsism; on the other, if he rejects solipsism, he cannot solve the problem of individuation. Of course, this predicament depends on accepting (C).

It is not idle to remark that Berkeley, though he rejects matter, the traditional *principium individuationis*, does not himself come to grips with that problem. This is merely another way of saying that he does not face up to the problem of choosing between (N) or (R).

---

[15] G. F. Stout uses much the same argument: He, too, analyzes a particular thing as a collection of qualities. To solve the problem of individuation, he argues the constituents of a collection must themselves be particulars. See his "The Nature of Universals and Particulars," *Proceedings of the British Academy,* X (1921–23), 157–172.

Much of what has been said in favor of Berkeley's realism depends upon the distinction that I have drawn between (P) and (N). To illustrate and sharpen that distinction, let us briefly examine Goodman's position. It is strikingly similar to Berkeley's.[16] (For example, both accept (C).) A particular thing—or as Goodman says, a concrete individual—is a bundle of *qualia*. Though he might be unhappy with its formulation, Goodman, like Berkeley, accepts (P). He does so for virtually the same reasons as Berkeley. Indeed, his paper "A World of Individuals"[17] is not too far from being a contemporary restatement of Berkeley's attack on abstract general ideas. At least it is safe to say that both were written in the same spirit. However, Goodman does what Berkeley does not do, viz. face the issue of deciding between (N) and (R). That is, he rejects (N), fittingly labeled *Particularism* by him, and accepts (R). Moreover, he does so without even arguing for the compatibility of (R) and (P). Nor need he; it is obvious that they are.

Goodman comes to grips with the problem of deciding between (N) and (R) because he clearly recognizes the problem of individuation. Berkeley did not recognize that problem; indeed, he may never have seen it. He was too busy with the task of establishing (C), avoiding Platonism and rejecting solipsism.

[16] Nelson Goodman, *The Structure of Appearance* (Cambridge: Harvard University Press, 1951). Here I summarize what I take to be one of the main "ontological themes" of that work. Especially recommended are pp. 30–35 (for a view of Goodman's nominalism) and pp. 107–110 (for his realism). Although Goodman allows that two concrete individuals may have some of their constituents in common, he stipulates that they cannot have *all* of them in common. It is not amiss to say that of the constituents of an individual, even though they are universals, one always "behaves" like a particular.

[17] Nelson Goodman, "A World of Individuals," in *The Problem of Universals*, ed. Bochenski, Church, and Goodman (South Bend, Ind.: University of Notre Dame Press, 1956), pp. 13–31. This paper provides an excellent account of Goodman's anti-Platonism.

G. E. Moore / The refutation

of idealism

Modern Idealism, if it asserts any general conclusion about the universe at all, asserts that it is *spiritual*. There are two points about this assertion to which I wish to call attention. These points are that, whatever be its exact meaning, it is certainly meant to assert (1) that the universe is very different indeed from what it seems, and (2) that it has quite a large number of properties which it does not seem to have. Chairs and tables and mountains *seem* to be very different from us; but, when the whole universe is declared to be spiritual, it is

From MIND, XII, No. 48 (October 1903), 433–453. Moore reprinted this article in his PHILOSOPHICAL STUDIES (London: Routledge and Kegan Paul Ltd., 1922, and New York: Humanities Press Inc., 1960). Reprinted by permission of Mrs. D. M. Moore, MIND, Routledge and Kegan Paul Ltd., and the Humanities Press Inc.

certainly meant to assert that they are far more like us than we think. The idealist means to assert that they are *in some sense* neither lifeless nor unconscious, as they certainly seem to be; and I do not think his language is so grossly deceptive, but that we may assume him to believe that they really are very different indeed from what they seem. And secondly when he declares that they are *spiritual,* he means to include in that term quite a large number of different properties. When the whole universe is declared to be spiritual, it is meant not only that it is in some sense *conscious,* but that it has what we recognise in ourselves as the *higher* forms of consciousness. That it is intelligent; that it is purposeful; that it is not mechanical; all these different things are commonly asserted of it. In general, it may be said, this phrase 'reality is spiritual' excites and expresses the belief that the *whole* universe possesses *all the qualities* the possession of which is held to make us so superior to things which seem to be inanimate: at least, if it does not possess exactly those which we possess, it possesses not one only, but several others, which, by the same ethical standard, would be judged equal to or better than our own. When we say it is *spiritual* we mean to say that it has quite a number of excellent qualities, different from any which we commonly attribute either to stars or planets or to cups and saucers.

Now why I mention these two points is that when engaged in the intricacies of philosophic discussion, we are apt to overlook the vastness of the difference between this idealistic view and the ordinary view of the world, and to overlook the number of *different* propositions which the idealist must prove. It is, I think, owing to the vastness of this difference and owing to the number of different excellences which Idealists attribute to the universe, that it seems such an interesting and important question whether Idealism be true or not. But, when we begin to argue about it, I think we are apt to forget what a vast number of arguments this interesting question must involve: we are apt to assume, that if one or two points be made on either side, the whole case is won. I say this lest it should be thought that any of the arguments which will be advanced in this paper would be sufficient to disprove, or any refutation of them sufficient to prove, the truly interesting and important proposition that reality is spiritual. For my own part I wish it to be clearly understood that I do not suppose that anything I shall say has the smallest tendency to prove that reality is not spiritual: I do not believe it possible to refute a single one of the many important propositions contained in the assertion that it is so. Reality may be spiritual, for all I know; and I devoutly hope it is. But I take 'Idealism' to be a wide term and to include not only this interesting conclusion, but a number of arguments which are supposed to be, if not sufficient, at least *necessary*, to prove it. Indeed I take it that modern Idealists are chiefly distinguished by certain arguments which they have in common. That reality is spiritual has, I believe, been the tenet of many theologians; and yet, for believing that alone, they should hardly be called Idealists. There are besides, I believe, many persons, not improperly called Idealists, who hold certain characteristic propositions, without venturing to think them quite sufficient to prove so grand a conclusion. It is, therefore, only with Idealistic *arguments* that I am concerned; and if any Idealist holds that *no* argument is necessary to prove that reality is spiritual, I shall certainly not have refuted him. I shall, however, attack at least one argument, which, to the best of my belief, is considered necessary to their position by *all* Idealists. And I wish to point out a certain advantage which this procedure gives me—an advantage which justifies the assertion that, if my arguments are sound, they will have refuted Idealism. If I can refute a single proposition which is a necessary and essential step in all Idealistic arguments, then, no matter how good the rest of these arguments may be, I shall have proved that Idealists have *no reason whatever* for their conclusion.

Suppose we have a chain of argument which takes the form: Since A is B, and B is C, and C is D, it follows A is D. In such an argument, though 'B is C' and 'C is D' may both be perfectly true, yet if 'A is B' be false, we have no more reason for asserting A is D than if all three were false. It does not, indeed, follow that A is D is false; nor does it follow that no other arguments would prove it to be true. But it does follow that, so far as this argument goes, it is the barest supposition, without the least bit of evidence. I propose to attack a proposition which seems to me to stand in this relation to the conclusion 'Reality is spiritual.' I do not propose to dispute that 'Reality is spiritual'; I do not deny that there may be reasons for thinking that it is: but I do propose to show that one reason upon which, to the best of my judgment, all other arguments ever used by Idealists depend is *false*. These other arguments may, for all I shall say, be eminently ingenious and true; they are very many and various, and different Idealists use the most different arguments to prove the same most important conclusions. Some of these *may* be sufficient to prove that B is C and C is D; but if, as I shall try to show, their 'A is B' is false, the conclusion A is D remains a pleasant supposition. I do not deny that to suggest pleasant and plausible suppositions may be the proper function of philosophy: but I am assuming that the name Idealism can only be properly applied where there is a certain amount of argument, intended to be cogent.

The subject of this paper is, therefore, quite uninteresting. Even if I prove my point, I shall have proved nothing about the Universe in general. Upon the important question whether Reality is or is not spiritual my argument will not have the remotest bearing. I shall only attempt to arrive at the truth about a matter, which is in itself quite trivial and insignificant, and from which, so far as I can see and certainly so far as I shall say, no conclusions can be drawn about any of the subjects about which we most want to know. The only importance I can claim for the subject I shall investigate is that it seems to me to be a matter upon which not Idealists only, but all philosophers and psychologists also, have been in error, and from their erroneous view of which they have inferred (validly or invalidly) their most striking and interesting conclusions. And that it has even this importance I cannot hope to prove. If it has this importance, it will indeed follow that all the most striking results of philosophy—Sensationalism, Agnosticism and Idealism alike— have, for all that has hitherto been urged in their favour, no more foundation than the supposition that a chimera lives in the moon. It will follow that, unless new reasons never urged hitherto can be found, all the most important philosophic doctrines have as little claim to assent as the most superstitious beliefs of the lowest savages. Upon the question what we have *reason* to believe in the most interesting matters, I do, therefore, think that my results will have an important bearing; but I cannot too clearly insist that upon the question whether these beliefs are true they will have none whatever.

The trivial proposition which I propose to dispute is this: that *esse* is *percipi*. This is a very ambiguous proposition, but, in some sense or other, it has been very widely held. That it is, in some sense, essential to Idealism, I must for the present merely assume. What I propose to show is that, in all the senses ever given to it, it is false.

But, first of all, it may be useful to point out briefly in what relation I conceive it to stand to Idealistic arguments. That wherever you can truly predicate *esse* you can truly predicate *percipi*, in some sense or other, is, I take it, a necessary step in all arguments, properly to be called Idealistic, and, what is more, in all arguments hitherto offered for the Idealistic conclusion. If *esse* is *percipi*, this is at once equivalent to saying that whatever is is experienced; and this, again, is equivalent, in a sense, to saying that whatever is is something mental. But this is not the sense in which the Idealist *conclusion* must maintain that Reality is *mental*. The Idealist *conclusion* is that *esse* is *percipere;* and hence, whether *esse* be *percipi* or not, a further and different discussion is needed to show whether or not it is also *percipere*. And again, even if *esse* be *percipere*, we need a vast quantity of further argument to show that what has *esse* has also those higher mental qualities which are denoted by spiritual. This is why I said that the question I should discuss, namely, whether or not *esse* is *percipi*, must be utterly insufficient either to prove or to disprove that reality is spiritual. But, on the other hand, I believe that every argument ever used to show that reality is spiritual has inferred this (validly or invalidly) from '*esse* is *percipere*' as one of its premisses; and that this again has never been pretended to be proved except by use of the premiss that *esse* is *percipi*. The type of argument used for the latter purpose is familiar enough. It is said that since whatever is, is experienced, and since some things are which are not experienced by the individual, these must at least form part of some experience. Or again that, since an object necessarily implies a subject, and since the whole world must be an object, we must conceive it to belong to some subject or subjects, in the same sense in which whatever is the object of our experience belongs to us. Or again, that, since thought enters into the essence of all reality, we must conceive behind it, in it, or as its essence, a spirit akin to ours, who thinks: that 'spirit greets spirit' in its object. Into the validity of these inferences I do not propose to enter: they obviously require a great deal of discussion. I only desire to point out that, however correct they may be, yet if *esse* is not *percipi*, they leave us as far from a proof that reality is spiritual, as if they were all false too.

But now: Is *esse percipi?* There are three very ambiguous terms in this proposition, and I must begin by distinguishing the different things that may be meant by some of them.

And first with regard to *percipi.* This term need not trouble us long at present. It was, perhaps, originally used to mean 'sensation' only; but I am not going to be so unfair to modern Idealists—the only Idealists to whom the term should now be applied without qualification—as to hold that, if they say *esse* is *percipi,* they mean by *percipi* sensation only. On the contrary I quite agree with them that, if *esse* be *percipi* at all, *percipi* must be understood to include not sensation only, but that other type of mental fact, which is called 'thought': and, whether *esse* be *percipi* or not, I consider it to be the main service of the philosophic school, to which modern Idealists belong, that they have insisted on distinguishing 'sensation' and 'thought' and on emphasizing the importance of the latter. Against Sensationalism and Empiricism they have maintained the true view. But the distinction between sensation and thought need not detain us here. For, in whatever respects they differ, they have at least this in common, that they are both forms of consciousness or, to use a term that seems to be more in fashion just now, they are both ways of experiencing. Accordingly, whatever *esse* is *percipi* may mean, it does *at least* assert that whatever is, is *experienced.* And since what I wish to maintain is, that even this is untrue, the question whether it be experienced by way of sensation or thought or both is for my purpose quite irrelevant. If it be not experienced at all, it cannot be either an object of thought or an object of sense. It is only, if being involves 'experience,' that the question, whether it involves sensation or thought or both, becomes important. I beg, therefore, that *percipi* may be understood, in what follows, to refer merely to what is *common* to sensation and thought. A very recent article states the meaning of *esse* is *percipi* with all desirable clearness in so far as *percipi* is concerned. 'I will undertake to show,' says Mr. Taylor,[1] 'that what makes [any piece of fact] real can be nothing but its presence as an inseparable aspect of *a sentient experience*.' I am glad to think that Mr. Taylor has been in time to supply me with so definite a statement that this is the ultimate premiss of Idealism. My paper will at least refute Mr. Taylor's Idealism, if it refutes anything at all: for I *shall* undertake to show that what makes a thing real cannot possibly be its presence as an inseparable aspect of a sentient experience.

But Mr. Taylor's statement, though clear, I think, with regard to the meaning of *percipi*, is highly ambiguous in other respects. I will leave it for the present to consider the next ambiguity in the statement: *Esse* is *percipi*. What does the copula mean? What can be meant by saying that esse *is* percipi? There are just three meanings, one or other of which such a statement *must* have, if it is to be true: and of these there is only one which it can have, if it is to be important. (1) The statement may be meant to assert that the word 'esse' is used to signify nothing either more or less than the word 'percipi': that the two words are precise synonyms: that they are merely different names for one and the same thing: that what is meant by *esse* is absolutely identical with what is meant by *percipi*. I think I need not prove that the principle *esse* is *percipi* is *not* thus intended merely to define a word; nor yet that, if it were, it would be an extremely bad definition. But if it does *not* mean this, only two alternatives remain. The second is (2) that what is meant by *esse*, though not absolutely identical with what is meant by *percipi*, yet *includes* the latter as *a part* of its meaning. If this were the meaning of 'esse is percipi,' then to say that a thing was real would not be the same thing as to say that it was experienced. That it

---

[1] A. E. Taylor's review of *The Problem of Conduct—A Study in the Phenomenology of Ethics* by J. B. Baille. The review appeared in the *International Journal of Ethics*, XXII (October 1902), 227 ff.

was *real* would mean that it was experienced and *something else besides:* 'being experienced' would be *analytically essential* to reality, but would not be the whole meaning of the term. From the fact that a thing was real we should be able to infer, by the law of contradiction, that it was experienced; since the latter would be *part* of what is meant by the former. But, on the other hand, from the fact that a thing was experienced we should *not* be able to infer that it was real; since it would not follow from the fact that it had one of the attributes essential to reality, that it *also* had the other or others. Now, if we understand *esse* is *percipi* in this second sense, we must distinguish *three* different things which it asserts. First of all, it gives a definition of the word 'reality': asserting that that word stands for a complex whole, of which what is meant by 'percipi' forms a part. And secondly it asserts that 'being experienced' forms a part of a certain whole. Both these propositions may be true, and at all events I do not wish to dispute them. I do not, indeed, think that the word 'reality' is commonly used to include 'percipi'; but I do not wish to argue about the meaning of words. And that many things which are experienced are also something else—that to be experienced forms part of certain wholes, is, of course, indisputable. But what I wish to point out is that neither of these propositions is of any importance, unless we add to them a *third.* That 'real' is a convenient name for a union of attributes which *sometimes* occurs, it could not be worth any one's while to assert: no inferences of any importance could be drawn from such an assertion. Our principle could only mean that when a thing happens to have *percipi* as well as the other qualities included under *esse,* it has *percipi:* and we should never be able to *infer* that it was experienced, except from a proposition which already asserted that it was both experienced and something else. Accordingly, if the assertion that *percipi* forms part of the whole meant by reality is to have any importance, it must mean that the whole is organic, at least in this sense, that the other constituent or constituents of it *cannot* occur without percipi, even if percipi can occur without them. Let us call these other constituents *x*. The proposition that *esse* includes *percipi*, and that therefore from *esse percipi* can be inferred, can only be important if it is meant to assert that *percipi* can be inferred from *x*. The only importance of the question whether the whole *esse* includes the part *percipi* rests therefore on the question whether the part *x* is necessarily connected with the part *percipi*. And this is (3) the third possible meaning of the assertion *esse* is *percipi*: and, as we now see, the only important one. *Esse* is *percipi* asserts that wherever you have *x* you also have *percipi*: that whatever has the property *x* also has the property that it is *experienced*. And this being so, it will be convenient if, for the future, I may be allowed to use the term *'esse'* to denote *x alone*. I do not wish thereby to beg the question whether what we commonly mean by the word 'real' does or does not include *percipi* as well as *x*. I am quite content that my definition of 'esse' to denote *x*, should be regarded merely as an arbitrary verbal definition. Whether it is so or not, the only question of interest is whether from *x percipi* can be inferred, and I should prefer to be able to express this in the form: can *percipi* be inferred from *esse*? Only let it be understood that when I say *esse*, that term will not for the future *include percipi*: it denotes only that *x*, which Idealists, perhaps rightly, include *along with percipi* under *their* term *esse*. That there is such an *x* they must admit on pain of making the proposition an *absolute* tautology; and that from this *x percipi* can be inferred they must admit, on pain of making it a perfectly barren analytic proposition. Whether *x* alone should or should not be called *esse* is not worth a dispute: what is worth dispute is whether *percipi* is necessarily connected with *x*.

We have therefore discovered the ambiguity of the copula in *esse* is *percipi*, so far as to see that this principle asserts two distinct terms to be so related, that whatever has the *one*, which I call *esse*, has *also* the property that it is experienced. It asserts a necessary connexion between *esse* on the one hand and *percipi* on the other; these two words denoting each a distinct term, and *esse* denoting a term in which that denoted by *percipi* is not included. We have, then, in *esse* is *percipi*, a *necessary synthetic* proposition which I have undertaken to refute. And I may say at once that, understood as such, it cannot be refuted. If the Idealist chooses to assert that it is merely a self-evident truth, I have only to say that it does not appear to me to be so. But I believe that no Idealist ever has maintained it to be so. Although this—that two distinct terms are necessarily related—is the only sense which 'esse is percipi' can have if it is to be true and important, it *can* have another sense, if it is to be an important falsehood. I believe that Idealists all hold this important falsehood. They do not perceive that *esse* is *percipi* must, if true, be *merely* a self-evident synthetic truth: they either identify with it or give as a reason for it another proposition which must be false because it is self-contradictory. Unless they did so, they would have to admit that it was a perfectly unfounded assumption; and if they recognised that it was *unfounded*, I do not think they would maintain its truth to be evident. *Esse* is *percipi*, in the sense I have found for it, *may* indeed be true; I cannot refute it: but if this sense were clearly apprehended, no one, I think, would *believe* that it was true.

Idealists, we have seen, must assert that whatever is experienced, is *necessarily* so. And this doctrine they commonly express by saying that 'the object of experience is inconceivable apart from the subject.' I have hitherto been concerned with pointing out what meaning this assertion must have, if it is to be an important truth. I now propose to show that it may have an important meaning, which must be false, because it is self-contradictory.

It is a well-known fact in the history of philosophy that *necessary* truths in general, but especially those of which it is said that the opposite is inconceivable, have been commonly supposed to be *analytic,* in the sense that the proposition denying them was self-contradictory. It was, in this way, commonly supposed, before Kant, that many truths could be proved by the law of contradiction alone. This is, therefore, a mistake which it is plainly easy for the best philosophers to make. Even since Kant many have continued to assert it; but I am aware that among those Idealists, who most properly deserve the name, it has become more fashionable to assert that truths are *both* analytic and synthetic. Now with many of their reasons for asserting this I am not concerned: it is possible that in some connexions the assertion may bear a useful and true sense. But if we understand 'analytic' in the sense just defined, namely, what is proved by the law of contradiction *alone*, it is plain that, if 'synthetic' means what is *not* proved by this alone, no truth can be both analytic and synthetic. Now it seems to me that those who do maintain truths to be both, do nevertheless maintain that they are so in this as well as in other senses. It is, indeed, extremely unlikely that so essential a part of the historical meaning of 'analytic' and 'synthetic' should have been entirely discarded, especially since we find no express recognition that it is discarded. In that case it is fair to suppose that modern Idealists have been influenced by the view that certain truths can be proved by the law of contradiction alone. I admit they also expressly declare that they can *not*: but this is by no means sufficient to prove that they do not also think they are; since it is very easy to hold two mutually contradictory opinions. What I suggest then is that Idealists hold the particular doctrine

in question, concerning the relation of subject and object in experience, because they think it is an analytic truth in this re-
stricted sense that it is proved by the law of contradiction alone.

I am suggesting that the Idealist maintains that object and
subject are necessarily connected, mainly because he fails to
see that they are *distinct*, that they are *two*, at all. When he
thinks of 'yellow' and when he thinks of the 'sensation of yellow,' he fails to see that there is anything whatever in the latter
which is not in the former. This being so, to deny that yellow
can ever *be* apart from the sensation of yellow is merely to deny
that yellow can ever be other than it is; since yellow and the
sensation of yellow are absolutely identical. To assert that yellow is necessarily an object of experience is to assert that yellow
is necessarily yellow—a purely identical proposition, and therefore proved by the law of contradiction alone. Of course, the
proposition also implies that experience is, after all, something
distinct from yellow—else there would be no reason for insist-
ing that yellow is a sensation: and that the argument thus both
affirms and denies that yellow and the sensation of yellow are
distinct, is what sufficiently refutes it. But this contradiction
can easily be overlooked, because though we are convinced, in
other connexions, that 'experience' does mean something and
something most important, yet we are never distinctly aware
what it means, and thus in every particular case we do not notice
its presence. The facts present themselves as a kind of antinomy:
(1) Experience *is* something unique and different from anything
else; (2) Experience of green is entirely indistinguishable from
green; two propositions which cannot both be true. Idealists,
holding both, can only take refuge in arguing from the one in
some connexions and from the other in others.

But I am well aware that there are many Idealists who
would repel it as an utterly unfounded charge that they fail
to distinguish between a sensation or idea and what I will call

its object. And there are, I admit, many who not only imply, as we all do, that green is distinct from the sensation of green, but expressly insist upon the distinction as an important part of their system. They would perhaps only assert that the two form an inseparable unity. But I wish to point out that many, who use this phrase, and who do admit the distinction, are not thereby absolved from the charge that they deny it. For there is a certain doctrine, very prevalent among philosophers now-adays, which by a very simple reduction may be seen to assert that two distinct things both are and are not distinct. A distinc-tion is asserted; but it is *also* asserted that the things distin-guished form an 'organic unity.' But, forming such a unity, it is held, each would not be what it is *apart from its relation to the other.* Hence to consider either by itself is to make an *ille-gitimate abstraction.* The recognition that there are 'organic unities' and 'illegitimate abstractions' in this sense is regarded as one of the chief conquests of modern philosophy. But what is the sense attached to these terms? An abstraction is illegiti-mate, when and only when we attempt to assert of *a part*—of something abstracted—that which is true only of the *whole* to which it belongs: and it may perhaps be useful to point out that this should not be done. But the application actually made of this principle, and what perhaps would be expressly acknowl-edged as its meaning, is something much the reverse of useful. The principle is used to assert that certain abstractions are *in all cases* illegitimate; that whenever you try to assert *anything whatever* of that which is *part* of an organic whole, what you assert can only be true of the whole. And this principle, so far from being a useful truth, is necessarily false. For if the whole can, nay *must*, be substituted for the part in all proposi-tions and for all purposes, this can only be because the whole is absolutely identical with the part. When, therefore, we are told that green and the sensation of green are certainly distinct but yet are not separable, or that it is an illegitimate abstraction to consider the one apart from the other, what these provisos are used to assert is, that though the two things are distinct yet you not only can but must treat them as if they were not. Many philosophers, therefore, when they admit a distinction, yet (following the lead of Hegel) boldly assert their right, in a slightly more obscure form of words, *also* to deny it. The principle of organic unities, like that of combined analysis and synthesis, is mainly used to defend the practice of holding *both* of two contradictory propositions, wherever this may seem convenient. In this, as in other matters, Hegel's main service to philosophy has consisted in giving a name to and erecting into a principle, a type of fallacy to which experience had shown philosophers, along with the rest of mankind, to be addicted. No wonder that he has followers and admirers.

I have shown then, so far, that when the Idealist asserts the important principle 'Esse is *percipi*' he must, if it is to be true, mean by this that: Whatever is experienced also *must* be experienced. And I have also shown that he *may* identify with, or give as a reason for, this proposition, one which must be false, because it is self-contradictory. But at this point I propose to make a complete break in my argument. '*Esse* is *percipi*,' we have seen, asserts of two terms, as distinct from one another as 'green' and 'sweet,' that whatever has the one has also the other: it asserts that 'being' and 'being experienced' are necessarily connected: that whatever *is* is *also* experienced. And this, I admit, cannot be directly refuted. But I believe it to be false; and I have asserted that anybody who saw that '*esse* and *percipi*' *were* as distinct as 'green' and 'sweet' would be no more ready to believe that whatever *is* is *also* experienced, than to believe that whatever is green is also sweet. I have asserted that no one would believe that '*esse* is *percipi*' if he saw how different *esse* is from *percipi*: but *this* I shall not try to prove. I have asserted that all who do believe that 'esse is percipi' identify with it or take as a reason for it a self-contradictory proposition: but this I shall not try to prove. I shall only try to show that certain propositions which I assert to be believed, are false. That they are believed, and that without this belief 'esse is percipi' would not be believed either, I must leave without a proof.

I pass, then, from the uninteresting question 'Is esse percipi?' to the still more uninteresting and apparently irrelevant question, 'What is a sensation or idea?'

We all know that the sensation of blue differs from that of green. But it is plain that if both are sensations they also have some point in common. What is it that they have in common? And how is this common element related to the points in which they differ?

I will call the common element 'consciousness' without yet attempting to say what the thing I so call is. We have then in every sensation two distinct terms, (1) 'consciousness,' in respect of which all sensations are alike; and (2) something else, in respect of which one sensation differs from another. It will be convenient if I may be allowed to call this second term the 'object' of a sensation: this also without yet attempting to say what I mean by the word.

We have then in every sensation two distinct elements, one which I call consciousness, and another which I call the object of consciousness. This must be so if the sensation of blue and the sensation of green, though different in one respect, are alike in another: blue is one object of sensation and green is another, and consciousness, which both sensations have in common, is different from either.

But, further, sometimes the sensation of blue exists in my mind and sometimes it does not; and knowing, as we now do, that the sensation of blue includes two different elements, namely consciousness and blue, the question arises whether, when the sensation of blue exists, it is the consciousness which exists, or the blue which exists, or both. And one point at least is plain: namely that these three alternatives are all different from one another. So that, if any one tells us that to say 'Blue exists' is the *same* thing as to say that 'Both blue and consciousness exist,' he makes a mistake and a self-contradictory mistake.

But another point is also plain, namely, that when the sensation exists, the consciousness, at least, certainly does exist; for when I say that the sensations of blue and of green both exist, I certainly mean that what is common to both and in virtue of which both are called sensations, exists in each case. The only alternative left, then, is that *either* both exist *or* the consciousness exists alone. If, therefore, any one tells us that the existence of blue is the same thing as the existence of the sensation of blue he makes a mistake and a self-contradictory mistake, for he asserts *either* that blue is the same thing as blue together with consciousness, *or* that it is the same thing as consciousness alone.

Accordingly to identify either 'blue' or any other of what I have called '*objects*' of sensation, with the corresponding sensation is in every case, a self-contradictory error. It is to identify a part either with the whole of which it is a part or else with the other part of the same whole. If we are told that the assertion 'Blue exists' is *meaningless* unless we mean by it that 'The sensation of blue exists,' we are told what is certainly false and self-contradictory. If we are told that the existence of blue is inconceivable apart from the existence of the sensation, the speaker *probably* means to convey to us, by this ambiguous expression, what is a self-contradictory error. For we can and must conceive the existence of blue as something quite distinct from the existence of the sensation. We can and must conceive that blue might exist and yet the sensation of blue not exist. For my own part I not only conceive this, but conceive it to be true.

Either therefore this terrific assertion of inconceivability means what is false and self-contradictory or else it means only that *as a matter of fact* blue never can exist unless the sensation of it exists also.

And at this point I need not conceal my opinion that no philosopher has ever yet succeeded in avoiding this self-contradictory error: that the most striking results both of Idealism and of Agnosticism are only obtained by identifying blue with the sensation of blue: that *esse* is held to be *percipi*, solely because *what is experienced* is held to be identical with *the experience of it*. That Berkeley and Mill committed this error will, perhaps, be granted: that modern Idealists make it will, I hope, appear more probable later. But that my opinion is plausible, I will now offer two pieces of evidence. The first is that language offers us no means of referring to such objects as 'blue' and 'green' and 'sweet,' except by calling them sensations: it is an obvious violation of language to call them 'things' or 'objects' or 'terms.' And similarly we have no natural means of referring to such objects as 'causality' or 'likeness' or 'identity,' except by calling them 'ideas' or 'notions' or 'conceptions.' But it is hardly likely that if philosophers had clearly distinguished in the past between a sensation or idea and what I have called its object, there should have been no separate name for the latter. They have always used the same name for these two different 'things' (if I may call them so); and hence there is some probability that they have supposed these 'things' *not* to be two and different, but one and the same. And, secondly, there is a very good reason why they should have supposed so, in the fact that when we refer to introspection and try to discover what the sensation of blue is, it is very easy to suppose that we have before us only a single term. The term 'blue' is easy enough to distinguish, but the other element which I have called 'consciousness'—that which sensation of blue has in common with sensation of green

—is extremely difficult to fix. That many people fail to distinguish it at all is sufficiently shown by the fact that there are materialists. And, in general, that which makes the sensation of blue a mental fact seems to escape us; it seems, if I may use a metaphor, to be transparent—we look through it and see nothing but the blue; we may be convinced that there *is something*, but *what* it is no philosopher, I think, has yet clearly recognised.

But this was a digression. The point I had established so far was that in every sensation or idea we must distinguish two elements, (1) the 'object,' or that in which one differs from another; and (2) 'consciousness,' or that which all have in common —that which makes them sensations or mental facts. This being so, it followed that when a sensation or idea exists, we have to choose between the alternatives that either object alone or consciousness alone or both exist; and I showed that of these alternatives one, namely that the object only exists, is excluded by the fact that what we mean to assert is certainly the existence of a mental fact. There remains the question: Do both exist? Or does the consciousness alone? And to this question one answer has hitherto been given universally: That both exist.

This answer follows from the analysis hitherto accepted of the relation of what I have called 'object' to 'consciousness' in any sensation or idea. It is held that what I call the object is merely the 'content' of a sensation or idea. It is held that in each case we can distinguish two elements and two only, (1) the fact that there is feeling or experience; and (2) *what* is felt or experienced; the sensation or idea, it is said, forms a whole, in which we must distinguish two 'inseparable aspects,' 'content' and 'existence.' I shall try to show that this analysis is false; and for that purpose I must ask what may seem an extraordinary question: namely what is meant by saying that one thing is 'content' of another? It is not usual to ask this question; the term is used as if everybody must understand it. But since I am going to maintain that 'blue' is *not* the content of the sensation of blue; and, what is more important, that, even if it were, this analysis would leave out the most important element in the sensation of blue, it is necessary that I should try to explain precisely what it is that I shall deny.

What then is meant by saying that one thing is the 'content' of another? First of all I wish to point out that 'blue' is rightly and properly said to be part of the content of a blue flower. If, therefore, we also assert that it is part of the content of the sensation of blue, we assert that it has to the other parts (if any) of this whole the same relation which it has to the other parts of a blue flower—and we assert only this: we cannot mean to assert that it has to the sensation of blue any relation which it does not have to the blue flower. And we have seen that the sensation of blue contains at least one other element beside blue—namely, what I call 'consciousness,' which makes it a sensation. So far then as we assert that blue is the content of the sensation, we assert that it has to this 'consciousness' the same relation which it has to the other parts of a blue flower: we do assert this, and we assert no more than this. Into the question what exactly the relation is between blue and a blue flower in virtue of which we call the former part of its 'content' I do not propose to enter. It is sufficient for my purpose to point out that it is the general relation most commonly meant when we talk of a thing and its qualities; and that this relation is such that to say the thing exists implies that the qualities also exist. The *content* of the thing is *what* we assert to exist, when we assert *that* the thing exists.

When, therefore, blue is said to be part of the content of the 'sensation of blue,' the latter is treated as if it were a whole constituted in exactly the same way as any other 'thing.' The 'sensation of blue,' on this view, differs from a blue bead or a blue beard, in exactly the same way in which the two latter differ from one another: the blue bead differs from the blue beard, in that while the former contains glass, the latter contains hair; and the 'sensation of blue' differs from both in that, instead of glass or hair, it contains consciousness. The relation of the blue to the consciousness is conceived to be exactly the same as that of the blue to the glass or hair: it is in all three cases the *quality* of a *thing*.

But I said just now that the sensation of blue was analysed into 'content' and 'existence,' and that blue was said to be *the* content of the idea of blue. There is an ambiguity in this and a possible error, which I must note in passing. The term 'content' may be used in two senses. If we use 'content' as equivalent to what Mr. Bradley calls the *'what'*—if we mean by it the *whole* of what is said to exist, when the thing is said to exist, then blue is certainly not *the* content of the sensation of blue: part of the *content* of the sensation is, in this sense of the term, that other element which I have called consciousness. The analysis of this sensation into the 'content' 'blue,' on the one hand, and mere existence on the other, is therefore certainly false; in it we have again the self-contradictory identification of 'Blue exists' with 'The sensation of blue exists.' But there is another sense in which 'blue' might properly be said to be *the* content of the sensation—namely, the sense in which 'content,' like εἶδος, is opposed to 'substance' or 'matter.' For the element 'consciousness,' being common to all sensations, may be and certainly is regarded as in some sense their 'substance,' and by the 'content' of each is only meant that in respect of which one differs from another. In this sense then 'blue' might be said to be *the* content of the sensation; but, in that case, the analysis into 'content' and 'existence' is, at least, misleading, since under 'existence' must be included *'what* exists' in the sensation other than blue.

We have it, then, as a universally received opinion that

blue is related to the sensation or idea of blue, as its *content*, and that this view, if it is to be true, must mean that blue is part of *what* is said to exist when we say that the sensation exists. To say that the sensation exists is to say both that blue exists and that 'consciousness,' whether we call it the substance of which blue is *the* content or call it another part of the content, exists too. Any sensation or idea is a '*thing*,' and what I have called its object is the quality of this thing. Such a 'thing' is what we think of when we think of a *mental image*. A mental image is conceived as if it were related to that of which it is the image (if there be any such thing) in exactly the same way as the image in a looking-glass is related to that of which it is the reflexion; in both cases there is identity of content, and the image in the looking-glass differs from that in the mind solely in respect of the fact that in the one case the other constituent of the image is 'glass' and in the other case it is consciousness. If the image is of blue, it is not conceived that this 'content' has any relation to the consciousness but what it has to the glass; it is conceived *merely* to be its *content*. And owing to the fact that sensations and ideas are all considered to be *wholes* of this description—things in the mind—the question: What do we know? is considered to be identical with the question: What reason have we for supposing that there are things outside the mind *corresponding* to these that are inside it?

What I wish to point out is (1) that we have no reason for supposing that there are such things as mental images at all—for supposing that blue *is* part of the content of the sensation of blue, and (2) that even if there are mental images, no mental image and no sensation or idea is *merely* a thing of this kind: that 'blue,' even if it is part of the content of the image or sensation or idea of blue, is always *also* related to it in quite another way, and that this other relation, omitted in the traditional analysis, is the *only* one which makes the sensation of blue a mental fact at all.

The true analysis of a sensation or idea is as follows. The element that is common to them all, and which I have called 'consciousness,' really *is* consciousness. A sensation is, in reality, a case of 'knowing' or 'being aware of' or 'experiencing' something. When we know that the sensation of blue exists, the fact we know is that there exists an awareness of blue. And this awareness is not merely, as we have hitherto seen it must be, itself something distinct and unique, utterly different from blue: it also has a perfectly distinct and unique relation to blue, a relation which is *not* that of thing or substance to content, nor of one part of content to another part of content. This relation is just that which we mean in every case by 'knowing.' To have in your mind 'knowledge' of blue, is *not* to have in your mind a 'thing' or 'image' of which blue is the content. To be aware of the sensation of blue is *not* to be aware of a mental image—of a 'thing,' of which 'blue' and some other element are constituent parts in the same sense in which blue and glass are constituents of a blue bead. It is to be aware of an awareness of blue; awareness being used, in both cases, in exactly the same sense. This element, we have seen, is certainly neglected by the 'content' theory: that theory entirely fails to express the fact that there is, in the sensation of blue, this unique relation between blue and the other constituent. And what I contend is that this omission is *not* mere negligence of expression, but is due to the fact that though philosophers have recognised that *something* distinct is meant by consciousness, they have never yet had a clear conception of *what* that something is. They have not been able to hold *it* and *blue* before their minds and to compare them, in the same way in which they can compare *blue* and *green*. And this for the reason I gave above: namely that the moment we try to fix our attention upon consciousness and to see *what*, distinctly, it is, it seems to vanish: it seems as if we had before us a mere emptiness. When we try to introspect the sensation of blue, all we can see is the blue: the other element is as if it were diaphanous. Yet it *can* be distinguished if we look attentively enough, and if we know that there is something to look for. My main object in this paragraph has been to try to make the reader *see* it: but I fear I shall have succeeded very ill.

It being the case, then, that the sensation of blue includes in its analysis, beside blue, *both* a unique element 'awareness' *and* a unique relation of this element to blue, I can make plain what I meant by asserting, as two distinct propositions, (1) that blue is probably not part of the content of the sensation at all, and (2) that, even if it were, the sensation would nevertheless not be the sensation *of* blue, if blue had only this relation to it. The first hypothesis may now be expressed by saying that, if it were true, then, when the sensation of blue exists, there exists a *blue awareness:* offence may be taken at the expression, but yet it expresses just what should be and is meant by saying that blue is, in this case, a *content* of consciousness or experience. Whether or not, when I have the sensation of blue, my consciousness or awareness is thus blue, my introspection does not enable me to decide with certainty: I only see no reason for thinking that it is. But whether it is or not, the point is unimportant, for introspection *does* enable me to decide that something else is also true: namely that I am aware *of* blue, and by this I mean, that my awareness has to blue a quite different and distinct relation. It is possible, I admit, that my awareness is blue *as well* as being *of* blue: but what I am quite sure of is that it is *of* blue; that it has to blue the simple and unique relation the existence of which alone justifies us in distinguishing knowledge of a thing from the thing known, and indeed in distinguishing mind from matter. And this result I may express by saying that what is called the *content* of a sensation is in very truth what I originally called it—the sensation's *object.*

But, if all this be true, what follows?

Idealists admit that some things really exist of which they

are not aware: there are some things, they hold, which are not inseparable aspects of *their* experience, even if they be inseparable aspects of some experience. They further hold that some of the things of which they are sometimes aware do really exist, even when they are not aware of them: they hold for instance that they are sometimes aware of other minds, which continue to exist even when they are not aware of them. They are, therefore, sometimes aware of something which is *not* an inseparable aspect of their own experience. They do *know some* things which are *not* a mere part or content of their experience. And what my analysis of sensation has been designed to show is, that whenever I have a mere sensation or idea, the fact is that I am then aware of something which is equally and in the same sense *not* an inseparable aspect of my experience. The awareness which I have maintained to be included in sensation is the very same unique fact which constitutes every kind of knowledge: 'blue' is as much an object, and as little a mere content, of my experience, when I experience it, as the most exalted and independent real thing of which I am ever aware. There is, therefore, no question of how we are to 'get outside the circle of our own ideas and sensations.' Merely to have a sensation is already to *be* outside that circle. It is to know something which is as truly and really *not* a part of *my* experience, as anything which I can ever know.

Now I think I am not mistaken in asserting that the reason why Idealists suppose that everything which *is* must be an inseparable aspect of some experience, is that they suppose some things, at least, to be inseparable aspects of *their* experience. And there is certainly nothing which they are so firmly convinced to be an inseparable aspect of their experience as what they call the *content* of their ideas and sensations. If, therefore, *this* turns out in every case, whether it be also the content or not, to be at least *not* an inseparable aspect of the experience of it, it will be readily admitted that nothing else which *we* experience ever is such an inseparable aspect. But if we never experience anything but what is *not* an inseparable aspect of *that* experience, how can we infer that anything whatever, let alone *everything*, is an inseparable aspect of *any* experience? How utterly unfounded is the assumption that '*esse* is *percipi*' appears in the clearest light.

But further I think it may be seen that if the object of an Idealist's sensation were, as he supposes, *not* the object but merely the content of that sensation, if, that is to say, it really were an inseparable aspect of his experience, each Idealist could never be aware either of himself or of any other real thing. For the relation of a sensation to its object is certainly the same as that of any other instance of experience to its object; and this, I think, is generally admitted even by Idealists: they state as readily that *what* is judged or thought or perceived is the *content* of that judgment or thought or perception, as that blue is the content of the sensation of blue. But, if so, then, when any Idealist thinks he is *aware* of himself or of any one else, this cannot really be the case. The fact is, on his own theory, that himself and that other person are in reality mere *contents* of an awareness, which is aware *of* nothing whatever. All that can be said is that there is an awareness in him, *with* a certain content: it can never be true that there is in him a consciousness *of* anything. And similarly he is never aware either of the fact that he exists or that reality is spiritual. The real fact, which he describes in those terms, is that his existence and the spirituality of reality are *contents* of an awareness, which is aware of nothing—certainly not, then, of its own content.

And further if everything, of which he thinks he is aware, is in reality merely a content of his own experience he has certainly no *reason* for holding that anything does exist except himself: it will, of course, be possible that other persons do exist; solipsism will not be necessarily true; but he cannot possibly infer from anything he holds that it is not true. That he himself exists will of course follow from his premiss that many things are contents of *his* experience. But since everything, of which he thinks himself aware, is in reality merely an inseparable aspect of that awareness; this premiss allows no inference that any of these contents, far less any other consciousness, exists at all except as an inseparable aspect of his awareness, that is, as part of himself.

Such, and not those which he takes to follow from it, are the consequences which *do* follow from the Idealist's supposition that the object of an experience is in reality merely a content or inseparable aspect of that experience. If, on the other hand, we clearly recognise the nature of that peculiar relation which I have called awareness of anything'; if we see that *this* is involved equally in the analysis of *every* experience—from the merest sensation to the most developed perception or reflexion, and that *this* is in fact the only essential element in an experience—the only thing that is both common and peculiar to all experiences—the only thing which gives us reason to call any fact mental; if, further, we recognise that this awareness is and must be in all cases of such a nature that its object, when we are aware of it, is precisely what it would be, if we were not aware: then it becomes plain that the existence of a table in space is related to my experience of *it* in precisely the same way as the existence of my own experience is related to my experience of *that*. Of both we are merely aware: if we are aware that the one exists, we are aware in precisely the same sense that the other exists; and if it is true that my experience can exist, even when I do not happen to be aware of its existence, we have exactly the same reason for supposing that the table can do so also. When, therefore, Berkeley supposed that the only thing of which I am directly aware is my own sensations and ideas, he supposed what was false; and when Kant supposed that the objectivity of things in space *consisted* in the fact that they were 'Vorstellungen' having to one another different relations from those which the same 'Vorstellungen' have to one another in subjective experience, he supposed what was equally false. I am as directly aware of the existence of material things in space as of my own sensations; and *what* I am aware of with regard to each is exactly the same—namely that in one case the material thing, and in the other case my sensation does really exist. The question requiring to be asked about material things is thus not: What reason have we for supposing that anything exists *corresponding* to our sensations? but: What reason have we for supposing that material things do *not* exist, since *their* existence has precisely the same evidence as that of our sensations? That either exist *may* be false; but if it is a reason for doubting the existence of matter, that it is an inseparable aspect of our experience, the same reasoning will prove conclusively that our experience does not exist either, since that must also be an inseparable aspect of our experience of *it*. The only *reasonable* alternative to the admission that matter exists *as well as* spirit, is absolute Scepticism—that, as likely as not *nothing* exists at all. All other suppositions—the Agnostic's, that something, at all events, does exist, as much as the Idealist's, that spirit does —are, if we have no reason for believing in matter, as baseless as the grossest superstitions.

W. T. Stace / The refutation

of realism

More than thirty years have now elapsed since Prof. Moore published in *Mind* his famous article, "The Refutation of Idealism." Therewith the curtain rose upon the episode of contemporary British realism. After three decades perhaps the time is now ripe for the inauguration of another episode. And it is but fitting that "The Refutation of Realism" should appear on the same stage as its famous predecessor.

I shall not gird at realism because its exponents disagree among themselves as to what precisely their philosophy teaches. But disagreements certainly exist, and they make it difficult for a would-be refuter to know precisely what is the proposition which he ought to refute. It is far from certain that all idealists

From MIND, XLIII (April 1934), 145–155. Reprinted by permission of the author and MIND.

would agree that the idealism which Prof. Moore purported to refute represented adequately, or even inadequately, their views. And it may be that a similar criticism will be urged by realists against what I shall here have to say. But I must take my courage in my hands. Realists, it seems to me, agree in asserting that "some entities sometimes exist without being experienced by any finite mind." This, at any rate, is the proposition which I shall undertake to refute.

I insert the word "finite" in this formula because if I wrote "some entities exist without being experienced by any mind," it might be objected that the proposition so framed would imply that some entities exist of which God is ignorant, if there is such a being as God, and that it is not certain that all realists would wish to assert this. I think that we can very well leave God out of the discussion. In front of me is a piece of paper. I assume that the realist believes that this paper will continue to exist when it is put away in my desk for the night, and when no finite mind is experiencing it. He *may* also believe that it will continue to exist even if God is not experiencing it. But he must *at least* assert that it will exist when no finite mind is experiencing it. That, I think, is essential to his position. And therefore to refute that proposition will be to refute realism. In what follows, therefore, when I speak of minds I must be understood as referring to finite minds.

Possibly I shall be told that although realists probably do as a matter of fact believe that some entities exist unexperienced, yet this is not the essence of realism. Its essence, it may be said, is the belief that the relation between knowledge and its object is such that the knowledge makes no difference to the object, so that the object *might* exist without being known, whether as a matter of fact it does so exist or not.

But it would seem that there could be no point in asserting that entities *might* exist unexperienced, unless as a matter of fact they at least sometimes do so exist. To prove that the universe *might* have the property X, if as a matter of fact the universe has no such property, would seem to be a useless proceeding which no philosophy surely would take as its central contribution to truth. And I think that the only reason why realists are anxious to show that objects are such, and that the relation between knowledge and object is such, that objects might exist unexperienced, is that they think that this will lead on to the belief that objects actually do exist unexperienced. They have been anxious to prove that the existence of objects is not dependent on being experienced by minds because they wished to draw the conclusion that objects exist unexperienced. Hence I think that I am correct in saying that the essential proposition of realism, which has to be refuted, is that "some entities sometimes exist without being experienced by any finite mind."

Now, lest I should be misunderstood, I will state clearly at the outset that I cannot prove that no entities exist without being experienced by minds. For all I know completely unexperienced entities may exist, but what I shall assert is that we have not the slightest reason for believing that they do exist. And from this it will follow that the realistic position that they do exist is perfectly groundless and gratuitous, and one which ought not to be believed. It will be in exactly the same position as the proposition "there is a unicorn on the planet Mars." I cannot prove that there is no unicorn on Mars. But since there is not the slightest reason to suppose that there is one, it is a proposition which ought not to be believed.

And still further to clarify the issue, I will say that I shall not be discussing in this paper whether sense-objects are "mental." My personal opinion is that this question is a pointless one, but that if I am forced to answer it with a "yes" or "no," I should do so by saying that they are not mental; just as, if I were forced to answer the pointless question whether the mind is an elephant, I should have to answer that it is not an elephant. I will, in fact, assume for the purposes of this paper that sense-objects, whether they be colour patches or other sense-data, or objects, are not mental. My position will then be as follows: There is absolutely no reason for asserting that these non-mental, or physical, entities ever exist except when they are being experienced, and the proposition that they do so exist is utterly groundless and gratuitous, and one which ought not to be believed.

The refutation of realism will therefore be sufficiently accomplished if it can be shown that we do *not* know that any single entity exists unexperienced. And that is what I shall in this paper endeavour to show. I shall inquire how we could possibly know that unexperienced entities exist, even if, as a matter of fact, they do exist. And I shall show that there is no possible way in which we could know this, and that therefore we do *not* know it, and have no reason to believe it.

For the sake of clearness, let us take once again the concrete example of the piece of paper. I am at this moment experiencing it, and at this moment it exists, but how can I know that it existed last night in my desk when, so far as I know, no mind was experiencing it? How can I know that it will continue to exist to-night when there is no one in the room? The knowledge of these alleged facts is what the realists assert that they possess. And the question is, Whence could such knowledge have been obtained, and how can it be justified? What I assert is that it is absolutely impossible to have any such knowledge.

There are only two ways in which it could be asserted that the existence of any sense-object can be established. One is by sense-perception, the other by inference from sense-perception. I know of the existence of this paper *now* because I see it. I am supposed to know of the existence of the other side of the moon, which no one has ever seen, by inference from various actual astronomical observations, that is, by inference from things actually experienced. There are no other ways of proving the existence of a sense-object. Is either of them possible in the present case?

1) *Sense-perception.* I obviously cannot know by perception the existence of the paper when no one is experiencing it. For that would be self-contradictory. It would amount to asserting that I can experience the unexperienced.

2) *Inference.* Nor is it possible to prove by inference the existence of the paper when no mind is experiencing it. For how can I possibly pass by inference from the particular fact of the existence of the paper now, when I am experiencing it, to the quite different particular fact of the existence of the paper yesterday or to-morrow, when neither I nor any other mind is experiencing it? Strictly speaking, the onus of proving that such an inference is impossible is not on me. The onus of proving that it is possible is upon anyone who asserts it, and I am entitled to sit back and wait until someone comes forward with such an alleged proof. Many realists who know their business admit that no valid inference from an experienced to an unexperienced existence is possible. Thus Mr. Russell says, "Belief in the existence of things outside my own biography must, from the standpoint of theoretical logic, be regarded as a prejudice, not as a well-grounded theory."[1]

I might therefore adopt the strategy of masterly inaction. But I prefer to carry the war into the enemy's camp. I propose to *prove* that no proof of the existence of unexperienced objects is possible.

It is clear in the first place that any supposed reasoning could not be inductive. Inductive reasoning proceeds always upon the basis that what has been found in certain observed

[1] Bertrand Russell, *Analysis of Mind* (London: G. Allen & Unwin Ltd., 1921), p. 133.

cases to be true will also be true in unobserved cases. But there is no single case in which it has been observed to be true that an experienced object continues to exist when it is not being experienced; for, by hypothesis, its existence when it is not being experienced cannot be observed. Induction is generalisation from observed facts, but there is not a single case of an unexperienced existence having been observed on which could be based the generalisation that entities continue to exist when no one is experiencing them. And there is likewise not a single known instance of the existence of an unexperienced entity which could lead me to have even the slightest reason for supposing that this paper ever did exist, or will exist, when no one is experiencing it.

Since inductive reasoning is ruled out, the required inference, if there is to be an inference, must be of a formal nature. But deductive inference of all kinds depends upon the principle of consistency. If $P \supset Q$, then we can only prove Q, *if* P is admitted. From $P \supset Q$, therefore, all that can be deduced is that P and not-Q are inconsistent, and that we cannot hold both P and not-Q together, though we may hold either of them separately.

Hence, if it is alleged that a deductive inference can be drawn from the existence of the paper now, when I am experiencing it, to its existence when no one is experiencing it, this can only mean that to assert together the two propositions, (1) that it exists now, and (2) that it does not exist when no one is experiencing it, is an internally inconsistent position. But there is absolutely no inconsistency between these two propositions. If I believe that nothing whatever exists or ever did or will exist, except my own personal sense-data, this may be a view of the universe which no one would ever hold, but there is absolutely nothing internally inconsistent in it. Therefore, no deductive inference can prove the existence of an unexperienced entity.

Therefore, by no reasoning at all, inductive or deductive, can the existence of such an entity be proved.

Nevertheless, arguments have been put forward from time to time by realists which are apparently intended to prove this conclusion. I will deal shortly with those with which I am acquainted. I am not bound to do this, since I have already proved that no proof of the realists' conclusion is possible. And for the same reason, if there are any arguments of this kind with which I am not acquainted, I am under no obligation to disprove them. But it will be better to meet at least the most well-known arguments.

a) It was Mr. Perry, I believe, who invented the phrase "egocentric predicament." The egocentric predicament was supposed to indicate where lay a fallacy committed by idealists. It consisted in arguing from the fact that it is impossible to discover anything which is not known to the conclusion that all things are known. That any competent idealist ever did use such an argument may well be doubted, but I will waive that point. Mr. Perry's comment was that the egocentric predicament, as employed by idealists, appeared to imply that from our ignorance of unexperienced entities we could conclude to their non-existence, and that to do so is a fallacy.

No doubt such a procedure would be a fallacy. But though Mr. Perry's argument may refute a supposed idealistic argument, *it does not prove anything whatever in favour of realism.* It would be a fallacy to argue that, because we have never observed a unicorn on Mars, therefore there is no unicorn there; but by pointing out this fallacy, one does not prove the existence of a unicorn there. And by pointing out that our ignorance of the existence of unexperienced entities does not prove their non-existence, one does nothing whatever towards proving that unexperienced entities do exist. As regards the unicorn on Mars, the correct position, as far as logic is concerned, is obviously that if anyone asserts that there is a unicorn there, the onus is on him to prove it; and that until he does prove it, we ought not to believe it to be true. As regards the unexperienced entities, the correct position, as far as logic is concerned, is that if realists assert their existence, the onus is on them to prove it; and that until they do prove it, we ought not to believe that they exist. Mr. Perry's argument, therefore, proves nothing whatever in favour of realism.

Possibly all this is admitted and understood by realists. But there seems, nevertheless, to have been a tendency to think that the overthrow of the supposed idealistic argument was a very important matter in forwarding the interests of realism. To point out, therefore, that it actually accomplishes nothing seems desirable.

b) Mr. Lovejoy, in his recent book, *The Revolt against Dualism*, argues that we can infer or at least render probable, the existence of things during interperceptual intervals by means of the law of causation. He writes, "The same uniform causal sequences of natural events which may be observed within experience appear to go on in the same manner when not experienced. You build a fire in your grate of a certain quantity of coal, of a certain chemical composition. Whenever you remain in the room there occurs a typical succession of sensible phenomena according to an approximately regular schedule of clock-time; in, say, half an hour the coal is half consumed; at the end of the hour the grate contains only ashes. If you build a fire of the same quantity of the same material under the same conditions, leave the room, and return after any given time has elapsed, you get approximately the same sense-experiences as you would have had at the corresponding moment if you had remained in the room. You infer, therefore, that the fire has been burning as usual during your absence, and that being perceived is not a condition necessary for the occurrence of the process."[2]

This argument is simply a *petitio principii*. It assumes that we must believe that the law of causality continues to operate in the universe when no one is observing it. But the law of causality is one aspect of the universe, the unobserved existence of which is the very thing to be proved.

Why must we believe that causation continues to operate during interperceptual intervals? Obviously, the case as regards unexperienced processes and laws is in exactly the same position as the case regarding unexperienced *things*. Just as we cannot perceive unexperienced things, so we cannot perceive unexperienced processes and laws. Just as we cannot infer from anything which we experience the existence of unexperienced things, so we cannot infer from anything we experience the existence of unexperienced processes and laws. There is absolutely no evidence (sense-experience) to show that the fire went on burning during your absence, nor is any inference to that alleged fact possible. Any supposed inference will obviously be based upon our belief that the law of causation operates continuously through time whether observed or unobserved. But this is one of the very things which has to be proved. Nor is there the slightest logical inconsistency in believing that, when you first observe the phenomena, unburnt coal existed, that there followed an interval in which nothing existed, not even a law, and that at the end of the interval ashes began to exist.

No doubt this sounds very absurd and contrary to what we usually believe, but that is nothing to the point. We usually believe that things go on existing when no one is aware of

[2] A. O. Lovejoy, *The Revolt against Dualism* (Chicago: The Open Court Publishing Co., 1930), p. 268.

them. But if we are enquiring how this can be *proved,* we must, of course, begin from the position that we do not know it, and therefore that it might not be true.

c) The distinction between sense-data and our awareness of them, which was first emphasised, so far as I know, by Prof. Moore, has been made the basis of an argument in favour of realism: Green, it is said, is not the same thing as awareness of green. For if we compare a green sense-datum with a blue sense-datum, we find a common element, namely awareness. The awareness must be different from the green because awareness also exists in the case of awareness of blue, and *that* awareness, at any rate, is not green. Therefore, since green is not the same thing as awareness of green, green might exist without awareness. Connected with this argument, too, is the assertion of a special kind of relationship between the awareness and the green.

Possibly this argument proves that green is not "mental." I do not know whether it proves this or not, but the point is unimportant, since I have already admitted that sense-data are not "mental." But whatever the argument proves, it certainly does *not* prove that unexperienced entities exist. For suppose that it proves that green has the predicate x (which may be "non-mental" or "independent of mind," or anything else you please), it still can only prove that green has the predicate x during the period when green is related to the awareness in the alleged manner, that is, when some mind is aware of the green. It cannot possibly prove anything about green when no mind is aware of it. Therefore, it cannot prove that green exists when no mind is aware of it.

For the sake of clearness, I will put the same point in another way. Suppose we admit that green and awareness of green are two quite different things, and suppose we admit that the relation between them is *r*—which may stand for the special relation asserted in the argument. Now it is not in any way inconsistent with these admissions to hold that green begins to exist only when awareness of green begins to exist, and that when awareness of green ceases to exist, green ceases to exist. It may be the case that these two quite different things always co-exist, always accompany each other, and are co-terminous in the sense that they always begin and end simultaneously, and that while they co-exist, they have the relation *r*. And this will be so *whatever* the relation *r* may be. And not only is this supposition that they always co-exist not at all absurd or arbitrary. It is on the contrary precisely the conclusion to which such evidence as we possess points. For we never have evidence that green exists except when some mind is aware of green. And it will not be asserted that awareness of green exists when green does not exist.

The argument from the distinction between green and the awareness of it, therefore, does nothing whatever towards proving the realist conclusion that some entities exist unexperienced.

d) It has also been argued that if we identify a green or a square sense-datum with our awareness of it, then, since awareness is admittedly a state of mind, we shall have to admit that there exist green and square states of mind.

This argument is merely intended to support the previous argument that a sense-datum is different from our awareness of it. And as it has already been shown that this proposition, even if admitted, proves nothing in favour of realism, it is not necessary to say anything further about the present argument.

I will, however, add the following. It is not by any means certain, as is here assumed, that awareness is a state of mind, or indeed that such a thing as a *state* of mind exists. For the mind is not static. It is active. And what exists in it are *acts* of mind.

Now the *attention* involved in being aware of a sense-datum is certainly an act of mind. But it is certainly arguable that *bare* awareness of a sense-datum (if there is such a thing as *bare* awareness) would be identical with the sense-datum and would not be an act of mind. For such bare awareness would be purely passive. In that case, the conclusion that there must exist green or square states of mind would not follow.

Moreover, even if we admit that there exist green and square states of mind, what then? I can see no reason why we should not admit it, except that (1) it is an unusual and unexplored view, and (2) it seems to smack of materialism, although I do not believe that it does really involve materialism. This shows that the whole argument is not really a logical argument at all. It is merely an attempt to throw dust in our eyes by appealing to the popular prejudices against (1) unfamiliar views, and (2) materialism.

It is not possible in the brief space at my disposal to make plausible the suggestions contained in the last two paragraphs. A full discussion of them would be necessary and this I have endeavoured to give elsewhere. In the present place, therefore, I must rely upon the strict logical position, which is, that this argument, since it is merely intended to support argument (c) above, and since argument (c) has already been refuted, proves nothing in favour of realism.

By the preceding discussion, I claim to have proved (1) that the existence of an unexperienced entity cannot be known by perception, (2) that it cannot be known by reasoning, and (3) that the arguments commonly relied upon by realists to prove it are all fallacies.

I think it is not worth while to discuss the possible suggestion that the arguments in favour of realism, although not proving their conclusion rigorously, render that conclusion probable. For what has been shown is that no valid reasoning of *any* kind can possibly exist in favour of this conclusion. Any conceivable reasoning intended to prove that unexperienced entities exist must, it has been shown, be *totally* fallacious. It cannot, therefore, lead even to a probable conclusion. The position, therefore, is that we have not even the faintest reason for believing in the existence of unexperienced entities.

That this is the correct logical position seems to be dimly perceived by many realists themselves, for it is common among them to assert that our belief in unexperienced existences is a "primitive belief," or is founded upon "instinctive belief," or upon "animal faith." This suggestion is obviously based upon the realisation that we cannot obtain a knowledge of unexperienced existences either from perception or from reasoning. Since this is so, realists are compelled to appeal to instinctive beliefs.

Such a weak position seems hardly to require discussion. A "primitive belief" is merely a belief which we have held for a long time, and may well be false. An "instinctive belief" is in much the same case. An "instinct," so far as I know, is some kind of urge to *action*, not an urge to believe a proposition. And it is therefore questionable whether there are such things as instinctive beliefs in any strict sense, although, of course, no one will deny that we have beliefs the grounds of which are only dimly, or not at all, perceived. Certainly the psychology of such alleged instinctive beliefs has not been adequately investigated. And certainly we have no good ground for supposing that an instinctive belief (if any such exists) might not be false.

And if we have such an instinctive or primitive belief in unexperienced existences, the question must obviously be asked How, When, and Why such a belief arose in the course of our mental evolution. Will it be alleged that the amoeba has this belief? And if not, why and when did it come into existence?

Or did it at some arbitrarily determined stage in our evolution descend suddenly upon us out of the blue sky, like the immortal soul itself?

Is it not obvious that to base our belief in unexperienced existences on such grounds is a mere gesture of despair, an admission of the bankruptcy of realism in its attempt to find a rational ground for our beliefs?

Strictly speaking, I have here come to the end of my argument. I have refuted realism by showing that we have absolutely no good reason for believing in its fundamental proposition that entities exist unexperienced. Nothing I have said, of course, goes any distance towards proving that entities do *not* exist unexperienced. That, in my opinion, cannot be proved. The logically correct position is as follows. We have no reason whatever to believe that unexperienced entities exist. We cannot prove that they do not exist. The onus of proof is on those who assert that they do. Therefore, as such proof is impossible, the belief ought not to be entertained, any more than the belief that there is a unicorn on Mars ought to be entertained.

It is no part of the purpose of this essay to do more than arrive at this negative result. But lest it should be thought that this thinking necessarily leads to nothing but a negative result, or to a pure scepticism, I will indicate in no more than a dozen sentences that there is the possibility of a positive and constructive philosophy arising from it. That positive philosophy I have attempted to work out in detail in another place. Here, I will say no more than the following. Since our belief in unexperienced existences is not to be explained as either (1) a perception, or (2) an inference, or (3) an "instinctive belief," how is it to be explained? I believe that it can only be explained as a mental construction or fiction, a pure assumption which has been adopted, not because there is the slightest evidence for it, but solely because it simplifies our view of the universe. How it simplifies our view of the universe, and by what detailed steps it has arisen, I cannot discuss in this place. But the resulting conception is that, in the last analysis, nothing exists except minds and their sense-data (which are not "mental"), and that human minds have, out of these sense-data, slowly and laboriously constructed the rest of the solid universe of our knowledge. Unexperienced entities can only be said to exist in the sense that minds have chosen by means of a fiction to project them into the void of interperceptual intervals, and thus to construct or create their existence in imagination.

Richard H. Popkin / Berkeley

and pyrrhonism

Berkeley laid great stress on the vital importance of refuting scepticism in his *Philosophical Commentaries (Commonplace Book)*, *Principles of Human Knowledge*, and *Dialogues Between Hylas and Philonous*, but very little attention has been given to this aspect of his thought. In this paper, I shall try to show that the exploration of this theme sheds some light on the aims, import, and possible origins of some of Berkeley's ideas.

The complete title of the *Principles* is *A Treatise Concerning the Principles of Human Knowledge, Wherein the chief causes of error and difficulty in the Sciences, with the grounds of Scepticism, Atheism, and Irreligion, are Inquired into.*[1] The

From the REVIEW OF METAPHYSICS, V (1951–52), 223–246. Reprinted by permission of the author and the REVIEW OF METAPHYSICS.
[1] George Berkeley, *The Principles of Human Knowledge* (hereafter re-

complete title of the *Dialogues* is *Three Dialogues Between Hylas and Philonous. The design of which is plainly to demonstrate the reality and perfection of human knowledge, the incorporeal nature of the soul, and the immediate providence of a Deity: in opposition to Sceptics and Atheists. Also to open a method for rendering the Sciences more easy, useful, and compendious.*[2] The introductions to each work, as well as various remarks in the *Philosophical Commentaries*, explain at greater length the author's intention of refuting the sceptics and atheists. In the initial section of the introduction to the *Principles*, Berkeley had said that the attempt to understand the nature of things had led men into all sorts of "uncouth paradoxes, difficulties, and inconsistencies, . . . till at length, having wander'd through many intricate mazes, we find ourselves just where we were, or, which is worse, sit down in a forlorn scepticism."[3] And a few sections later, Berkeley stated that his intention was to discover the sources of the absurdities and contradictions that have entered philosophy, and to eliminate them.[4]

The Preface to the *Dialogues* is almost entirely devoted to stating and restating that the author's intention is to destroy atheism and scepticism. Scepticism arises from distinguishing the real nature of things from their apparent nature, and such

---

ferred to as *Principles*), in *The Works of George Berkeley, Bishop of Cloyne*, ed. A. A. Luce and T. E. Jessop (9 vols.; London and Edinburgh: Thomas Nelson and Sons, 1948–1957), II, 1. (All references to Berkeley's *Principles, Dialogues, Philosophical Commentaries*, and *Theory of Vision Vindicated* are to the text in this edition.)

[2] George Berkeley, *Three Dialogues Between Hylas and Philonous*, p. 147. (This work is hereafter referred to as *Dialogues*.)

[3] Berkeley, *Principles*, Introduction, par. 1, p. 25. In the original draft of this introduction, Berkeley had said, "[men] are often by their principles lead into a necessity of admitting the most irreconcilable opinion or (which is worse) of sitting down in a forlorn scepticism." *Ibid.*, p. 121.

[4] *Ibid.*, Introduction, pars. 4–5, p. 26.

a distinction leads to all kinds of paradoxes and perplexities. Berkeley's principles will rescue mankind from these difficulties. *"If the principles, which I here endeavour to propagate, are admitted for true; the consequences which, I think, evidently flow from thence, are, that atheism and scepticism will be utterly destroyed, many intricate points made plain, great difficulties solved, several useless parts of science retrenched, speculation referred to practice, and men reduced from paradoxes to common sense."*[5]

In his notebooks, the *Philosophical Commentaries*, Berkeley noted several times that scepticism was the view he was opposing, or, that it was the direct opposite of what he was advocating. "The Reverse of the Principle [Berkeley's] I take to have been the chief source of all that scepticism and folly, all those contradictions and inextricable puzzling absurdities, that have in all ages been a reproach to Human Reason."[6] "I am the farthest from Scepticism of any man."[7] And finally, in a letter Berkeley wrote to Sir John Percival on September 6, 1710, regarding the initial reaction to the *Principles*, he said "whoever reads my book with due attention will plainly see that there is a direct opposition between the principles contained in it and those of the sceptics."[8]

In the letter to Percival quoted above, Berkeley revealed

---

[5] *Dialogues*, Preface, p. 168. See also p. 167. The point is reiterated again on p. 168 when Berkeley claimed that the main virtue of his theory, if it is correct, would be that *"the discouragements that draw to scepticism [would be] removed."*

[6] George Berkeley, *Philosophical Commentaries (Commonplace Book)*, in *Works of Berkeley* (London and Edinburgh: Thomas Nelson and Sons, 1948), I, 52, entry 411.

[7] *Ibid.*, p. 70, entry 563. See also p. 15, entry 79, p. 38, entry 304, and pp. 61–62, entry 491.

[8] Benjamin Rand, *Berkeley and Percival, The Correspondence of George Berkeley and Sir John Percival* (Cambridge: Cambridge University Press, 1914), p. 83.

that one of his great fears when he published the *Principles* was that he might be considered a sceptic. Percival's letter of August 26, 1710, indicated that such a consideration was already being presented.[9] And, of course, it is ironic but true that many times in the eighteenth century Berkeley was interpreted as the greatest sceptic of them all, by figures like Andrew Baxter and David Hume.[10]

With all this emphasis on the sceptics and scepticism, it seems reasonable to inquire why Berkeley was so upset about such a view. Whom was he attacking? Why do such people require such a strong refutation?[11] Some scholars, like G. A. Johnston, have stressed the fact that Berkeley wanted to prove that Locke and Descartes, and possibly Malebranche, were sceptics.[12] But apparently little or no attention has been given to the questions of what scepticism represented for Berkeley, why he considered it so horrendous, why he considered it to be in complete opposition to common sense, what part the identification of Cartesianism and Lockeanism with scepticism played in Berkeley's thought, and what the relation of the Berkeleian concept of an attitude towards scepticism was to the conception of scepticism in Berkeley's time. In this paper I shall try to answer these questions at least in part. The answer that I shall offer is a way of interpreting Berkeley in the light of his views about scepticism and the development of Pyrrhonian scepticism at the time. Such an interpretation makes it possible to explain rather

---

[9] *Ibid.*, pp. 80–83.
[10] Cf. Andrew Baxter, *An Enquiry into the Nature of the Human Soul* (2nd ed.; London: [the author,] 1737), Vol. II, Section II, especially pp. 258–260, 267, 270–272, 279–280, 284, and 310; and David Hume, *An Enquiry Concerning Human Understanding* (La Salle, Ill.: Open Court, 1949), Section XII, p. 173*n*.
[11] The same problems could be raised with regard to atheism and atheists, but these are not the concern of this paper.
[12] See for example, G. A. Johnston, *The Development of Berkeley's Philosophy* (London: Macmillan, 1923), pp. 57–59 and 70.

than ignore the emphasis on scepticism in the *Principles, Dialogues,* and *Philosophical Commentaries.* It seems probable that an author who devotes so much time to discussing such a view must have some reason for so doing. In offering my explanation of this reason, I shall also present a hypothesis regarding part of the development of Berkeley's views, in terms of his having had what Pierre Villey has called "la crise pyrrhonnienne"[13]— the realization of the force and consequences of Pyrrhonism. Such a crisis, I believe, must have happened to Berkeley on reading certain passages in Pierre Bayle's *Dictionary,* and led Berkeley to discover his "refutation" of scepticism.

First of all, what did Berkeley mean by scepticism? This doctrine is defined either explicitly or implicitly in the *Philosophical Commentaries,* the *Principles,* and the *Dialogues.* Altogether Berkeley attributes three doctrines to the sceptics: (1) the sceptic doubts everything;[14] (2) the sceptic doubts the validity of sensible things;[15] (3) the sceptic doubts the existence of real objects like bodies or souls.[16] These three different views

---

[13] Cf. Pierre Villey-Desmeserets, *Les Sources et l'Evolution des Essais de Montaigne* (Paris, 1908), II, 230. This is what he believes happened to Montaigne on reading Sextus Empiricus.

[14] Rand, *op. cit.,* p. 83, "the sceptics, who are not positive as to any one truth." Also, in the *Dialogues,* p. 173, Hylas explains that what he means by a sceptic is "one that doubts of everything."

[15] Cf. *Philosophical Commentaries,* p. 61, entry 491. Also in the *Dialogues,* p. 173, Hylas offers as a second definition of a sceptic, "What think you of distrusting the senses, of denying the real existence of sensible things, or pretending to know nothing of them. Is not this sufficient to denominate a man a *sceptic?*" And, in the letter to Percival referred to above, Berkeley stated that he did not wish to be confused with the sceptics, who doubt of the existence of things (Rand, *op. cit.,* p. 83).

[16] Cf. *Philosophical Commentaries,* p. 15, entry 79, "Mem. that I take notice that I do not fall in wth Sceptics Fardella etc, in y^t I make bodies to exist certainly, wch they doubt of." See also entries 304–305, p. 38. This meaning of scepticism is made most clear in the *Principles,* par. 86 ff., p. 78 seq.

constitute the core of the sceptical view for Berkeley. The second and third are corollaries of the first, and were for Berkeley the most interesting features of the position.

Before considering Berkeley's analysis of scepticism at length, let us see how it is related to the discussions of scepticism in the seventeenth and eighteenth centuries.

There are two articles in Pierre Bayle's *Dictionnaire Historique et Critique* which seem to form the basis, or at least part of the basis of Berkeley's conception of scepticism. These are the articles on Pyrrho of Elis and on Zeno the Eleatic. There is much evidence in the *Philosophical Commentaries* that Berkeley was acquainted with these articles. If we examine some of the material in these articles and the way in which Berkeley apparently used this material, and the evidence that Berkeley was referring to this material in the *Philosophical Commentaries*, I believe we shall have found the key to Berkeley's interest in scepticism, and will then be able to interpret Berkeley's discussions and refutations of scepticism in the *Principles* and *Dialogues*.

The first passage from Bayle that is relevant here is in the famous remark B in the article on Pyrrho, where Bayle related a discussion between two abbots about the dangers of Pyrrhonism to religion. One of the abbots is showing the force of Pyrrhonism against Christian theology, and digresses to show the further support that Pyrrhonists might gain from the new Philosophers, and the relation of Pyrrhonism and modern philosophy. Since the development of Cartesianism, we are told,

> none among good Philosophers doubt now but the Sceptics are in the right to maintain, that the qualities of bodies which strike our senses are only meer appearances. Every one of us may say, *I feel heat before a fire,* but not *I know that fire is such in itself as it appears to me.* Such was the style of the ancient Pyrrhonists. But now the new Philosophy speaks more positively:

heat, smell, colours, etc, are not in the objects of our senses; they are only some modifications of my soul; I know that bodies are not such as they appear to me. They were willing to except extension and motion, but they could not do it; for if the objects of our senses appear to us coloured, hot, cold, smelling, tho' they are not so, why should they not appear extended and figured, at rest, and in motion, though they had no such thing. Nay, the objects of my senses cannot be the cause of my sensations: I might therefore feel cold and heat, see colours, figures, extension, and motion, tho' there was not one body in the world. I have not therefore one good proof of the existence of bodies.[17]

Then, after referring to Malebranche for support of this last point, the abbot goes on to demolish the Cartesian argument for the existence of bodies from the fact that God is not a deceiver. Thus, all qualities, both primary and secondary, are reduced to mere appearances, subjective conditions of the mind. The reality of sensible things is denied. Further, since there is no need for real bodies to produce appearance, and there is no proof of the existence of real bodies, the reality of bodies is denied. And this is what Bayle offered as Pyrrhonism developed from the new philosophy, or the new philosophy developed from Pyrrhonism.

In the article on Zeno, in remark G, Bayle argues against the real existence of extension. Once again, he claimed that the sort of Pyrrhonism or sceptical arguments that led philosophers

[17] Pierre Bayle, The Dictionary Historical and Critical (2nd ed.; London, 1737), IV, 654. The reduction of primary qualities to the same status as secondary qualities had already been suggested as Bayle noted here, by the Abbé Foucher in his Critique de la Recherche de la Vérité (Paris, 1675), pp. 44–80, especially pp. 78–80. In Foucher the point is neither made as clearly as in Bayle's writings, nor is as sweeping a conclusion drawn. Foucher's intention was to show how easily the Academic and Pyrrhonian sceptics could destroy Malebranche's and Descartes' philosophy. Bayle's aim was to reduce all modern philosophy to Pyrrhonism.

to deny the reality of secondary qualities should lead them to deny the reality of primary qualities.

Add to this [a set of previous arguments], that all the *ways of suspension* which destroy the reality of corporeal qualities, overthrows the reality of extension. Since the same bodies are sweet to some men, and bitter to others, it may reasonably be inferred that they are neither sweet nor bitter in their nature, and absolutely speaking: The modern Philosophers, though they are no Sceptics, have so well apprehended the foundation of the epoch [epoche, suspense of judgment] with relation to sounds, odours, heat, and cold, hardness, and softness, ponderosity, and lightness, savours and colours, etc., that they teach that all these qualities are perceptions of our mind, and do not exist in the objects of our senses. Why should we not say the same thing of extension? If a being, void of colour, yet appears to us under a colour determined as to its species, figure and situation, why cannot a being, without any extension, be visible to us, under an appearance of determinate extension, shaped, and situated in a certain manner? Observe, also, that the same body appears to us little or great, round or square, according to the place from whence we view it: and certainly, a body which seems to us very little, appears very great to a fly. It is not therefore by their proper, real, or absolute extension that objects present themselves to our mind: whence we may conclude that in themselves they are not extended. Would you at this day argue thus: *Since certain bodies appear sweet to one man, sowre* [sic] *to another, and bitter to another, etc. I must affirm, that in general they are savoury, though I do not know the savour proper to them, absolutely, and in themselves?* All the modern philosophers would explode you. Why then would you venture to say, *since certain bodies appear great to this animal, middle sized to that, and very little to a third, I must affirm, that in general they are extended, though I do not know their absolute extension.*[18]

18 *Ibid.*, V, 612.

This same theme was discussed again in remark H in the article on Zeno, where Bayle asserted:

> There are two Philosophical axioms which teach us, one that nature does nothing in vain; the other, that things are done in vain by more means which might have been as commodiously done by fewer. By these two axioms the Cartesians, whom I am speaking of [Malebranche, Fardella, etc.] may maintain that no such thing as matter exists; for whether it doth or doth not exist, God could equally communicate to us all the thoughts which we have. To say that our senses assure us, with the utmost evidence that matter exists, is not proving it. Our senses deceive us with respect to all the corporeal qualities, not excepting the magnitude, figure, and motion of bodies, and when we believe them, we are persuaded that out of our mind there exists a great number of colours, savours, and other beings, which we call hardness, fluidity, cold, heat, etc, yet it is not true that any such thing exists out of our mind. Why then should we rely on our senses with respect to extension? It may very well be reduced to appearance in like manner with colours.[19]

Bayle then went on to cite passages from Malebranche and Fardella in support of this thesis, and as evidence that the Cartesian proof of the existence of an external world is invalid. Next Arnauld's objections to Malebranche were considered in which Arnauld charged Malebranche with holding *"some extravagant propositions, which strictly taken, tend to the establishment of a very dangerous Pyrrhonism."*[20]

These three passages in Bayle present a basis for a scepticism which denies both the reality of sensible objects, that is, the independent existence of sense objects, and also the reality of the sort of real objects posited by the "new" philosophies of Descartes and Locke, that is, objects consisting of primary

[19] *Ibid.*, V, 614.
[20] *Ibid.*, V, 615.

qualities. All qualities, whether primary or secondary are reduced to the status of appearances or modifications of the soul. A world of real objects which produces the world of appearances is unknown, and possibly unknowable. There is no rational evidence for the existence of an independent reality.

This presentation of Bayle's was apparently intended to offer a new version of Pyrrhonian scepticism, developed from the arguments of the seventeenth-century rationalists. An earlier version had appeared in the writings of Montaigne and Gassendi, based on the classical statement of Pyrrhonism of Sextus Empiricus. In these presentations, the Pyrrhonist was said to believe that only appearances were known, that we had no means of discovering the nature of reality, and that all that was known was only an affection of the mind.[21] Rationalists like Descartes had tried to found their certitude about the nature of the real world on the basis of this new Pyrrhonian theory about appearances, by introducing the distinction between primary and secondary qualities; real qualities of real objects and apparent qualities of unreal objects. The "new" philosophy was thoroughly in keeping with seventeenth-century Pyrrhonism about secondary qualities, and employed many of the stock Pyrrhonian arguments from the ten tropes of classical Pyrrhonism to defend this denial of the reality of secondary qualities. The "new" philosophy was opposed to what Hume later called "the most extravagant scepticism," the view that there

---

[21] Cf. Sextus Empiricus, *Outlines of Pyrrhonism*, Book I, chaps. x–xi, and Book II, chaps. v–vii especially par. 72; Michel de Montaigne, "Apology for Raimond Sebond," in *The Essays of Montaigne*, trans. E. J. Trechmann (New York and London, n.d.), II, 16–17 and 45–50; and Petrus Gassendi, *Syntagma philosophicum, De Logicae fine*, Caput III, "Modi Epoches Scepticorum circa Veritatem, ipsiusque Criteria," in *Opera*, Vol. I (Lyon, 1658).

Seventeenth-century Pyrrhonism is a movement that has been almost completely neglected.

is nothing that can be said of real objects with continued and independent existence outside of our minds,[22] since this "new" doctrine always maintained that there was a real external world composed of objects possessing primary qualities.

Bayle's novel presentation of seventeenth-century Pyrrhonism is original mainly in that the great sceptic had made all the "new" philosophers his allies in Pyrrhonism. The same sort of sceptical arguments that they accepted about secondary qualities applied to the allegedly real primary qualities as well, and hence the "new" philosophy, in spite of all its brave attempts was just a disguised form of that most extravagant scepticism—Pyrrhonism.[23]

Malebranche, Fardella, Lannion, and others had already shown that there were grave difficulties in the Cartesian attempt to establish a demonstration of the existence of a real physical world. However, they had not been willing to accept the sceptical conclusion. Bayle, armed not only with their arguments, but also with his great discovery of the equal ontological status of primary and secondary qualities, was ready to herald and propound the triumph of seventeenth-century Pyrrhonism, that no external reality can be known, and that all that we know is only a set of modifications of our own mind.

Bayle had succeeded in showing that those who denied the reality of sensible things were really complete Pyrrhonists, since

[22] Cf. David Hume, *A Treatise of Human Nature*, Selby-Bigge edition (Oxford: Oxford University Press, 1949), pp. 214 and 228. Arnauld, in *La Logique ou l'Art de Penser*, treated this doubt of whether a real world exists as one of the more fantastic features of Pyrrhonism. See the 1724 edition, pp. xx–xxi.

[23] Cf. Francisque Bouillier, *Histoire de la Philosophie Cartesienne* (3rd ed.; Paris, 1868), II, 487; François Picavet, "Bayle," in *La Grande Encyclopédie* (Paris, 1888), V, 951; Jean Delvolvé, *Religion, Critique et Philosophie Positive chez Pierre Bayle* (Paris, 1906), pp. 252–253 and 256; and F. Pillion, "Le Scepticisme de Bayle," *L'Année Philosophique*, VI (1895), 193–194.

once the objects of our perception are denied any reality, the alleged real world of primary qualities is also denied and destroyed.

I believe it can be shown in two ways that Bayle's type of Pyrrhonism was what Berkeley had in mind when he set out to refute the sceptics: (1) by examining Berkeley's refutation, and (2) by producing evidence that Berkeley had knowledge of, and was aroused by, Bayle's scepticism.

One of Berkeley's themes in the *Philosophical Commentaries, Principles,* and *Dialogues* is that he has discovered the source of scepticism, and can show us how to avoid falling into such an horrendous view. His own position he presents as that one which is farthest from scepticism.[24] The sceptics doubt that we can know if anything really exists. All we can ever be acquainted with are appearances, which are "in the mind." Berkeley claims to have found the basis for this extravagant theory in the distinction between appearances and real objects, or between what is perceived and what exists. And finally, Berkeley tries to show us that all philosophers who believe in the absolute existence of matter will be reduced to scepticism, since their views are always based on such a distinction.

At the beginning of the third dialogue between Hylas and Philonous, Berkeley presents us with the picture of the man who has arrived at "la crise pyrrhonienne." Hylas starts the discussion with a pitiful picture of the limits of human knowledge. He is "plunged into the deepest and most deplorable *scepticism* that ever man was."[25] Hylas informs Philonous that we can know of nothing in this world, we can know naught of the real nature of things, not even if real objects exist. As far as we can tell it is impossible for real objects to exist in Nature.

24 Berkeley, *Principles,* par. 40, p. 57.
25 *Dialogues,* p. 229.

All that we are ever acquainted with are ideas or appearances in our own minds, and no real object could exist with the qualities that we perceive in the appearances.[26]

The dangers of falling into the sort of sceptical despair in which we find poor Hylas are that it is a flagrant violation of our ordinary commonsensical views and practices, and that it paves the way of doubt of the principles of religion. The normal members of the human race have no sceptical doubts of the real existence of the objects they perceive. Every sane man would consider a sceptical view like Hylas's as ridiculous.[27] Thus the philosopher who ends as a sceptic is making a farce of his profession by spending his life *"in doubting of those things which other men evidently know, and believing those things which they laugh at, and despise."*[28] If philosophy is to be more than a useless comedy it must return to the views of the vulgar, and reject as absurd any view that ordinary mortals could not possibly believe. Otherwise, Berkeley believes, philosophy will have no contribution to make to the actual life of man.[29]

In addition there is the danger that the sceptic who doubts if anything exists will lead people to doubt the principles of true religion. When people see the most learned men professing an ignorance of everything, or advancing absurd theories, this may lead to a suspicion that the most sacred and important truths are dubitable. The same sort of reasoning that has ended in scepticism has also led to atheism.[30]

The error on which scepticism is always based, Berkeley

---

[26] *Ibid.*, pp. 227–228.

[27] Cf. *Ibid.*, pp. 172, 211, 229, 237, and 246.

[28] *Ibid.*, Preface, p. 167.

[29] See, for example, *ibid.*, Preface, pp. 167–168.

[30] See *ibid.*, pp. 171–172, and *Principles*, pars. 92–93, pp. 81–82. In Baxter, *op. cit.*, the author, who interprets Berkeley as a sceptic, feels that one main reason for refuting him is that scepticism leads to irreligion. Cf. pp. 280 and 293.

claims, is the distinction between ideas and things, between *percipi* and *esse*. It is this which leads the sceptic to declare that the absolute existence of any object apart from the mind is unknowable.

> All this scepticism follows, from our supposing a difference between *things* and *ideas,* and that the former have a subsistence without the mind, or unperceived. It were easy to dilate on the subject; and show how the arguments urged by *sceptics* in all ages, depend on the supposition of external objects.

> So long as we attribute a real existence to unthinking things, distinct from their being perceived, it is not only impossible for us to know with evidence the nature of any real unthinking being, but even that it exists. Hence, it is, that we see philosophers distrust their senses, and doubt of the existence of heaven and earth, of every thing they see or feel, even of their own bodies.[31]

Berkeley's point here is that the classical Pyrrhonian arguments about illusions, the round tower, the bent oar, the pigeon's neck, etc, are decisive if ideas are distinguished from things. Our ideas vary, and if the variations are attributed to an external reality, contradictions follow. Our ideas are the only things we know, hence we cannot tell what things are like, or if they exist.[32]

All of modern philosophy, from Descartes to Locke and Malebranche, reduces to scepticism. This *does not* mean that modern philosophy is sceptical, since Berkeley is well aware that Descartes, Locke and Malebranche all hold that an unper-

---

31 *Principles*, pars. 87–88, p. 79. See also par. 86, p. 78, par. 92, p. 81, par. 101, p. 85; *Dialogues*, pp. 228–229, 246, and 258; and *Philosophical Commentaries*, entry 606, p. 75. The latter states, "The supposition that things are distinct from Ideas takes away all real Truth, & consequently brings in Universal Scepticism, since all our knowledge & contemplation is confin'd barely to our Ideas."

32 See *Dialogues*, pp. 174–207 and 258.

ceived external world of things exists. They all deny the reality of sensible things, but maintain that a real corporeal world of objects composed of primary qualities actually exists. However, the distinction between primary and secondary qualities is untenable, and besides not a shred of evidence or meaning can be given to the contention that an unperceived corporeal world exists. Thus, in spite of the titanic efforts of Descartes, Locke and Malebranche to support their denial of the existence of sensible qualities without advocating the Pyrrhonian doubt if anything exists, by means of appealing to God's perfection, a *je ne sais quoi,* or the authority of Scriptural revelation, they are all turned into advocates of Pyrrhonism.

This transformation of dogmatists into sceptics is accomplished not by sleight-of-hand, but by Berkeley's appealing to Baylean type arguments about primary qualities, and Malebranchian type attacks on Descartes' proof of the existence of an external world. Besides contending that no one has an abstract general idea of primary qualities, Berkeley attempts to show that the same type of sceptical arguments about the variability of appearances that have led all modern philosophers to deny the real existence of secondary qualities will lead them to deny the reality of primary ones. Figures, extension, solidities and motions all vary according to our state and circumstances. Things appear large to a mite which can hardly be seen at all by us, objects appear to be moving to one observer, and to be stationary to another, etc. "In short, let anyone consider those arguments, which are thought manifestly to prove that colours and tastes exist only in the mind, and he shall find they may with equal force, be brought to prove the same thing of extension, figure and motion."[33]

Hence, as Bayle had already pointed out, the "new" philosophy, in building on the Pyrrhonian arguments about sec-

[33] *Principles,* par. 15, p. 47. See also the first *Dialogue,* pp. 188–192, and *Principles,* pars. 10–14, pp. 45–47.

ondary qualities, would be forced into an unholy alliance with the sceptics on the status of primary qualities. Everything would become only appearance.

To show that there is no evidence or meaning to the claim that material substance exists, Berkeley develops the thesis that matter is undefinable and the contention of Malebranche and Bayle that there is no demonstration of the existence of matter. To show that we can have no idea of matter, Berkeley first appeals to the fact that material substance conceived of as a substratum supporting qualities and causing our perceptions makes no sense if primary qualities have been shown to be mental in the same sense as secondary ones. How can matter "support" extension if it cannot be extended (because extension is "in the mind, too")? How can matter cause perceptions if it does not move (since motion is "in the mind")? Thus, the Baylean claim that there is no difference in ontological status between primary and secondary qualities destroys the conception of matter of the new philosophy. Further, since matter is not perceived, we know nothing of it.[34]

Finally, Berkeley shows that we cannot know of an external material reality by reason. Here he builds on the type of argument of Malebranche and Bayle that the existence of matter is not demonstrable. From this, Berkeley goes on to point out that there is no classification into which matter falls, neither accident, occasion, instrument, etc.[35] When Hylas says that all this does not prove the impossibility of matter's existence, Philonous

[34] Cf. *Principles*, pars. 16–18, pp. 47–48, and *Dialogues*, pp. 198 and 215–217.
[35] Cf. *Principles*, pars. 18–20, pp. 48–49, and *Dialogues*, pp. 217–225. See also Nicolas Malebranche, *De la Recherche de la Vérité*, ed. Geneviève Lewis (Paris: Urin, 1945), III, Éclaircissement vi, 24–33; Nicolas Malebranche, *Dialogues on Metaphysics and Religion*, trans. Morris Ginsberg (New York: Macmillan, 1923), I, v, 75–77; and VI, v–vi, 167–168; and Pierre Bayle, *Dictionary*, art. *Pyrrho*, Remark B, and art. *Zeno*, Remarks G and H.

replies sharply, "You are not therefore to expect I should prove a repugnancy between ideas where there are no ideas; or the impossibility of matter taken in an *unknown* sense, that is no sense at all. My business was only to shew, you meant *nothing;* and this you were brought to own. So that in all your various senses, you have been shewed either to mean nothing at all, or if anything, an absurdity. And if this be not sufficient to prove the impossibility of a thing, I desire you will let me know what is."[36]

At this point the sceptic seems to have triumphed in casting in doubt the view that a real world exists. Once a distinction has been made between appearance and reality, the Pyrrhonist is able to conquer all by showing that anything that we ever come to know is appearance. Rather than trying, as his predecessors did, to stem the onrushing tide of Pyrrhonism by stoutly defending an unperceived reality as a last bulwark against the menace of scepticism, Berkeley follows the sage political advice of our day, "if you can't beat them, join them." After joining forces with the Pyrrhonists, Berkeley is able to show that their attack is innocuous if *esse est percipi.* The others who tried to oppose scepticism by denying the reality of sensible things have been captured by the sceptics.

In order to accomplish this revolution from within, of changing the Pyrrhonian denial of the reality of anything into an affirmation of the reality of the entire sensible universe, Berkeley merely places together two views, one of the vulgar and the other of the seventeenth-century Pyrrhonists which the new philosophers had accepted—"the former being of opinion that *those things they immediately perceive are the real things;* and the latter, *that the things immediately perceived, are ideas which exist only in the mind.* Which two notions put together,

[36] *Dialogues,* p. 226.

do in effect constitute the substance of what I advance."[37] Once Berkeley's criterion of reality is joined to the sceptic's thesis, the latter is completely overturned, and a commonsensical realism results.[38] And from this Berkeley derives, by means of his causal theory of perception, his entire theory of immaterialism.[39]

Thus, the sceptical overthrowing of the believers in material substance is only half of the tale. Once the unseen material world is removed, then we can find the real world right before us where previous philosophers had simply failed to look. The world of sensible things really exists, even though the sceptics have shown that it is only in the mind. The world of appearance is the world of reality. And thus Berkeley can say in triumph in his notebooks, "I am more for reality than any other Philosophers, they make a thousand doubts and know not certainly but we may be deceiv'd. I assert the direct contrary," and "In ye immaterial hypothesis, the wall is white, fire hot, etc."[40] Only Berkeley with his insistence that the world of appearance is the real world could defend common sense realism and challenge Pyrrhonism on its own battlefield, the world of sensible things. Only Berkeley could accept the sceptical arguments and not their nihilistic conclusions and thus overcome "la crise pyrrhonienne." In this way Berkeley overturns the arguments from illusion or variety of experience. Berkeley sees that the Pyrrhonian tropes are only forceful if one assumes a real

---

37 *Ibid.*, p. 262.

38 That Berkeley's theory is a defense of common sense realism has been most forcefully pointed out in F. J. E. Woodbridge's essay, "Berkeley's Realism," in *Studies in the History of Ideas*, ed. the Department of Philosophy, Columbia University (New York, 1918), I, 188–215.

39 See, for example, *Dialogues*, pp. 211 ff.

40 *Philosophical Commentaries*, entry 517a, p. 64, and entry 19, p. 10. See also *Principles*, pars. 3–4, p. 42, pars. 34–35, p. 55 and par. 40, p. 57; *Dialogues*, pp. 229–230, 237–238, 244, 249, 260, and 262; and *Philosophical Commentaries*, entry 305, p. 38.

world apart from sensation. If, instead, one adopts the view that *esse est percipi*, then there are no examples of sense illusions. The only possibility of error with regard to perception is the inference that is drawn from experience. The experiences of the bent rod or the tower that is round at a distance are not illusory experiences, but sensible things. If we infer from these experiences that we will perceive other sensible things, then we may make an incorrect inference. In this manner, what was traditionally the strongest part of Pyrrhonism is rendered harmless by Berkeley's revolution within the citadel of Pyrrhonism.[41]

The secret of this conquest of scepticism, Berkeley is always willing to admit, is the examination of the nature of existence. All previous philosophers, sceptical or otherwise, distinguished things and ideas, *esse* and *percipi*. Hence when the sceptics showed that sensible things were ideas, this appeared to be a devastating result. However, once we understand that *esse est percipi*, Berkeley claimed no sceptical objections can be dangerous. Thus he could make his remark in his notebooks,

> Mem: Diligently to set forth how that many of the Ancient philosophers run into so great absurdity as even to deny the existence of motion and those other things they perceiv'd actually by their senses, this sprung from their not knowing w[t] existence was and wherein it consisted this is the source of all their Folly, 'tis on the discovering of the nature & meaning & import of existence that I chiefly insist. This puts a wide difference between the Sceptics & me. This I think wholly new. I am sure 'tis new to me.[42]

This discovery of the source of the strength of seventeenth-century Pyrrhonism, I believe, follows out of the discoveries of Bayle and Malebranche. All modern philosophers prior to

[41] Cf. *Dialogues*, p. 238.
[42] *Philosophical Commentaries*, entry 491, pp. 61–62.

Berkeley had fallen into the sceptic's trap, and had distinguished appearance from reality. Berkeley alone had been able to accept the sceptics at their word and still offer a theory of the reality of sensible things. Descartes, Locke and Malebranche had all reduced the sensible world to appearance and had struggled valiantly, albeit unsuccessfully, to defend a theory of the real existence of a material world. Berkeley had refused to follow their lead after seeing that the Baylean and Malebranchian type of analysis reduced such attempts to scepticism. Instead Berkeley chose to turn the Baylean type of Pyrrhonism inside out, and use it to defend the reality of sensible things, rather than of an unperceived material substance. Bayle had shown that we only know the existence of sensible things. This, Berkeley showed, was knowing the existence of a real world. This dialectical victory over Pyrrhonism is neatly put in the closing passages of the *Dialogues*. Hylas says, "You set out upon the same principles that Academics, Cartesians, and the like sects, usually do; and for a long time it looked as if you were advancing their philosophical *scepticism*; but in the end your conclusions are directly opposite to theirs."

Philonous replies in his closing speech, "You see, Hylas, the water of yonder fountain, how it is forced upwards, in a round column, to a certain height; at which it breaks and falls back into the basin from whence it rose: to ascent as well as descent, proceeding from the same uniform law or principle of *gravitation*. Just so, the same principles which at first view lead to *scepticism*, pursued to a certain point, bring men back to common sense."[43]

Descartes had accepted a partial Pyrrhonism, a denial of the reality of sensible things, to defend his view of the true nature of things. Bayle, employing his discovery about primary

[43] *Dialogues*, pp. 262–263.

qualities and Malebranche's view about the evidence for the existence of a material world, had unleashed a new "crise pyrrhonienne" by showing that this partial Pyrrhonism quickly becomes a complete scepticism, a denial of all reality. Berkeley with his new principle was able to overcome the crisis by following Bayle to a certain point and then adding a new ending to the sceptic's tale.

Seeing Berkeley in relation to Pyrrhonism also aids in observing the originality of his metaphysics. In his *Berkeley and Malebranche*,[44] A. A. Luce defends the originality of Berkeley's immaterialism, maintaining that such a view was not "in the air" at the beginning of the eighteenth century, but that materialism was. This view has been attacked recently by Anita D. Fritz, in her article, "Malebranche and the Immaterialism of Berkeley,"[45] her main argument being that Malebranche's principles logically imply an immaterialist theory, which was developed by Berkeley. In terms of the interpretation of Berkeley's views on scepticism that I have been presenting in this paper, I think a more precise delineation of Berkeley's originality can be given. At the beginning of the eighteenth century two types of theories were current, one advocating that some sort of material reality existed (Descartes, Locke and Malebranche), the other doubting if anything outside the mind really existed (Baylean Pyrrhonism). Malebranche's "seeing all things in God" tended in the direction of ignoring rather than denying materialism, and making the real world one of essences in God's Mind. Berkeley's immaterialism is a radical innovation in this battle of ideas, based on the Malebranchian theory that God's Mind is the source of all that exists, and the Pyrrhonian insistence

[44] A. A. Luce, *Berkeley and Malebranche* ([Oxford: Oxford University Press,] 1934), pp. 47–48.
[45] Anita Dunlevy Fritz, "Malebranche and the Immaterialism of Berkeley," *Review of Metaphysics*, III (1949–50), 59–80.

that we only know appearances. The innovation is that the real world, produced and sustained by some spiritual substance or substances, is the world of appearance. Though Berkeley and Malebranche might agree that the source of all was immaterial, and that only spirit can be efficacious in this universe, they would never agree on the status of appearance. Malebranche's *esse est concepi* is from another universe than Berkeley's *esse est percipi*. The immaterialism Malebranche was tending to was one of essences supported by Spirit, while Berkeley pictured a world of appearances supported by Spirit. Malebranche saw reality as radically different from appearance, and hence relegated appearances to being mere "modifications of the soul" unlike the real natures that existed in God's Mind. Berkeley refused to give up the Pyrrhonian thesis that all we can ever know is appearance, and in offering a foundation for appearance, offers one that makes appearance real, not unreal. In his notebooks, Berkeley insists that he, unlike Malebranche, has no doubts of the existence of bodies.[46] Malebranche's doctrines

---

[46] *Philosophical Commentaries*, entry 686a, p. 84, and entries 800–801, p. 96. In connection with this difference between the views of Berkeley and Malebranche, and what I claim is the originality of the former, some mention must be made of the thesis of John Wild concerning the nature of Berkeley's philosophy. Professor Wild, in his interesting work, *George Berkeley* (Cambridge, Mass.: Harvard University Press, 1936), attempted to show that Berkeley's philosophical career represented the development of a "concrete logic," which discarded abstractions, and fragmentary pictures of reality, and pointed to a transcendental reality towards which reason was constantly groping. In this interpretation the *Siris* is seen as the culmination of the neo-Platonic or Hegelian philosophy which Berkeley was creating through his dissatisfaction and disillusionment with the philosophy of the times.

It is impossible in the scope of this paper to do justice to Wild's views, but in terms of my contention regarding Berkeley's relation to Pyrrhonism, I think that Wild's interpretation gives too little importance to Berkeley's major contribution to the seventeenth- and eighteenth-century war against Pyrrhonism. Rather than applying a "concrete logic" to

may lead logically to a type of immaterialism, but certainly not to Berkeley's, since the former is still in the Pyrrhonian trap of distinguishing the real from the perceived. The uniqueness of Berkeley's immaterialism is that it provides a basis for the Pyrrhonian world of appearances in the mind.

Reading Berkeley as a challenge to Bayle's Pyrrhonism gives some basis for Berkeley's claim to being the refuter of scepticism. If the passages that I quoted from Bayle's *Dictionary* were known to Berkeley, they might have led him to see that Bayle's monumental discovery about primary qualities and Malebranche and Bayle's destruction of the arguments to prove that a real external world exists, meant that if one denied the reality of sensible things, the reality of all things would follow therefrom. Hence Descartes, Locke and Malebranche would be forced into scepticism. And this in turn might have led to Berkeley's analysis of the sources of scepticism, and his discovery of the new principle by which he escaped the Pyrrhonian conclusion.

When one comes to proving historically that this is what happened, one finds that there is much evidence to make this

---

the issue, Berkeley advanced a common-sense realism, and came out with the startling discovery that in this way the Pyrrhonian arguments could be accepted and rendered innocuous. The Malebranchian philosophy, by rejecting such a realism, could never defeat the sceptical menace. Berkeley certainly deserves recognition for offering this new way out of some of the basic difficulties of modern philosophy.

Berkeley's views about the nature of the reality behind the common-sense world, or on which the common-sense world depended, may have led him on to his later views in the *Siris*. This however does not destroy or detract from the initial originality of the *Principles* and the *Dialogues*. Regardless of what Berkeley's views may have later become, or how his later views may be related ones, one of his main contributions to eighteenth-century philosophy was his new way of dealing with old problems through admitting the force of scepticism, and then showing the harmlessness of the attack if the sense world is the real world.

probable, if not certain. Two great experts on Berkeley, A. A. Luce and T. E. Jessop, have examined the evidence that links Bayle and Berkeley and have apparently come to a growing recognition that it is more than probable that there was a direct connection between Bayle's *Dictionary* and Berkeley's philosophy. In his *Berkeley and Malebranche*, published in 1934, A. A. Luce pointed out that a copy of Bayle's *Dictionary* was sold at the auction of Berkeley's library; Luce said that "I suspect that Bayle exerted considerable influence upon Berkeley, but I cannot prove it."[47] After discussing some of the evidence, Luce concluded his discussion of Bayle by suggesting that Bayle was probably one of Berkeley's important sources ranking next in importance after Malebranche and Locke.[48] In 1944, Luce stated in a note to his edition of the *Philosophical Commentaries* that Berkeley was probably influenced by Bayle, especially by the articles on Pyrrho and Zeno.[49] More recently in his notes to the *Philosophical Commentaries* in a different edition, Luce states categorically that Bayle's *Dictionary*, and especially the articles on Pyrrho and Zeno, "had considerable influence on Berkeley's thought."[50] No reason is offered for coming to this definite conclusion of the matter. Jessop, in his notes to the *Principles*, suggests three places where Berkeley may have been influenced by Bayle's articles on Pyrrho and Zeno.[51]

What evidence there is supports Luce's more definite stand on the matter. As far as I know, Berkeley mentions Bayle only three times in his writings. There are two almost identical references to Bayle in the *Philosophical Commentaries*, entries 358

---

47 Luce, *Berkeley and Malebranche*, p. 53.
48 *Ibid.*, p. 55.
49 George Berkeley, *Philosophical Commentaries*, ed. A. A. Luce (Edinburgh: Thomas Nelson and Sons, 1944), note to entry 358, p. 388.
50 *Philosophical Commentaries*, in *Works of Berkeley*, I, note to entry 358, p. 122.
51 *Principles*, notes on pp. 44, 76, and 95.

and 424, which read, "Malebranche's & Bayle's arguments do not seem to prove against Space, but onely Bodies," and "Bayle's Malebranche's etc. arguments do not seem to prove against space, but only against Bodies."[52] In *The Theory of Vision Vindicated,* Bayle is referred to along with Hobbes, Leibniz and Spinoza as a dangerous enemy of religion.[53] This last reference is of little value here since it appears in a work written long after the *Principles* and the *Dialogues.* It does suggest however that Berkeley had Bayle in mind when he listed as one of the dangers of scepticism that it lead to a denial of the principles of religion.

The two entries in the *Philosophical Commentaries* can easily be read as references to Bayle's discussion in the Pyrrho and Zeno articles, in which case the coupling of the names of Bayle and Malebranche would make sense, since Bayle introduces Malebranche's arguments in both articles.[54] Also, in the Zeno article the discussion starts off with Zeno's arguments about space, before it arrives at a discussion of the status of primary qualities and the existence of bodies and the arguments of Bayle and Malebranche there relate only to bodies and not to space.

Further evidence in the *Philosophical Commentaries* that Berkeley had read Bayle's articles on Pyrrho and Zeno can be

---

[52] *Philosophical Commentaries,* pp. 43 and 53.

[53] George Berkeley, *The Theory of Vision Vindicated,* in *Works,* I, 254. Luce hints in *Berkeley and Malebranche* that Bayle's anti-religious views may be responsible for the almost complete omission of Bayle's name in Berkeley's writings.

[54] In Mrs. Fritz's article, "Malebranche and the Immaterialism of Berkeley," it is suggested that Berkeley is referring to Bayle's *Recueil de Quelques Pièces Curieuses Concernant la Philosophie de Monsieur Descartes.* See Fritz, *op. cit.,* p. 77. However I think this is unlikely since Bayle's interest in that work is in the religious opposition to Descartes, and Bayle makes no arguments there to which Berkeley's remarks are appropriate.

found in entry 79 referring to Fardella, and many of the entries
on infinite divisibility, e.g. number 26. Besides the few entries
that seem almost certainly to refer to Bayle's articles, there are a
tremendous number that are in agreement with Bayle's text. The
Fardella entry states "Mem. that I take notice that I do not fall
in wth Sceptics Fardella, etc., in y^t I make bodies to exist certainly, wch they doubt of."[55] There is no evidence that Berkeley
read Fardella, and he is quoted in Bayle's article on Zeno, Remark H, in a context that could lead to his being coupled with
sceptics.[56] As to infinite divisibility, almost all of Berkeley's
arguments on the subject appear in Bayle's article on Zeno. In
entry 26 Berkeley connects the problem of infinite divisibility
with the problem of external existence, just as Bayle does in the
Zeno article.[57]

The last piece of direct evidence linking Bayle and Berkeley is one that neither Luce nor Jessop seems to have noticed,
that is that the same type of illustrations are used by both Bayle
and Berkeley on the primary quality issue. In showing the extension of things varies as color does both philosophers appeal
to what objects will look like to tiny animals, flies or mites, and
how objects appear under magnification. They also both appeal
to the change in size and shape of objects as we change position.[58] It might be a coincidence that Bayle and Berkeley discovered the same fact about primary qualities, but it could
hardly be a coincidence that they used the same type of illustrations to prove their case.

Thus, considering the popularity of Bayle's *Dictionary*, the

[55] *Philosophical Commentaries*, p. 15.
[56] Bayle, *Dictionary*, V, 614.
[57] *Philosophical Commentaries*, p. 10, and Luce's note in his 1944 edition
of the *Philosophical Commentaries* to entries 26 and 258, pp. 325 and 388.
[58] Bayle, *Dictionary*, art. *Zeno*, remark G, V, 612; and *Dialogues*, pp.
188–189.

fact that a copy was auctioned off from Berkeley's library, the two references in the notebooks to Bayle, the mention of Fardella in the notebooks, the same arguments about infinite divisibility in the notebooks, and the Zeno article, the same theory about primary qualities, and the similarity of illustrations on the matter, I think that we have more than just probable evidence of a historical connection between Berkeley's philosophy and Bayle's *Dictionary*.

As a last bit of evidence in support of interpreting Berkeley as an antagonist of Baylean Pyrrhonism, I should like to appeal to the way it was read by Andrew Baxter and Thomas Reid. Baxter sees Berkeley as a terrible Pyrrhonist, in a class with Bayle or Pyrrho. Berkeley's type of reasoning in denying the material world would lead in turn to denying the spiritual world too, and thus to complete Pyrrhonism. Berkeley's attempt to refute scepticism only leads to the "wildest and unbounded scepticism." Baxter treats Berkeley's view as being a denial that there is a real world anywhere, and such a view he places in the Pyrrhonian tradition. Thus Baxter considers that Berkeley's scepticism is no antidote but actually a worse form of the disease. He says of Berkeley's claim to have refuted scepticism, "This is, I think, as if one should advance, that the best way for a woman to silence those who may attack her reputation, is to turn a common prostitute. He puts us into a way of denying all things, that we may get rid of the absurdity of those who deny some things."[59] Throughout his answer to Berkeley, Baxter keeps developing the relation of Pyrrhonism to modern philosophy, and placing Berkeley in the absurd position of the man who tried to answer Pyrrhonism by advocating it.[60]

[59] Baxter, *Enquiry into the Nature of the Human Soul*, II, 284. The discussion of Berkeley occurs in Section II, pp. 256–344.
[60] A somewhat similar point is made in James Beattie's *An Essay on the Nature and Immutability of Truth, in Opposition to Sophistry and Scep-*

Reid is careful never to accuse Berkeley of being a sceptic like Hume, but treats him as the first to see that the systems of Descartes and Locke lead to scepticism, and that this may be avoided by eliminating the material world from the system. Unfortunately, Reid observes, Hume showed that Berkeley's system, in spite of all attempts to avoid it, led to scepticism too. So that Reid sees Berkeley's historical role in the collapse of the Cartesian type of philosophy as one who saw that it was tending to scepticism, and who thought he could avoid it by his immaterialism.[61]

Thus both of these readings, Baxter's and Reid's, place Berkeley in the context of an opponent of the sceptical tendencies in modern philosophy, and both of these see him, unfortunately, plunging headlong into the greatest of all sceptical debacles.

---

ticism, in *Essays* (Edinburgh, 1776), Part II, chap. ii, sec. 2, pp. 187–189.

Also in Jean Pierre de Crousaz's *Examen du Pyrrhonisme* (La Haye, 1733), p. 97, and *A New Treatise of the Art of Thinking* (London, 1724), I, 42. Berkeley was apparently alluded to by the remark, "Un auteur moderne prétend renverser le Pyrrhonisme, en niant l'Existence des Corps, & n'admettant que celle des Esprits." This view is then shown to be fantastic and unbelievable.

61 Cf. Thomas Reid, *Inquiry into the Human Mind*, I, v and vii, and VII; and Thomas Reid, *Essays on the Intellectual Powers of Man*, II, 10–11. It is interesting to note what Hume says of Berkeley in a footnote after stating Berkeley's argument against general ideas. "This argument is drawn from Dr. Berkeley; and indeed most of the writings of that very ingenious author form the best lessons of scepticism, which are to be found either among the ancient or modern philosophers, Bayle not excepted. He professes, however, in his title-page (and undoubtedly with great truth) to have composed his book against the sceptics as well as against the atheists and free-thinkers. But that all his arguments, though otherwise intended, are, in reality, merely sceptical, appears from this, *that they admit of no answer and produce no conviction.* Their only effect is to cause that momentary amazement and irresolution and confusion, which is the result of scepticism." David Hume, *An Enquiry Concerning Human Understanding*, Section XII, Part I, p. 173n.

The contention of this paper is, then, that Berkeley set out to refute scepticism because of "la crise pyrrhonienne" that Bayle had just brought to light. Bayle, like his later follower, Hume, had turned the whole enterprise of modern philosophy into a new Pyrrhonism—a doubting of the real existence of everything, and an asserting that all that we could ever be acquainted with were mental appearances. This Baylean type of Pyrrhonism was in flagrant violation of common sense, and led, even in the hands of its creator, to free thought and doubt of Christian principles. Berkeley saw, as Reid later did too, that this type of Pyrrhonian scepticism reaches its disastrous conclusions through a distinction between the real and the perceived. The Pyrrhonian contention that all that we ever came in contact with was a set of appearances in the mind, Berkeley believed, was undeniable. But one could avoid the horrendous consequence of this by a new theory of the nature of reality. The theory of the "new" philosophers, that real objects were constituted of primary qualities, was shown to be untenable by Bayle's argument. Their contention that a world of reality was inferable from the world of appearances was shown to be untenable by Malebranche's, Fardella's and Bayle's arguments. Hence the sceptical challenge had to be met by a new theory of reality—the world of appearance is the real world. This thesis coupled with the theory of immaterialism to explain the cause and status of the world of appearance, would provide a new foundation for human knowledge. Baylean Pyrrhonism destroyed the world of the seventeenth-century philosophers. Berkeley tried to construct a new world out of Baylean Pyrrhonism, with scepticism paving the way of truth. Unfortunately, Hume turned the sceptical attack against the new realism of Berkeley and reduced it again to Pyrrhonism, and Reid followed once again with an attempt to find a more material reality safe from the attacks of the sceptics.

Karl R. Popper / A note on

Berkeley as precursor

of Mach and Einstein

I had only a very vague idea who Bishop Berkeley was, but was thankful to him for having defended us from an incontrovertible first premise.

SAMUEL BUTLER

I

The purpose of this note is to give a list of those ideas of Berkeley's in the field of the philosophy of physics which have a strik-

This article first appeared under the title, "A Note on Berkeley as Precursor of Mach," in the BRITISH JOURNAL FOR THE PHILOSOPHY OF SCIENCE, IV (1953–54), 26–36. From CONJECTURES AND REFUTATIONS (New York: Basic Books, Inc., 1962, and London: Routledge and Kegan Paul Ltd., 1963, 1965). © Karl R. Popper 1962, 1963, and 1965. Reprinted by permission of the author, Basic Books, Inc., and Routledge and Kegan Paul Ltd.

ingly new look. They are mainly ideas which were rediscovered and reintroduced into the discussion of modern physics by Ernst Mach and Heinrich Hertz, and by a number of philosophers and physicists, some of them influenced by Mach, such as Bertrand Russell, Philip Frank, Richard von Mises, Moritz Schlick,[1] Werner Heisenberg and others.

I may say at once that I do not agree with most of these positivistic views. I admire Berkeley without agreeing with him. But criticism of Berkeley is not the purpose of this note, and will be confined to some very brief and incomplete remarks in section V.[2]

Berkeley wrote only one work, *De Motu*, devoted exclusively to the philosophy of physical science; but there are passages in many of his other works in which similar ideas and supplementary ones are represented.[3]

The core of Berkeley's ideas on the philosophy of science is in his *criticism of Newton's dynamics*. (Newton's mathematics were criticized by Berkeley in *The Analyst* and its two sequels.) Berkeley was full of admiration for Newton, and no

---

[1] Schlick, under the influence of Wittgenstein, suggested an instrumentalist interpretation of universal laws which was practically equivalent to Berkeley's 'mathematical hypotheses'; see *Naturwissenschaften*, 19 (1931), 151 and 156. For further references see my *Conjectures and Refutations*, n. 23 to section iv of ch. 3.

[2] I have since developed these ideas more fully in my *Conjectures and Refutations*, ch. 3, especially section V.

[3] Apart from *DM* (= *De Motu*, 1721) I shall quote *TV* (= *Essay Towards a New Theory of Vision*, 1709); *Pr* (= *Treatise Concerning the Principles of Human Knowledge*, 1710); *HP* (= *Three Dialogues Between Hylas and Philonous*, 1713); *Alc* (= *Alciphron*, 1732); *An* (= *The Analyst*, 1734); and *S* (= *Siris*, 1744). As far as I know, there does not exist an English translation of *DM* which succeeds in making clear what Berkeley meant to say; and the editor of the latest edition of the *Works* even goes out of his way to belittle the significance of this highly original and in many ways unique essay.

doubt realized that there could have been no worthier object for
his criticism.

II

The following twenty-one theses are not always expressed in
Berkeley's terminology; their order is not connected with the
order in which they appear in Berkeley's writings, or in which
they might be presented in a systematic treatment of Berkeley's
thought.

For a motto, I open my list with a quotation from Berkeley
(*DM*, 29).

1) *'To utter a word and mean nothing by it is unworthy
of a philosopher.'*

2) The meaning of a word is the idea or the sense-quality
with which it is associated (as its name). Thus the words 'absolute space' and 'absolute time' are without any empirical (or
operational) meaning; Newton's doctrine of absolute space and
absolute time must therefore be rejected as a physical theory.
(Cf. *Pr*, 97, 99, 116; *DM*, 53, 55, 62; *An*, 50, Qu. 8; *S*, 271:
'Concerning absolute space, that phantom of the mechanical
and geometrical philosophers, it may suffice to observe that it is
neither perceived by our sense, nor proved by our reason . . .';
DM, 64: 'for . . . the purpose of the philosophers of mechanics
. . . it suffices to replace their "absolute space" by a relative
space determined by the heavens of the fixed stars. . . . Motion
and rest defined by this relative space can be conveniently used
instead of the absolutes. . . .')

3) The same holds for the word 'absolute motion.' The
principle that all motion is relative can be established by appealing to the meaning of 'motion,' or to operationalist arguments.

(Cf. *Pr* as above, 58, 112, 115: 'To denominate a body "moved" it is requisite . . . that it changes its distance or situation with regard to some other body . . .'; *DM*, 63: 'No motion can be discerned or measured, except with the help of sensible things'; *DM*, 62: '. . . the motion of a stone in a sling or of water in a whirled bucket cannot be called truly circular motion . . . by those who define [motion] with the help of absolute space. . . .')

4) The words 'gravity' and 'force' are misused in physics; to introduce force as the cause or 'principle' of motion (or of an acceleration) is to introduce 'an occult quality' (*DM*, 1–4, and especially 5, 10, 11, 17, 22, 28; *Alc*, vii, 9). More precisely, we should say 'an occult metaphysical substance'; for the term 'occult quality' is a misnomer, in so far as 'quality' should more properly be reserved for observable or observed qualities— qualities which are given to our senses, and which, of course, are never 'occult.' (*An*, 50, Qu. 9; and especially *DM*, 6: 'It is plain, then, that it is useless to assume that the principle of motion is gravity or force; for how could this principle be known any more clearly through [its identification with] what is commonly called an *occult quality?* That which is itself occult explains nothing; not to mention that an unknown acting cause might more properly be called a [metaphysical] *substance* rather than a *quality.*')

5) In view of these considerations Newton's theory cannot be accepted as an explanation which is truly *causal,* i.e., based on true natural causes. The view that gravity causally explains the motion of bodies (that of the planets, of free-falling bodies, etc.), or that Newton discovered that gravity or attraction is 'an essential quality' (*Pr,* 106), whose inherence in the essence or nature of bodies explains the laws of their motion, must be discarded (*S,* 234; see also *S,* 246, last sentence). *But it must be admitted that Newton's theory leads to the correct results (DM, 39, 41).* To understand this, 'it is of the greatest importance . . . to dis-

tinguish between *mathematical hypotheses* and the *natures [or essences] of things*.[4] . . . If we observe this distinction, then all the famous theorems of mechanical philosophy which . . . make it possible to subject the world system [i.e., the solar system] to human calculations, may be preserved; and at the same time, the study of motion will be freed of a thousand pointless trivialities and subtleties, and from [meaningless] abstract ideas' (*DM*, 66).

6) In physics (mechanical philosophy) there is no causal explanation (cf. *S*, 231), i.e., no explanation based upon the discovery of the hidden nature or essence of things (*Pr*, 25). '. . . real efficient causes of the motion . . . of bodies do not in any way belong to the field of mechanics or of experimental science. Nor can they throw any light on these . . .'(*DM*, 41).

7) The reason is, simply, that physical things have no secret or hidden, 'true or real nature,' no 'real essence,' no 'internal qualities' (*Pr*, 101).

8) There is nothing physical *behind* the physical bodies, no occult physical reality. *Everything is surface,* as it were; physical bodies are nothing but their qualities. *Their appearance is their reality* (*Pr*, 87, 88).

9) The province of the scientist (of the 'mechanical philosopher') is the discovery, 'by experiment and reasoning' (*S*, 234), of *Laws of Nature*, that is to say, of the regularities and uniformities of natural phenomena.

10) The Laws of Nature are, in fact, regularities or similarities or analogies (*Pr*, 105) in the perceived motions of physical bodies (*S*, 234); '. . . these we learn from experience' (*Pr*, 30); they are observed, or inferred from observations (*Pr*, 30, 62; *S*, 228, 264).

11) 'Once the Laws of Nature have been formed, it be-

---

[4] Concerning the equivalence of '*natures*' and '*essences*' see my *The Open Society and Its Enemies* (Princeton, N. J.: Princeton University Press, 1963), ch. 5, section vi.

comes the task of the philosophers to show of each phenomenon that it is in conformity with these laws, that is, necessarily follows from these principles.' (*DM*, 37; cf. *Pr*, 107; and *S*, 231: 'their [i.e., the "mechanical philosophers' "] province being . . . to account for particular phenomena by reducing them under, and showing their conformity to, such general rules.')

12) This process *may* be called, if we like, 'explanation' (even 'causal explanation'), so long as we distinguish it clearly from the truly causal (i.e., metaphysical) explanation based upon the true nature or essence of things. *S*, 231; *DM*, 37: 'A thing may be said to be mechanically explained if it is reduced to those most simple and universal principles' (i.e., 'the primary laws of motion which have been proved by experiments . . .' *DM*, 36) 'and proved, by accurate reasoning, to be in agreement and connection with them. . . . This means to *explain* and solve the phenomena, and to assign them their *cause*. . . .' This terminology is admissible (cf. *DM*, 71) but it must not mislead us. We must always clearly distinguish (cf. *DM*, 72) between an 'essentialist'[5] explanation with appeals to the nature of things and a 'descriptive' explanation which appeals to a Law of Nature, i.e., to the description of an observed regularity. Of these two kinds of explanation only the latter is admissible in physical science.

13) From both of these we must now distinguish a third kind of 'explanation'—an explanation which appeals to *mathematical hypotheses*. A mathematical hypothesis may be described as a procedure for calculating certain results. It is a mere formalism, a mathematical tool or instrument, comparable to a calculating machine. It is judged merely by its efficiency. It may not only be admissible, it may be useful and it may be admir-

---

[5] The term 'essentialist' (and 'essentialism') is not Berkeley's but was introduced by me in *The Poverty of Historicism* (Boston: Beacon, 1957), and in *The Open Society and Its Enemies*.

able, yet it is *not science:* even if it produces the correct results, it is only a trick, 'a knack' (*An,* 50, Qu. 35). And, as opposed to the explanation by essences (which, in mechanics, are simply false) and to that by laws of nature (which, if the laws 'have been proved by experiment,' are simply true), the question of the *truth* of a mathematical hypothesis does not arise—only that of its *usefulness as a calculating tool.*

14) Now, those principles of the Newtonian theory which 'have been proved by experiment'—those of the laws of motion which simply describe the observable regularities of the motion of bodies—are true. But the part of the theory involving the concepts which have been criticized above—absolute space, absolute motion, force, attraction, gravity—is not true, since these are 'mathematical hypotheses.' As such, however, they should not be rejected, if they work well (as in the case of force, attraction, gravity). Absolute space and absolute motion have to be rejected because they do not work (they are to be replaced by the system of fixed stars, and motion relative to it). ' "Force," "gravity," "attraction,"[6] and words such as these are useful for purposes of reasoning and for computations of motions and of moving bodies; but they do not help us to understand the simple nature of motion itself, nor do they serve to designate so many distinct qualities. . . . As far as attraction is concerned it is clear that it was not introduced by Newton as a true physical quality but merely as a mathematical hypothesis' (*DM,* 17).[7]

15) Properly understood, a mathematical hypothesis does not claim that anything exists in nature which corresponds to it—neither to the words or terms with which it operates, nor to

[6] The italics in the Latin original function here as quotation marks.
[7] This was more or less Newton's own opinion; cf. Newton's letters to Bentley, 17th January, and especially 25th February 1692–93, and my *Conjectures and Refutations,* section iii of ch. 3.

the functional dependencies which it appears to assert. It erects, as it were, a fictitious mathematical world behind that of appearance, but without the claim that this world exists. 'But what is said of forces residing in bodies, whether attracting or repelling, is to be regarded only as a mathematical hypothesis, and not as anything really existing in nature' (S, 234; cf. DM, 18, 39 and especially Alc, vii, 9; An, 50, Qu. 35). It claims only that from its assumptions the correct consequences can be drawn. But it can easily be misinterpreted as claiming more, as claiming to describe a real world behind the world of appearance. But no such world *could* be described; for the description would necessarily be meaningless.

16) It can be seen from this that the same appearances *may* be successfully calculated from more than one mathematical hypothesis, and that two mathematical hypotheses which yield the same results concerning the calculated appearances may not only differ, but even contradict each other (especially if they are misinterpreted as describing a world of essences behind the world of appearances); nevertheless, there may be nothing to choose between them. 'The foremost of men proffer . . . many different doctrines, and even opposite doctrines, and yet their conclusions [i.e., their calculated results] attain the truth. . . . Newton and Torricelli seem to disagree with one another, . . . but the thing is well enough explained by both. For all forces attributed to bodies are merely mathematical hypotheses . . . ; thus the same thing may be explained in different ways' (DM, 67).

17) The analysis of Newton's theory thus yields the following results:

We must distinguish

a) Observations of concrete, particular things.
b) Laws of Nature, which are either observations of regularities, or which are proved ('comprobatae,' DM, 36; this may

perhaps mean here 'supported' or 'corroborated'; see *DM,*
31) by experiments, or discovered 'by a diligent observation
of the phenomena' (*Pr,* 107).

c) Mathematical hypotheses, which are not based on observation but whose consequences agree with the phenomena (or
'save the phenomena,' as the Platonists said).

d) Essentialist or metaphysical causal explanations, which have
no place in physical science.

Of these four, (*a*) and (*b*) are based on observation, and
can, from experience, be known to be true; (*c*) is not based on
observation and has only an instrumental significance—thus
more than one instrument may do the trick (cf. (16), above); and
(*d*) is known to be false whenever it constructs a world of
essences behind the world of appearances. Consequently (*c*) is
also known to be false whenever it is interpreted in the sense
of (*d*).

18) These results clearly apply to cases other than Newtonian theory, for example to atomism (corpuscular theory). In
so far as this theory attempts to explain the world of appearances by constructing an invisible world of 'inward essences'
(*Pr,* 102) behind the world of appearances, it must be rejected.
(Cf. *Pr,* 50; *An,* 50, Qu. 56; *S,* 232, 235.)

19) The work of the scientist leads to something that may
be called 'explanation,' but it is hardly of great value for *understanding* the thing explained, since the attainable explanation is
not one based upon an insight into the nature of things. But it is
of practical importance. It enables us to make both *applications*
and *predictions.* '. . . laws of nature or motions direct us how to
act, and teach us what to expect' (*S,* 234; cf. *Pr,* 62). Prediction
is based merely upon regular sequence (not upon causal sequence—at least not in the essentialist sense). A sudden darkness at noon may be a 'prognostic' indicator, a warning 'sign,' a
'mark' of the coming downpour; nobody takes it as its cause.
Now *all* observed regularities are of this nature even though

'prognostics' or 'signs' are usually mistaken for true causes (*TV*, 147; *Pr*, 44, 65, 108; *S*, 252–254; *Alc*, iv, 14, 15).

20) A general practical result—which I propose to call 'Berkeley's razor'—of this analysis of physics allows us *a priori* to eliminate from physical science all essentialist explanations. If they have a mathematical and a predictive content they may be admitted *qua* mathematical hypotheses (while their essentialist interpretation is eliminated). If not, they may be ruled out altogether. This razor is sharper than Ockham's: *all* entities are ruled out except those which are perceived.

21) The ultimate argument for these views, the reason why occult substances and qualities, physical forces, structures of corpuscles, absolute space, and absolute motion, etc. are eliminated, is this: we know that there are no entities such as these because we know that the words professedly designating them must be meaningless. *To have a meaning, a word must stand for an 'idea'*; that is to say, for a perception, or the memory of a perception; in Hume's terminology, for an impression or its reflection in our memory. (It may also stand for a 'notion,' such as God; but the words belonging to physical science cannot stand for 'notions.') Now the words here in question do not stand for ideas. 'Those who assert that active force, action, and the principle of motion are in reality inherent in the bodies, maintain a doctrine that is based upon no experience, and support it by obscure and general terms, and so do not themselves understand what they want to say' (*DM*, 31).

III

Everybody who reads this list of twenty-one theses must be struck by their modernity. They are surprisingly similar, especially in the criticism of Newton, to the philosophy of physics which Ernst Mach taught for many years in the conviction that it was new and revolutionary; in which he was followed by, for example, Joseph Petzold; and which had an immense influence on modern physics, especially on the Theory of Relativity. There is only one difference: Mach's 'principle of the economy of thought' (*Denkoekonomie*) goes beyond what I have called 'Berkeley's razor,' in so far as it allows us not only to discard certain 'metaphysical elements,' but also to distinguish in some cases between various competing hypotheses (of the kind called by Berkeley 'mathematical') with respect to their *simplicity*. (Cf. (16) above.) There is also a striking similarity to Hertz's *Principles of Mechanics* (1894), in which he tried to eliminate the concept of 'force,' and to Wittgenstein's *Tractatus*.

What is perhaps most striking is that Berkeley and Mach, both great admirers of Newton, criticize the ideas of absolute time, absolute space, and absolute motion, on very similar lines. Mach's criticism, exactly like Berkeley's, culminates in the suggestion that all arguments for Newton's absolute space (like Foucault's pendulum, the rotating bucket of water, the effect of centrifugal forces upon the shape of the earth) fail because these movements are relative to the system of the fixed stars.

To show the significance of this anticipation of Mach's criticism, I may cite two passages, one from Mach and one from Einstein. Mach wrote (in the 7th edition of the *Mechanics*, 1912, ch. ii, section 6, § 11) of the reception of his criticism of *absolute motion*, propounded in earlier editions of his *Mechanics*: 'Thirty years ago the view that the notion of "absolute motion" is meaningless, without any empirical content, and scientifically without use, was generally felt to be very strange. Today this view is upheld by many well-known investigators.' And Einstein said in his obituary notice for Mach ('Nachruf auf Mach,' *Physikalische Zeitschr.*, 1916) referring to this view of Mach's: 'It is not improbable that Mach would have found the Theory of Relativity if, at a time when his mind was still young, the problem of the constancy of velocity of light had agitated the physicists.' This remark of Einstein's is no doubt more than generous.[8] Of the bright light it throws upon Mach some reflection must fall upon Berkeley.[9]

IV

A few words may be said about the relation of Berkeley's philosophy of science to his metaphysics. It is very different indeed from Mach's.

While the positivist Mach was an enemy of all traditional, that is non-positivistic, metaphysics, and especially of all theology, Berkeley was a Christian theologian, and intensely interested in Christian apologetics. While Mach and Berkeley agreed that such words as 'absolute time,' 'absolute space' and 'absolute motion' are meaningless and therefore to be eliminated from science, Mach surely would not have agreed with Berkeley on the reason why physics cannot treat of real causes. Berkeley believed in causes, even in 'true' or 'real' causes; but all true or real causes were to him 'efficient or final causes' (*S*, 231), and therefore *spiritual* and utterly beyond physics (cf. *HP*, ii). He also believed in true or real causal *explanation* (*S*, 231)or, as I

---

[8] Mach survived Einstein's Special Theory of Relativity by more than eleven years, at least eight of which were very active years; but he remained strongly opposed to it; and though he alluded to it in the preface to the last (seventh) German edition (1912) of the *Mechanik* published during his lifetime, the allusion was by way of compliment to the opponent of Einstein, Hugo Dingler: Einstein's name and that of the theory were not mentioned.

[9] This is not the place to discuss other predecessors of Mach, such as Leibniz.

may perhaps call it, in 'ultimate explanation.' This, for him, was God.

All appearances are truly caused by God, and explained through God's intervention. This for Berkeley is the simple reason why physics can only describe regularities, and why it cannot find true causes.

It would be a mistake, however, to think that the similarity between Berkeley and Mach is by these differences shown to be only superficial. On the contrary, Berkeley and Mach are both convinced that there is no physical world (of primary qualities, or of atoms; cf. *Pr*, 50; *S*, 232, 235) behind the world of physical appearances (*Pr*, 87, 88). Both believed in a form of the doctrine nowadays called phenomenalism—the view that physical things are bundles, or complexes, or constructs of phenomenal *qualities*, of particular experienced colours, noises, etc.; Mach calls them 'complexes of elements.' The difference is that for Berkeley, these are directly caused by God. For Mach, they are just there. While Berkeley says that there can be nothing physical behind the physical phenomena, Mach suggests that there is nothing at all behind them.

V

The great historical importance of Berkeley lies, I believe, in his protest against essentialist explanations in science. Newton himself did not interpret his theory in an essentialist sense; he himself did not believe that he had discovered the fact that physical bodies, by their nature, are not only extended but endowed with a force of attraction (radiating from them, and proportional to the amount of matter in them). But soon after him the essentialist interpretation of his theory became the ruling one, and remained so till the days of Mach.

In our own day essentialism has been dethroned; a Berkeleian or Machian positivism or instrumentalism has, after all these years, become fashionable.

Yet there is clearly a third possibility—a 'third view' (as I call it).

Essentialism is, I believe, untenable. It implies the idea of an *ultimate* explanation, for an essentialist explanation is neither in need of, nor capable of, further explanation. (If it is in the nature of a body to attract others, then there is no need to ask for an explanation of this fact, and no possibility of finding such an explanation.) Yet we know, at least since Einstein, that explanation may be pushed, unexpectedly, further and further.

But although we must reject essentialism, this does not mean that we have to accept positivism; for we may accept the 'third view.'

I shall not here discuss the positivist dogma of meaning, since I have done so elsewhere. I shall make only six observations. (i) One can work with something like a world 'behind' the world of appearance without committing oneself to essentialism (especially if one assumes that we can never know whether there may not be a further world behind that world). To put it less vaguely, one can work with the idea of hierarchical levels of explanatory hypotheses. There are comparatively low level ones (somewhat like what Berkeley had in mind when he spoke of 'Laws of Nature'), higher ones such as Kepler's laws, still higher ones such as Newton's theory, and, next, Relativity. (ii) These theories are not mathematical hypotheses, that is, *nothing but* instruments for the prediction of apearances. Their function goes very much further; for (iii) there is no pure appearance or pure observation: what Berkeley had in mind when he spoke of these things was always the result of interpretation, and (iv) it had therefore a theoretical or hypothetical admixture. (v) New theories, moreover, may lead to re-interpretation of old appearances, and in this way change the world of appearances. (vi) The multiplicity of explanatory theories which Berkeley noted (see Section II (16), above) is used, wherever possible, to construct, for any two competing theories, conditions in which they yield different observable results, so that we can make a crucial test to decide between them, winning in this way new experience.

A main point of this third view is that science aims at *true* theories, even though we can never be sure that any particular theory is true; and that science *may* progress (and know that it does so) by inventing theories which compared with earlier ones may be described as better approximations to what is true.

So we can now admit, without becoming essentialist, that in science we always try *to explain the known by the unknown,* the observed (and observable) by the unobserved (and, perhaps, unobservable). At the same time we can now admit, without becoming instrumentalist, what Berkeley said of the nature of hypotheses in the following passage (S, 228), which shows both the weakness of his analysis—its failure to realize the conjectural character of all science, including what he calls the 'laws of nature'—and also its strength, its admirable understanding of the logical structure of hypothetical explanation.

'It is one thing,' Berkeley writes, 'to arrive at general laws of nature from a contemplation of the phenomena; and another to frame an hypothesis, and from thence deduce the phenomena. Those who suppose epicycles, and by them explain the motions and appearances of the planets, may not therefore be thought to have discovered principles true in fact and nature. And, albeit we may from the premises infer a conclusion, it will not follow that we can argue reciprocally, and from the conclusion infer the premises. For instance, supposing an elastic fluid, whose constituent minute particles are equidistant from each other, and of equal densities and diameters, and recede one from another with a centrifugal force which is inversely as the distance of the centres; and admitting that from such supposition it must follow that the density and elastic force of such fluid are in the inverse proportion of the space it occupies when compressed by any force; yet we cannot reciprocally infer that a fluid endowed with this property must therefore consist of such supposed equal particles.'

Colin Murray Turbayne / Berkeley's

two concepts of mind

Some moderns have thought fit to deride all that is said of æthereal vehicles as mere jargon or words without a meaning. But they should have
considered that all speech concerning the soul is altogether, or for the
most part, metaphorical.

GEORGE BERKELEY, Siris 171

I

Very little attention has been given to Berkeley's doctrine of
mind either by Berkeley himself or by his critics. This is strange,
because mind is the central concept in his system. He planned a
book on the subject. It was to have been Part II of his *Principles*.

From PHILOSOPHY AND PHENOMENOLOGICAL RESEARCH, *XX (1959–60), 85–92,
and XXII (1962), 577–580. Reprinted, with minor omissions, by permission of* PHILOSOPHY AND PHENOMENOLOGICAL RESEARCH.

In his notebook he wrote: "In Book 2 I shall at large show the difference there is betwixt the Soul and Body." He began this book, but then, as he said later, "I had made a considerable progress in it, but the manuscript was lost about fourteen years ago during my travels in Italy, and I never had leisure since to do so disagreeable a thing as writing twice on the same subject." He published Part I of the *Principles* in 1710, then, because of its poor reception, rewrote it in dialogue form. These books, however, are merely summaries of his whole project. He had planned Parts II, III, and IV to deal with mind, physics, and mathematics, respectively. None was written, but *De Motu* (1721) and *The Analyst* (1734) are substitutes for Parts III and IV. He never produced a substitute for Part II. Why? Was it solely lack of leisure?

Berkeley's account of the mind is disappointingly brief. The mind is "a thing entirely distinct" from ideas. It is a substance in which ideas exist. Ideas are passive. Mind alone is active. Its essence is indefinitely either "*percipere* or *agere*, i.e., *velle*." The word "mind" does "not denote any one of my ideas," but I have "some notion" of the mind and its operations such as willing and loving, that is, "I understand the meaning of those words." I am immediately aware of my own mind, but I have only mediate knowledge of others. Here Berkeley's account peters out. He says nothing more about the relation between mind and body and nothing about memory.

But this concept of mind is inconsistent with the rest of Berkeley's system. He should have suffered the gravest embarrassment in retaining mental substance, although it is unperceivable, and in rejecting material substance, because it is unperceivable: mind, like matter, is nothing but an abstract idea, i.e., *merum nihil*.

There is, however, latent in Berkeley's system, when correctly interpreted, another concept of mind. Had Berkeley developed it in Part II of his *Principles,* he would have avoided the inconsistency just described. But he would have suffered embarrassment of another kind.

To say this, however, is to go too far too soon. My problem is: How can I discover his *real* view of the nature of mind, given that his only systematic treatment of it is lost? I think that a clue is provided, if I reinterpret his "entire scheme." To this I now turn.

II

Berkeley's philosophy, in my view, needs re-examination from a new starting point. Since his death, one way of interpreting his doctrine has hardened into a common attitude. When the *Principles* first appeared, people fixed their attention on Berkeley's paradox—the *esse* of the common things of daily life is *percipi*—and on its related phenomenalism. During the subsequent two hundred and fifty years the place of emphasis has not altered. While it is true that these problems bequeathed to us in their modern form by Berkeley are important, our attention to them has led us to ignore others that Berkeley fathered. It is a mistake to treat Berkeley's paradox as though it were the title of his philosophy. G. E. Moore's "Refutation of Idealism" (1903) [p. 57, above] and W. T. Stace's "Refutation of Realism" (1934) [p. 85, above] have crystallized the common attitude. My indirect purpose is to shift the place of emphasis. For the truth is that Berkeley's paradox and his phenomenalism are only fragments of a doctrine, the great bulk of which is independent of their truth or falsity.

My point of departure is Berkeley's early note: "To behold the deformity of error we need only undress it." I treat his philosophy as an analysis of error—an attempt to extirpate prejudice, rather than to discover new truth. "I do not, therefore, pretend that my books can teach truth," he wrote in middle age, but he did pretend that he had cleared the ground for the discovery of truth by others. His fundamental purpose was "to inquire into the source of [our] perplexities." Moreover, he regarded our perplexities and prejudices as maladies or ailments which are curable. Finally, he had the conception of "levels of error" or "layers of deformity" such that when any "deformity" was "undressed," another could usually be found beneath it. There are, for example, sources of sources of sources of skepticism. From all this, once we put together—as he did not—what he called "the entire scheme," much becomes plain and more can be inferred. We are able, for example, to place in their proper categories such concepts as skepticism, atheism, matter, mind, cause, abstract ideas, metaphors, and proper nouns. And we are able to infer what a large part of Berkeley's philosophy of mind would have been had he written nothing at all on it.

I now hold, therefore, that Berkeley's philosophy can be correctly interpreted only if it is realized that his exposure of our delusions is, in effect, an etiology of a modern malady containing different levels or layers. At each level Berkeley provides a diagnosis of a set of doctrines or attitudes held either explicitly or implicitly by philosophers. He indicates what their consequences or symptoms will be in the minds of plain men. Then he traces their causes through levels of delusion to their ultimate sources. Thus, these levels form a hierarchy such that a doctrine found at any one level, except the last or deepest, has its immediate cause in a corresponding doctrine at the next deeper, and its ultimate origin at the deepest level. (I use the spatial metaphors "deeper," "analysis-in-depth," and "level," because of Berkeley's own use of the metaphors, "found at bottom," "rooted in," etc.) In this analysis-in-depth, four main levels are clearly distinguishable.

At the *first level* are the consequences or symptoms, predicted or noticed by Berkeley as skepticism, atheism, and vice.

These consequences "spring from" the official doctrine of the philosophers which, in Berkeley's diagnosis, is materialism. Materialism occurs at the *second level* of error. It contains three main doctrines. Two of these, at least, by the time Berkeley wrote, had already stiffened into dogma. The first I name "the dogma of the two worlds." This may be described as the doctrine according to which the everyday world is merely a representation of the real world of physical objects that science investigates. This doctrine leads inevitably to skepticism. The second doctrine I call "hylopsychism," because it involves the supposition that personal characteristics such as forces or causes or active powers reside in physical objects. In Berkeley's analysis, this supposition leads by psychological transition to atheism. For the third doctrine, whose essence is the inadvertent ascription of physical properties to the mind, I have coined the title, "psychohylism." In particular Berkeley noticed that, although the philosophers regarded the mind as immaterial, they subscribed, nevertheless, to a doctrine of the embodied self. The mind is located, said Henry More, "in the fourth ventricle of the brain." To this view Descartes, Malebranche, Newton, and others attested. Berkeley was aware also of the common opinion that the mind and its operations are sufficiently explicable in physical terms. In my view, the correct account of Berkeley's philosophy of mind must stress his attempt to exorcize the prejudices inherent in psychohylism.

In exposing the errors present in the official doctrine, Berkeley reveals that the three dogmas depend, although not quite "at bottom," on corresponding errors at the *third level*. These errors are the fallacy of abstract ideas and certain fallacies of composition or category mistakes. The former is conveniently characterized by Newton. In a passage from which Berkeley often quotes, Newton manifests the deep-seated delusion of the age about abstractions: "In philosophical disquisitions . . . we ought to abstract from our senses and consider things themselves, distinct from what are only sensible measures of them." Berkeley's analysis of the doctrine reduces to: (*a*) abstracting things-in-themselves, (*b*) mistaking abstractions for concrete things. Omitting details, the chief abstractions on which the three dogmas depend are absolute space, time, and motion, material substance, and force. The category mistakes at this level involve confusing psychology with physics and geometry, facts with theories, and supposed qualities ("occult qualities") with explaining devices ("mathematical hypotheses").

The delusions present in the doctrine of abstract ideas and in the categorial errors are rooted in errors in our use of language. Two fallacies occur at this *fourth and deepest level* of error. They are the ultimate source of all "the inextricable puzzling absurdities" that philosophers commit. They are:

   i) Treating general names as proper names.
   ii) Treating metaphors literally.

These two fallacies define the phrase "the mist or veil of words" in Berkeley's unpublished remark, "The chief thing I do or pretend to do is only to remove the mist or veil of words. This has occasioned ignorance and confusion." How do these idols-in-chief of the market place cause that idol of the theater, psychohylism?

The first is the source of "that strange doctrine" of abstract ideas, a doctrine manifested in every subject treated by the philosophers. Words like "will," "force," and "action" are nouns. There is, therefore, a disposition to regard them as names of things. Accordingly, realists and conceptualists were deluded to think that they could make a "division of things truly inseparable" (*De Motu* 47), and then could inspect or introspect respectively, such precise, naked, and discrete "things-in-them-selves" as the will, force, and action. Then, on the analogy of persons who can act or will or do things, the philosophers ascribed action or power to the corporeal world and used it as a mechanical principle of explanation. But the power to act or to do things belongs only to persons. The view that mind is part of the physical causal scheme was thus difficult to escape.

The second has made us prone to what may be called "the fallacy of composition" (*De Motu* 47), or "the category mistake," defined by Ryle as "the presentation of facts belonging to one category in the idioms appropriate to another." Berkeley noticed that the philosophers used the "person" language in physics: " 'Solicitation' and 'effort' or 'conation' [I may add from other passages, 'force,' 'cause,' 'action'] belong properly to animate beings. When they are attributed to other things, they must be taken in a metaphorical sense" (*De Motu* 3). He noticed also that they used the physical language in psychology: "But nothing seems more to have contributed towards engaging men in controversies and mistakes with regard to the nature and operations of the mind, than the being used to speak of those things in terms borrowed from sensible ideas. For example, the will is termed the 'motion' of the soul: this infuses the belief that the mind of man is as a ball in motion" (*Principles* 144).

Berkeley correctly did not object to the use of metaphor by philosophers. "Common custom," he said, "hath authorized" it. What he did object to was ignorance of its use. We must be constantly aware that we deal in metaphor, not in literal truth: "Most part of the mental operations being signified by words borrowed from sensible things; as is plain in the terms 'comprehend,' 'reflect,' 'discourse,' etc., which being applied to the mind must not be taken in their gross original sense" (*Three Dialogues* III 20).

Thus the use of words like "force" and "action" in physics,

and "motion" and "in the mind" in psychology, is legitimate and, in the latter case, unavoidable. But in such matters it was the lot of Berkeley's precursors—as it has been the lot of many of his successors—not only to speak with the vulgar, but to think with them. Unaware that they were using metaphors, the metaphors then used them. They believed that real forces reside in bodies, that bodies can really act or do things (Locke even wondered whether they could think), that the human mind has the physical properties of location in space and size, or that it is like a box or a room containing furniture. Berkeley himself was largely able to extricate his thinking from the physical connotations of "in the mind"—his favorite metaphor. In forgetting that they spoke in metaphor the philosophers not only denuded the mind of its defining property, but ascribed to it properties of the corporeal world.

Three strands run through the levels of error. Skepticism arises from the two-worlds dogma which in turn depends on the doctrine of abstract ideas. This in turn depends on the linguistic error that every noun names a thing. The other two strands are intertwined, which suggests that Berkeley's philosophy of science and his doctrine of mind should be considered together. Atheism and vice are traceable through hylopsychism and psychohylism to abstract ideas and categorial errors. But these have their roots in the literal use of metaphors. To invent a metaphor like attraction is an achievement. It is also an achievement to "undress" a dead one and to indicate that it can at most be a "mathematical hypothesis" and not the name of an occult quality. In one manner of speaking, Berkeley's philosophies of science and mind amount to the "undressing" of certain dead metaphors. Berkeley's brief treatment of metaphor does not forbid the use of models in our understanding of the mind. That models are useful and even necessary can be deduced from his account. We must merely be on guard against treating models of the mind as the mind. The Id, Ego, and Superego of Freud are no better and no worse off in this regard than the Self-love, Benevolence, and Conscience of Bishop Butler.

III

Let us see what is the nature of the theory of mind that follows from the preceding destructive analysis. Berkeley made the following points in three important fields:

In physics, the philosophers used such words as "force," "attraction," and "velocity" as names for entities. In Berkeley's analysis, their supposed referents are occult qualities, but though they name nothing they are, nevertheless, of great use in reasoning as explanatory devices, that is, as mathematical hypotheses.

In psychology, the philosophers used words like "reason," "the will," "appetite," and "pure intellect" as names for "distinct" entities. Berkeley cannot himself "abstract and distinguish so many beings in the soul" (*Alciphron* VII 18).

In theology, there are words used that look like names, such as "Grace," "the Trinity," "Substance," "Personality." But in Berkeley's view, if these are treated as names, then their referents are abstract ideas, that is, no things. He adds, however, that we can "assent to a proposition" although its terms name nothing. Thus, the doctrine of the Trinity can become for a man "a lively operative principle influencing his life and actions" (*Alciphron* VII 8) on the analogy with force and velocity and $\sqrt{-1}$. All these symbols are "instruments to direct our practice" (*Alciphron* VII 11). Men cannot find things lurking beneath the names "Trinity," "the will," "time," etc., although they "believe, know, argue, and dispute" about them (*Alciphron* VII 9).

According to Berkeley, then: (*a*) some words are cashed immediately in things; (*b*) some words, although cashable in things on demand, are like counters in gambling, not cashed immediately; (*c*) other words are not cashable at all in things. Their meaning lies not in objects, but in actions of an actor. "I may be puzzled to define or conceive a notion of freedom in general and abstract," but "it is evident to me, in the gross and concrete, that I am a free agent" (*Alciphron* VII 18). Berkeley is often treated as though he holds that all words are like those in (*a*). This was a stage that he climbed through in early life. Some critics have noticed that he holds (*b*). But his view about (*c*) has been ignored, and, in consequence, much of his doctrine (e.g., his philosophy of mathematics) has been misinterpreted.

Where do mental words fit in this scheme? Clearly the words "mind," "will," "understanding" cannot belong in the (*a*) and (*b*) categories on Berkeley's own showing. In other words, the mind, the will, and the understanding cannot be things at all. The mind cannot be called a substance—a thing in which ideas inhere—in any literal sense. To say that these entities are things or substances is, accordingly, to speak in metaphor. To think that they are is to fall into the philosophers' traps about metaphors, proper names, abstract ideas, and category mistakes. To think that they are not is to think with the learned. Thus, that the mind is not a substance, that the word "mental substance" denotes nothing, that to say that mind is a substance is to speak in metaphor, all this follows from Berkeley's destructive analysis-in-depth.

The question now is: Did Berkeley entertain this second concept of mind? I think that he did for the following reasons:

First, even in his official account of the mind he treats the will and the understanding, considered as faculties, as abstract ideas. But he is all for retaining the words "the will" and "the understanding" (*Principles* 27).

Second, it is difficult to conceive that Berkeley with his acute logical sense failed to notice the inconsistency involved in holding his official theory of mind.

Third, to hold the second concept of mind in reserve, as it were, to be given to the world in *Principles*, Part II, would be typical of Berkeley the tactician. Could he not have retained mind as literally a substance in Part I just as he retained matter in his *Essay on Vision*, "because it was beside my purpose to examine and refute it" in a mere summary?

Fourth, the last few pages of Berkeley's private notebooks —the *Philosophical Commentaries*—suggest that he was approaching a different theory of mind: There is no need for "a thinking substance, something unknown" (637); "No thing at all that wills" (658); "The substance of Spirit we do not know, it not being knowable" (701); "There must be a disposition to act" (777); "Substance of a Spirit is that it acts, causes, wills, operates, or, if you please (to avoid the quibble y^t may be made on ye word it), to act, cause, will, operate its' substance is not knowable not being an Idea" (829); "I must not say the Will and Understanding are all one, but that they are both Abstract Ideas, i.e., none at all" (871). In addition to entries of this nature, Berkeley writes that he must use the word "Mind" instead of "person," "lest offence be given" (713), and, two entries later, "N.B. to use utmost Caution not to give the least Handle of offence to the Church or Church-men" (715).

From these considerations, I suggest that there is latent in Berkeley's writings another theory of mind whose elements are sketched independently of any motive of prudence. His official theory is a brilliant attempt to superadd elements compatible with Christian theology, notably the doctrine of the self as substance, soul, or spirit. The second secret doctrine merely hints at a theory of mind which is the inevitable conclusion of an argument that Berkeley has been following wherever it might lead, no matter how much "Handle of offence to the Church or Church-men" it would, most assuredly, give.

IV

In a recent paper,[1] S. A. Grave has objected that I do not say what Berkeley's secret theory was. My labels "official" and "secret" were, perhaps, inappropriate, but they represent a distinction which is, I think, easy to grasp. Berkeley was interested in metaphor. As a philosopher of science he tried to show that contemporary physicists and psychologists were victimized by certain metaphors. As a scientist within the science of optics it can be argued that he practiced what he preached, for he showed how to use the language metaphor to set up a theory of vision.

When he came to present his own psychology, however, he gave the impression that he too was a victim, that he took the assertion "Mind is a substance" in a literal sense, that he thought the soul was actually a "substance" "in" which ideas "inhere" and which "supports" the ideas, etc., hence the expression "in the mind." This account I called Berkeley's "official doctrine."

But let us suppose that he practiced in his psychology what he preached in his philosophy of science and had practiced in his optics. We get an account in which the substance metaphor is used to make a theory of mind. This is what I supposed. Insofar as I argued, in addition, that this was Berkeley's real view, I called it his "secret doctrine."

Mr. Grave objects, however, that if Berkeley held that to say "The mind is a substance" is to speak in metaphor, then he

[1] S. A. Grave, "A Note on Berkeley's Conception of the Mind," *Philosophy and Phenomenological Research*, XXII (1962), 574–576.

could not have regarded his "official theory" of the mind as a theory at all, but merely as a way of speaking. This is strange. I cannot see why, for example, Plato and Berkeley must regard their theories of man and vision as not really theories but merely ways of speaking even though they regard the assertions "Man is a state" and "Vision is a language" as metaphorical. Nor can I see why Berkeley cannot hold both that "we speak of spirits in a figurative style" (*Alciphron* VII 13) and that we make our theories of spirits from such figures.

Mr. Grave says that I really argued for the view that Berkeley had a "purely anti-substantivalist conception" of the mind which he expressed literally in private (The mind is not a substance) and metaphorically in public (The mind is a substance). This is a peculiar correction. He would have been nearer the mark if he had said that I argued that Berkeley had a "purely substantivalist conception" of the mind confirmed by his private utterances. If I had argued that Churchill was using the phrase "the iron curtain" metaphorically, and then had had the good fortune to find him saying in his memoirs, posthumously published, that he thought the Russian boundary was really neither a curtain nor made of iron, my view would have been not a little confirmed. I should then have been inclined to say not that Sir Winston held an "anti-iron curtain" concept but rather an "iron curtain" concept of the Russian boundary. I did argue, however, that Berkeley was speaking metaphorically when he said "The mind is a substance." In which case, the passages that I (and, happily, Mr. Grave) quoted from Berkeley's posthumously published private notebook to the effect that the mind is not a substance confirm my view.

Finally, Mr. Grave rejects my theory because of its "moral improbability": We have "what amounts to Berkeley's word for it that he did adopt the substantivalist conception." In other words, if Berkeley believed that mind is not a substance and said it was, then he was a liar: We must take Berkeley literally when he said that the mind is a substance because he said that the mind is a substance. Now it is true that Berkeley adopted the substance conception of mind just as he adopted the linguistic conception of vision, but this does not mean that we must take him literally, and, if not, that he was a liar. Although most metaphors come unlabelled, their users need tell no lies. Churchill did not say: "Mussolini is a utensil, metaphorically speaking," but he did say that Mussolini was a utensil, metaphorically speaking, and what he said was no lie.

While I cannot be sure that Berkeley had the awareness I ascribe to him, there are two factors which I think Mr. Grave has ignored. The first is this. Among philosophers Berkeley is notorious for his sharp distinction between speaking strictly or literally and speaking metaphorically, and for pressing this distinction further than most. "Speech is metaphorical more than we imagine" (*Commentaries* 175). We speak strictly or literally when we attribute energy, effort, force, action to persons, for "they belong properly to animate beings." But, astonishingly enough from our prejudiced point of view, "when they are attributed to other things, they must be taken in a metaphorical sense" (*De Motu* 3). Such attribution is metaphorical because "it transfers the principle of action from the human soul to things outward and foreign" (*Alciphron* VII 16), that is, it represents the facts about bodies in the idioms appropriate to souls or minds. Now the physicists did attribute force, action, etc., to bodies. Berkeley said to them: You suppose bodies in a literal sense to be forceful, active, energetic, and powerful. Thus, from his point of view, they took metaphors literally. Again, according to Berkeley, we speak literally when we attribute motion to bodies, and metaphorically when we attribute it to the mind. The psychologists fell into the same trap as the physicists. Berkeley said to them: "You suppose the mind in a literal sense to be

moved and its volitions to be mere motions" (*Alciphron* VII 16).
Thus, they, too, were victims. Were the physicists and psychologists to give up their theories because they involved metaphor?
Certainly not, if they worked. Let these scientists merely become
aware that they dealt in metaphor, not in literal truth. Let them
retain their metaphors as "instruments to direct action" or as
"operative principles." Nevertheless, from Berkeley's point of
view, they did not choose the best metaphors.

The second is this. A man discloses that he is using a metaphor if he spells out both its literal and its metaphorical meanings. Let me illustrate. If Sir Winston Churchill, confronted with
a recalcitrant audience in Fulton, Missouri, and forced to explicate what he meant by "iron curtain," had replied: "It is
evident 'support' cannot here be taken in its usual or literal
sense—as when we say that bars are made of iron; nevertheless,
I know what I mean when I affirm that there is an iron curtain
or screen between the East and the West, that is, that the
boundary between the East and the West is impenetrable," he
would have disclosed that he was using "iron curtain" metaphorically. In similar fashion, Berkeley first gave the literal
meaning of "substance" or "substratum that supports": "It is
evident 'support' cannot here be taken in its usual or literal
sense—as when we say that pillars support a building" (*Principles* 16). Then, confronted with a recalcitrant audience, he gave
the metaphorical meaning: "I know what I mean when I affirm
that there is a spiritual substance or support of ideas, that is,
that a spirit knows and perceives ideas" (*Three Dialogues* III 4).
But then, just a few pages later, he gave the same type of analysis for that auxiliary metaphor of "substance," namely, "ideas
exist in the mind": first, "the gross literal sense—as when bodies
are said to exist in a place," and then his vain attempt to say
what he really meant, that is, to give the metaphorical meaning:
"My meaning is only that the mind comprehends or perceives

them." I say "vain attempt" because, ten lines later, we learn that "comprehend" is also a metaphor, and not a good one in its present context because it suggests the mind as active. Mind as "sub-stance" or "under-standing," the passive container and support of ideas, i.e., the passive perceiver of ideas, demands a "passive," not an "active" metaphor. He was saying in effect: "The mind is passively active in perception."

From these considerations it still seems likely to me that Berkeley was looking for the best possible metaphors to illustrate the mind. "Sub-stance" with all of its associated idioms would have met many of his tests.

James W. Cornman / Theoretical terms, Berkeleian notions, and minds

Consider the following quotations from the beginning of Berkeley's *Principles*. First:

> It is evident to anyone who takes a survey of the *objects* of human knowledge that they are either ideas actually imprinted on the senses, or else such as are perceived by attending to the passions and operations of the mind, or lastly, ideas formed by help of memory and imagination—either compounding, dividing, or barely representing those originally perceived in the aforesaid ways (*Principles* 1).*

This essay appears for the first time in this volume.

* All quotations from the *Principles*, *Dialogues*, and *Correspondence* are from *Principles, Dialogues, and Philosophical Correspondence*, ed. C. M. Turbayne (Indianapolis and New York: Bobbs-Merrill, 1965). All other quotations from Berkeley are from *The Works of George Berkeley*, ed. A. A. Luce and T. E. Jessop, Vols. I and IV (Edinburgh: Thomas Nelson and Sons, 1948–1957).

And also:

> This perceiving, active being is what I call "mind," "spirit,"
> "soul," or "myself." By which words I do not denote any one
> of my ideas, but a thing entirely distinct from them, wherein
> they exist or, which is the same thing, whereby they are per-
> ceived—for the existence of an idea consists in being perceived
> (*Principles* 2).

From these two quotations it seems we can derive two statements:

> 1) All objects of human knowledge are ideas;
> 2) No idea is denoted by the word 'mind';

which taken together allow us to deduce:

> 3) No objects of human knowledge are denoted by 'mind.'

An apparent contradiction in Berkeley's philosophy

This conclusion would seem to be unpalatable to Berkeley because his whole philosophy is so intimately dependent upon the
existence of minds. Nevertheless, in his earlier writings there is
evidence that he did accept the conclusion at some time. In the
Philosophical Commentaries, written before the *Principles* and
the *Dialogues*, he says in entry 581:

> Say you the Mind is not the Perceptions. but that thing w^{ch}
> perceives. I answer you are abus'd by the words that & thing
> these are vague empty words wthout a meaning.

In this entry it certainly seems that Berkeley is claiming that
the word 'mind' does not denote some thing. Indeed, even to
talk of 'mind' denoting some thing is to misuse the word 'thing.'
And, clearly, if it is without meaning to talk of some thing denoted by 'mind,' then there can be no human knowledge of

what thing 'mind' denotes. Later, in the *Commentaries*, Berkeley again agrees with (3):

> The substance of Body we know, the substance of Spirit we do not know it not being knowable. it being purus actus (*Commentaries* 701).

It would make a consistent interpretation of Berkeley's position easier if he had continued to hold the theory of mind expressed in the *Commentaries*.[1] His later and what seems to be his final position, however, the position stated in both the *Principles* and *Dialogues*, is quite different:

> We may be said to have some knowledge or notion of our own minds, of spirits and active beings, whereof in a strict sense we have not ideas (*Principles* 89).[2]

This by itself seems inconsistent with (3), yet it need not be. Statement (3) asserts there is no knowledge of things denoted by 'mind,' but the quotation implies nothing about whether or not 'mind' is a denoting term. Indeed, Berkeley's claim in the quotation would be compatible with (3) if, as some commentators have claimed, Berkeley considered the word 'mind' to be more like the word 'number' than like the word 'apple.'[3] According to Berkeley, 'number' is not a denoting term. He says that

[1] For a view that the concept of mind found in the *Commentaries* is closer to Berkeley's final position than the one expressed in this paper, cf. C. M. Turbayne, "Berkeley's Two Concepts of Mind," *Philosophy and Phenomenological Research*, XX (1959), 85–92; and XXII (1962), 577–580. These articles are reprinted in part in this volume, pp. 145–160, above. Turbayne claims that Berkeley continued to maintain the non-denoting view of 'mind' found in the *Commentaries*, but that he gave up his view in the *Commentaries* that talk of 'mind' denoting things is meaningless. Rather, Turbayne says, it is metaphorical.

[2] See also *Dialogues* III 4.

[3] Cf. Turbayne, *op. cit.*, and, for an article pursuing the line Turbayne takes, J. Murphy, "Berkeley and the Metaphor of Mental Substance," *Ratio*, 7 (1965), 170–179.

there are no ideas of number in abstract denoted by numerical names and figures. The theories therefore in arithmetic, if they are abstracted from the names and figures, as likewise from all use and practice, as well as from the particular things numbered, can be supposed to have nothing at all for their object (*Principles* 120).

Nevertheless, Berkeley would not deny we can have arithmetical knowledge, knowledge we might call knowledge of numbers, and surely knowledge which in the strict sense does not involve ideas.

Thus Berkeley could avoid contradicting (3) by taking an instrumental or non-denoting view of mental terms, but it seems quite clear that this is not his position in the *Dialogues* and *Principles* where, in addition to the second quotation above, he says:

For by the word "spirit" we mean only that which thinks, wills, and perceives; this, and this alone, constitutes the signification of that term. . . . What I am myself, that which I denote by the term "I," is the same with what is meant by "soul," or "spiritual substance" (*Principles* 138, 139).

From this and the quotation from *Principles* 89 we can conclude from what Berkeley asserted in these two major works:

4) Some objects of human knowledge are denoted by 'mind,'

and this statement flatly contradicts (3).

Berkeley's way to avoid the contradiction: two kinds of objects of knowledge

Can Berkeley be saved from this contradiction? It is clear, I think, how he would claim to avoid it: by modifying premise (1). In the *Principles* he says that

human knowledge may naturally be reduced to two heads—
that of *ideas* and that of *spirits* (*Principles* 86).

This adjustment may seem to contradict the quotation from
which we extracted premise (1), but, although in that passage
it may seem Berkeley calls all objects of knowledge "ideas,"
the section relevant to minds does not mention ideas:

> or else such as are perceived by attending to the passions and
> operations of the mind. . . .

Here 'such' may seem to refer to ideas, but if we take it to refer
to objects of knowledge and take seriously Berkeley's repeated
claims that we have no idea of, i.e., no idea represents, either
minds or operations of the mind, then even in this initial quotation there is a hint of two quite disparate objects of knowledge.[4]

Another contradiction avoided by Berkeley: notions and minds

We have not yet dissipated all traces of contradiction, however,
for the following argument must first be rebutted:

> 5) If humans have knowledge about some object, then they
> have an idea of it, i.e., they think about the object by means
> of an idea which represents the object.
> 6) A mind "being an agent, cannot be like unto, or repre-
> sented by, any idea whatsoever" (*Principles* 27).

Therefore,

> 7) There is no human knowledge of minds.

---

[4] This position has been stated by A. A. Luce, *Berkeley's Immaterialism*
(Edinburgh: Thomas Nelson and Sons, 1945), pp. 39–40.

Clearly Berkeley cannot accept (7), which is even a stronger claim than (3), and is inconsistent with even an instrumental theory of mind. Consequently because he accepts (6), Berkeley must reject (5). This is what he does:

> We may not, I think, strictly be said to have an *idea* of an active being, or of an action, although we may be said to have a *notion* of them. I have some knowledge or notion of my mind, and its acts about ideas, in as much as I know or understand what is meant by those words. What I know, that I have some notion of (*Principles* 142).

Given the addition of notions to ideas, it is easy to absolve Berkeley of being committed to the inconsistent conjunction of (4) and (7). As often interpreted, instead of holding (5) as it first seems, Berkeley would agree to:

> 5a) If humans have knowledge about some object, then they have either an idea or notion that represents the object,

which does not entail (7) when taken with (6). Berkeley, then, by the introduction of notions can avoid holding (3) and (7), and his philosophy avoids contradiction. But to many it surely seems he avoids contradiction only by the sudden *ad hoc* introduction of something like an idea in all respects except that it does what ideas cannot do: represents active rather than inert entities. If this is the most plausible interpretation, then it surely seems Berkeley avoids contradiction only at the price of making his theory rest upon an *ad hoc* assumption so tenuous and so little developed that it makes his whole position implausible.

A defense of notions: theoretical terms and notions

My aim in this paper is to show that although Berkeley has hardly given us enough to conclude that notions are any more than a weak *ad hoc* addition to his thesis, and although, as he presented it, his position has an important weakness, it is possible, nevertheless, to build upon what little Berkeley said a viable theory of notions which complements and makes plausible his whole position. Whether Berkeley held anything remotely like the theory I shall propose is something I'm afraid we shall never know because it seems his more detailed writings on mind are irreparably lost.[5] My aim, then, is not to speculate about what Berkeley thought, but rather to flesh out the little Berkeley gave us in a plausible way.

Berkeley, like many contemporary philosophers, was keenly interested in language and its importance for philosophical problems, particularly the problems of what kind of words are denoting words and what kinds of objects are denoted. For example, as previously quoted, he claims that arithmetical terms do not denote objects. They, as many other terms, have a different function. Berkeley realized that "the communication of ideas marked by words is not the chief and only end of language, as is commonly supposed" (*Principles,* Introduction 20). And, although many general terms do denote objects, none denote abstract ideas, but rather they "signify indifferently a great number of particular ideas" (*Principles,* Introduction 18).

Berkeley claims that words such as 'apple' denote collections of ideas, but, as we have seen above, that mental substance words such as 'mind,' 'soul' or 'spirit,' which I shall call "mind-terms" to distinguish them from the broader class of mental terms, denote things that are not ideas and not constituted of ideas. My claim in this paper is that if we understand terms such as 'apple' to be observation terms but mind-terms to be theoretical terms, and couple this with an empiricist view of the meaning of theoretical terms, we shall arrive at a distinction between

---

[5] This seems to be the most plausible interpretation of the subject matter of a manuscript lost by Berkeley. Cf. *Correspondence* II 6.

ideas and notions which is neither vague nor baseless. What results will be the view that our idea of apple is expressed by the observation term 'apple' and is what we use to think about particular apples. In this regard, the idea of an apple can be said to represent or picture particular apples, themselves bundles of particular ideas, and, derivatively, the term 'apple,' which refers to particular apples, can be said to represent or picture apples.[6] Similarly, our *notion* of mind is expressed by the theoretical term 'mind' and is what we use to think about minds which are not like ideas and therefore cannot be represented by ideas. Whereas apples, stones, trees, and other sensible things are observable entities, minds and the like are unobservable theoretical entities.

Elaboration of the defense: empiricism and the meaning of theoretical terms

But there is still the question of what reason there can be for distinguishing ideas from notions in this way. It will not do to answer that the reason is that, because ideas can represent only ideas, something else is needed to represent minds. A much more plausible answer will come from considering a currently

[6] I have here interpreted Berkeley as claiming that each particular object consists of sensible ideas that are themselves particulars. R. J. Van Iten disagrees. Cf. "Berkeley's Alleged Solipsism," *Revue internationale de Philosophie*, XVI, No. 61–62 (1962), 447–452, reprinted in this volume, pp. 47–56, above. He claims that Berkeley can consistently escape solipsism only if he construes the constituent ideas as universals, because if the constituents of each object are particular ideas, then, because no two minds can perceive the same particular idea, it follows that no two minds can perceive the same object. But there is a missing premise here, namely, if no two minds can perceive the same constituents of an object, then no two minds can perceive the same object. This premise is debatable and surely not a necessary truth.

widely accepted empiricist theory of the meaning of theoretical terms and observation terms. Like all empiricist theories of meaning, it requires that any non-logical term derives whatever meaning it has from certain of its relationships to observable situations. It differs from other empiricist theories, however, in having less restrictive requirements about what this relationship must be. This theory, as expounded by Carnap, distinguishes between the vocabulary, V_o, of an observation language, L_o, and the vocabulary, V_t, of a theoretical language, L_t. He first considers the observation vocabulary:

> The terms of V_o are predicates designating observable properties of events or things (e.g., "blue," "hot," "large," etc.) or observable relations between them (e.g., "x is warmer than y," "x is contiguous to y," etc.).[7]

Because all these terms designate properties we are aware of by observation, there is no problem of their applicability to what they designate. In this respect, their role in language is completely determined by what can be observed. That is, their meaning can be completely and clearly determined by specifying the observable conditions of their application. Thus, as Carnap says, "L_o is intended for the description of observable events and therefore is meant to be completely interpreted."[8] Observation terms, then, are completely meaningful according to this or, in-

[7] R. Carnap, "The Methodological Character of Theoretical Concepts" in *Minnesota Studies in the Philosophy of Science*, ed. H. Feigl and M. Scriven (Minneapolis: University of Minnesota Press, 1956), I, 41. It should be noted that Berkeley would not agree that there are observable relations. Cf. *Principles* 142. Furthermore, while Berkeley would seem to claim that sensation words such as 'pleasure' and 'pain' are part of the observation vocabulary because they, like 'blue' and 'hot,' refer to ideas, Carnap would now disagree. For Berkeley, the observation language would be a phenomenal language, but for Carnap it would be the thing-language.

[8] *Ibid.*

deed, any empiricist theory of meaning. Using Berkeley's terminology, we can say that such terms are used to express the
ideas we have of observable properties, ideas which represent,
by being images or pictures, these properties. And, we could also
say, the observation terms picture in some derivative way these
same observable properties.

Theoretical terms, on the other hand, have always raised
problems for empiricist theories of meaning. Previous theorists
have asserted that, if a term is not an observation term, it is
meaningful only if and only insofar as it is definable by observation terms. Empiricists have tried to construe theoretical entities
as logical constructions out of observables by using observation
terms to provide explicit definitions of theoretical terms. When
this procedure failed, however, they turned to partial definitions
in reduction sentences to give the terms a clear although incomplete meaning. This procedure also failed and it is now generally
agreed that many theoretical terms are not observation terms,
and not definable—either explicitly or partially—by observation
terms.[9] The relationship of theoretical terms to what is observable is much more tenuous, and, consequently, on an empiricist
theory of meaning they have at best both unclear and incomplete
meaning. The problem for the empiricist, however, is to show
that they have any meaning at all.

Carnap's solution of this problem is to construe the theoretical vocabulary, V_t, the vocabulary containing only theoretical terms, and, therefore, no observation terms, as connected by
correspondence rules, C-rules, to the observation vocabulary,
V_o. For example, let us assume that we have a very simple theoretical system T with two purely theoretical statements,
$(x)[T_1x \supset T_2x]$ and $(x)[T_2x \supset T_3x]$, and two C-rules $(x)[O_1x \supset T_1x]$ and $(x)[T_3x \supset O_2x]$. According to Carnap, whatever

---

[9] *Ibid.*, pp. 66–69.

significance the theoretical terms T_1, T_2, and T_3 have is provided by the contingent connections they have to the fully and clearly meaningful observation terms O_1 and O_2. That is:

There is no independent interpretation for L_t. The system T is in itself an uninterpreted postulate system. The terms of V_t obtain only an indirect and incomplete interpretation by the fact that some of them are connected by the rules C with observational terms, and the remaining terms of V_t are connected with the first ones by the postulates of T. Thus it is clear that the rules C are essential; without them the terms of V_t would not have any observational significance. These rules must be such that they connect sentences of L_o with certain sentences of L_t, for instance, by making derivation in the one or the other direction possible.[10]

On this empiricist view of theoretical terms, they are meaningful, but, because they are neither completely nor partially definable by observation terms, have only an incomplete and unclear meaning. We cannot, therefore, be said to have a complete and clear understanding of whatever a theoretical term might refer to. Instead of a full and clear understanding, or idea, we have at best something like a Berkeleian notion of what it signifies. Strictly speaking, then, for theoretical terms, unlike observation terms, we do not have an idea of—an idea that represents or pictures—anything at all. While we can "visualize" those things that 'apple' or 'stone' denote we cannot imagine in the same way what 'electron' or 'mind' might denote. Nevertheless we do have a conception of, an understanding of, what an electron or mind is. It is true that a grasp of theoretical entities is often aided by a picture, such as a tinker toy "picture" of an atomic structure. But this is picturing only in the sense of using something observable, something we can have an idea of, as a

10 *Ibid.* p. 47.

model to help us better understand what we cannot visualize or completely understand.

I have suggested that Berkeleian notions be construed as what we can call "theoretical concepts," concepts which we use in thinking about theoretical explanations of what we observe and which we express using theoretical terms. I have suggested that such concepts are, as required by one empiricist theory of meaning, neither completely nor clearly understood and do not represent whatever they might denote. On this view of notions, therefore, premise (5a) is false, for the function of notions is not to represent what ideas cannot represent. Their function in thinking is not a representative one at all; it is rather to explain what we observe. To add to ideas, which function descriptively, something quite different that functions to explain, is not to make a mere *ad hoc* adjustment. It is to take into account something essential for any adequate theory of mind, because any such theory must be able to account for explanatory thinking, as exemplified in science, as well as descriptive thinking.

An objection: the term 'mind' is not a theoretical term

We have not reached the end of the matter, however, because construing 'mind' and other mind-terms as theoretical terms immediately gives rise to two objections. The first is that although 'mind' is surely not an observation term, because minds are not observable, that is, no ideas can represent them, it is surely not a theoretical term either because it is always used to refer to what someone is aware of, unlike theoretical terms such as 'electron.' It is both true and recognized by Berkeley that 'mind' refers to what someone is aware of. In *Principles* 89, he says, "We comprehend our own existence by inward feeling or reflection, . . ." and in *De Motu* 21, "the sentient, percipient, thinking thing we know by a certain internal consciousness." We should, consequently, construe 'mind' as what we can call a "reporting term," i.e., a term used to refer to what someone is aware or conscious of. In this way it is like 'apple,' but it differs from 'apple' because we do not observe its referent through the senses. Rather, we are aware of it through "internal consciousness." But, having granted this much, must we conclude that Berkeley could not consistently hold that 'mind' is a theoretical term? And, because of this, must we agree after all that Berkeley's notions can have no function in thinking except the one forced on him by his own theory, i.e., that of representing what ideas cannot represent?

We can avoid these conclusions, but in so doing we must draw a distinction between mind-terms that are theoretical terms and certain other theoretical terms such as 'electron.' This distinction will not only allow us to avoid this objection, but will prepare the way for the answer to the second and more serious objection.

Reply: two kinds of theoretical terms

There are two reasons why mind-terms should be construed as theoretical terms, albeit a unique kind, and why it is plausible to fill out Berkeley's view in this way. The first reason is that whether or not mind-terms have a reporting use, surely one of their primary roles is to explain various sorts of observable human behavior. And, since they are clearly not observation terms, they meet what is generally accepted as a sufficient condition for being a theoretical term.[11] That is, they are non-logical

---

[11] See Carnap, *Meaning and Necessity* (Chicago: University of Chicago Press, 1958), p. 230.

constants in an explanatory vocabulary that are neither observation terms nor definable by observation terms. Because
terms that meet this sufficient condition can also be reporting
terms, we can distinguish between theoretico-reporting terms
such as 'mind' and non-reporting or "pure" theoretical terms
such as 'electron.'

The second reason for construing mind-terms as theoretical terms is that, although it is true that when someone uses
them self-ascriptively—in their first-person use—they are, like
observation terms, used to refer to what the person is aware of,
this is not true when someone uses them other-ascriptively.
When so used they function very similarly to 'electron' because
in both these cases when I make an assertion using either term, I
am not aware of whatever the term refers to, but rather must
justify my assertion by inference from what I observe. It might
be concluded from this that when used other-ascriptively, mind-
terms are pure theoretical terms, but that when used self-ascriptively they are non-theoretical or "pure" reporting terms. But
the claim that mind-terms, contrary to appearances, are ambiguous in their first and other-person uses seems reasonable
to me only if there are grounds for concluding that no theoretical terms are reporting terms. I can think of no reason for
this, however.[12] Let us conclude, consequently, that Berkeley
can agree with what seems reasonable: Mind-terms are, in both
their first and other-person uses, theoretico-reporting terms.
They differ, therefore, from both the pure theoretical term
'electron' and the observation term 'apple.'

It is interesting to note at this point how Berkeley's view
of mind on the above extrapolation both differs from and is, I
think, more plausible than either Locke's or Hume's. For Locke,

---

[12] I have discussed theoretico-reporting terms in more detail in "Mental
Terms, Theoretical Terms, and Materialism," *The Philosophy of Science*,
35 (1968), 45–63.

a mind is a mental substance, something like a material substance,

> the one being supposed to be (without knowing what it is) the
> *substratum* to those simple ideas we have from without; and
> the other supposed (with a like ignorance of what it is) to be
> the *substratum* to those operations which we experiment in
> ourselves within.[13]

That is, minds are pure theoretical entities postulated because
they are needed to "support" mental activities. If, however,
Locke is right about mental substance and Berkeley is right
about the inadmissibility of material substance, then it seems
we should conclude with Hume, and with those words Berkeley
put into the mouth of Hylas against his defender Philonous:

> It should follow that you are only a system of floating ideas
> without any substance to support them. Words are not to be
> used without a meaning. And, as there is no more meaning in
> *spiritual* substance than in *material* substance, the one is to be
> exploded as well as the other (*Dialogues* III 4).

But Philonous' answer stresses the important differences between the two kinds of substance:

> I know or am conscious of my own being, as that I *myself* am
> not my ideas, but somewhat else, a thinking, active principle
> that perceives, knows, wills, and operates about ideas. . . . But
> I am not in like manner conscious either of the existence or
> essence of matter (*Dialogues* III 4).

As Berkeley realizes, someone is aware of himself when he
is active, as in willing, just as surely as he is aware of any idea.
Someone's mind, an active entity, is not, therefore, merely a
postulated theoretical entity, but rather a theoretical entity he is
aware of when he is active. Thus, Locke is wrong, but not com-

[13] *An Essay Concerning Human Understanding*, Bk. II, ch. 23, sec. 5.

pletely, because someone's mind, unlike his ideas, is more than what he is aware of. To paraphrase Locke, a mind is a something I do not know *completely* what. For one thing, as Berkeley says in a letter to the American Samuel Johnson, "That the mind is passive as well as active I make no doubt" (*Correspondence* IV 3). Thus, reinforcing what was previously claimed, we have at best an incomplete and unclear understanding of our minds.

Hume is also wrong, and on two counts. First I am not, as Hume says, merely:

> a bundle or collection of different perceptions, which succeed each other with an inconceivable rapidity, and are in a perpetual flux and movement.[14]

I am an active being and no collection of ideas is active. Furthermore, when I am active I am aware of myself, so Hume is also wrong in claiming:

> when I enter most intimately into what I call *myself,* I always stumble on some particular perception or other. . . .[15]

Sometimes I "stumble on" myself which is not a perception. Hume, like Locke, however, may not be completely wrong, for when I introspect it may well be I come across only ideas. What Hume overlooked, however, is that self-awareness comes primarily, if not exclusively, when I am active; it is not some object I find by introspection.

Another objection: Berkeley's instrumental view of theoretical terms

The second objection is more serious, for it is aimed at the claim that the view of the mind stated is consistent with the rest of

---

[14] *A Treatise of Human Nature*, Bk. I, Part iv, sec. 6.
[15] *Ibid.*

Berkeley's philosophy. By construing mind-terms as theoretical terms and by claiming that for Berkeley they are denoting terms, what results is a realistic interpretation of theoretical terms whereas Berkeley actually maintained an instrumental view of theoretical terms. Consequently, according to this objection, the elaborated construal of Berkeley's position offered in this paper may help save him from one inconsistency only by involving him in another.

It must be admitted that there is good reason to claim Berkeley adopts instrumentalism. This is the view that the sentences that formulate the purely theoretical part of science are merely complex linguistic devices used to warrant inferences from certain factual claims expressed in the observation vocabulary to certain other factual claims also expressed in the observation vocabulary. And, according to instrumentalism, because theoretical terms function merely as integral parts of these nonformal rules of inference, they are, like the terms used to express formal rules of inference, non-denoting "auxiliary marks, which serve as convenient symbolic devices in the transition from one set of experiential statements to another."[16] We have already seen that Berkeley is an instrumentalist regarding mathematical terms. One reason to think he has the same view about theoretical terms is his comparison of the two:

> And just as geometers for the sake of their art make use of many devices which they themselves cannot describe nor find in the nature of things, even so the mechanician makes use of certain abstract and general terms, imagining in bodies force, action, attraction, solicitation, *etc.* which are of first utility for theories and formulations, as also for computations about motion, even if in the truth of things, and in bodies actually existing, they would be looked for in vain, just like the

16 C. Hempel, "The Theoretician's Dilemma" in *Minnesota Studies in the Philosophy of Science*, ed. H. Feigl and M. Scriven (Minneapolis: University of Minnesota Press, 1958), II, 86.

geometers' fictions made by mathematical abstraction (*De Motu* 39).

Reply: causal explanations, theoretical terms, and realism

There is, then, good reason to think Berkeley an instrumentalist —at least for some theoretical terms.[17] But, I think, not for all, in particular not for those we have previously called theoretico-reporting terms. Berkeley might be an instrumentalist regarding all pure theoretical terms; they, then, would not be denoting terms. But, by definition, a reporting term is a denoting term so that some theoretical terms are also denoting terms, indeed, just those theoretical terms that are mind-terms. The others, e.g., the theoretical terms of physics, which are surely not reporting terms, are not denoting terms either. There is, therefore, nothing in the view of mind-terms presented here that is inconsistent with the rest of Berkeley's philosophy, for he can be an instrumentalist regarding the pure theoretical terms of science because they denote nothing we are aware of, and be a realist regarding theoretico-reporting terms because they do denote things we are aware of.

We have not done enough yet, however, for although the above account works for terms such as 'myself,' 'mind,' 'spirit,' and 'soul' which are clearly reporting terms and can, therefore, be distinguished from pure theoretical terms, this does not seem true of 'God,' 'Creator,' and 'Author of Nature.' They are not reporting terms and, thus, if we are to construe them as theoretical terms, it seems we must admit they are pure theoretical

[17] For more textual evidence of Berkeley's instrumentalism, cf. K. R. Popper, "A Note on Berkeley as Precursor of Mach and Einstein," *Conjectures and Refutations*, second edition (London: Routledge & Kegan Paul, 1965), pp. 166–174, a revised version of which is reprinted in this volume, pp. 129–144, above.

terms and, contrary to Berkeley, non-denoting terms. It is true that we are not aware of what such terms might denote so we should claim they are pure theoretical terms. Someone might try to resolve this problem by claiming these particular pure theoretical terms denote on Berkeley's view because the notions I have corresponding to these terms are "obtained by reflecting on my soul, heightening its powers, and removing its imperfections" (*Dialogues* III 4). But, although this may explain how I can have a notion of God, I do not think it sufficient to establish that 'God' is a denoting term.

Fortunately, there is another way to justify that 'God' as well as all other mind-terms are denoting terms, whether or not they are reporting terms. We can divide theoretical terms in another way, according to the kind of explanatory role they play. As Berkeley puts it when discussing the physical sciences:

> It is not, however, in fact the business of physics or mechanics to establish efficient causes, but only the rules of impulsions or attractions, and, in a word, the laws of motions, and from the established laws to assign the solution, not the efficient cause of particular phenomena. . . . The true, efficient and conserving cause of all things by supreme right is called their fount and principle. But the principles of experimental philosophy are properly to be called foundations and springs, not of their existence but of our knowledge of corporeal things, both knowledge by sense and knowledge by experience, foundations on which that knowledge rests and springs from which it flows. . . . These laws of motion are conveniently called principles, since from them are derived both general mechanical theorems and particular explanations of the phenomena. A thing can be said to be explained mechanically then indeed when it is reduced to those most simple and universal principles, and shown by accurate reasoning to be in agreement and connection with them (*De Motu* 35–37).

One explanatory role, the role of the pure theoretical terms of the physical sciences, is to warrant the derivation of inferential relationships, both deductive and inductive, among observable facts.[18] This is an important kind of explanation because it allows us to make inferences beyond our present observations and thereby attain the knowledge needed to guide the course of our lives. For this explanatory role, Berkeley's instrumentalist or "inference ticket" construal of theoretical terms is plausible. But it is not plausible for the other role, the role Berkeley assigns to mind-terms.

The second explanatory role described by Berkeley is that of explaining the causation, or production, of the various observable phenomena. It is clear why Berkeley thinks that the physical sciences cannot deal with these causes. The subject matter of science is observable phenomena. These are nothing but ideas, and no ideas, being inert, can cause anything. Only active entities, i.e., minds, can be causes and, consequently, the second kind of explanation requires mind-terms, and, clearly, denoting terms, because the terms used to explain the production of ideas must denote active entities. They cannot, therefore, be merely non-denoting parts of inference tickets. Consequently, any theoretical term, whether pure or not, whose explanatory role is the explanation of the production of ideas, rather than the establishment of inferential relations among ideas, must be a denoting term.

Conclusion

We can conclude that 'God,' as well as all other mind-terms, are, on Berkeley's view, denoting theoretical terms, unlike other

18 Cf. Hempel, p. 87.

theoretical terms, and that this distinction can be made on the basis of the differences in the kind of explanatory roles they play. Whether all these terms, e.g., 'God,' actually denote, is, of course, another question, one I think Berkeley failed to answer satisfactorily. But, regardless of that, we have finished the task of this paper. We have, I think, arrived at a full-bodied and plausible theory of mind-terms, notions, and minds that fits with and supplements what little Berkeley has given us. Whether we would be justfied in accepting this theory is another and much longer story.

Paul J. Olscamp / Does Berkeley

have an ethical theory?

The answer to the title question depends upon the meaning of "theory." If we mean a set of arguments, grouped together in Berkeley's writings and deductively organized, then, with the possible exception of *Passive Obedience,* the answer is negative. But if we mean that the principles for an ethical system, supported by an analysis of their foundations, together with conclusions constituting solutions for traditional ethical problems are to be found in his writings, then the answer is affirmative. In what follows, I shall try to prove three claims: 1) that the principles of an ethical system are to be found in Berkeley's works; 2) that they are established in such a way that they are integrally related to the principles of Berkeley's epistemology

This essay appears for the first time in this volume.

and ontology; 3) that from these principles, "practical propositions" are deduced by Berkeley.

Berkeley began a second part to the *Principles of Human
Knowledge,* but he lost it in Italy in 1716. The subjects discussed
were apparently moral philosophy, metaphysics, and philosophy of mind. Referring to this second part, Berkeley lists his
"two great principles of morality" as the "Being of a God and
the freedom of Man" (*PC* 508).* There is an obvious relationship between these principles and the reasons he offers for the
entire philosophical endeavor: to refute scepticism and to vindi-
cate theism. In order to fulfill the latter purposes, he had to
establish the first of the two moral principles, and his epistemo-
logical and ontological investigations are an attempt to do just
that. But since he saw that there is no morality without freedom,
he also argues that man is a free agent. These arguments are
integrally related to his epistemology and ontology, for they
rest upon his radical bifurcation of the world into mind and
body and his elimination of motion in the traditional sense from
the natural world, thereby, in his view, destroying the basis for
determinism.

The principles of Berkeley's moral philosophy

Here are the principles of Berkeley's moral philosophy:

1) God exists.

* Abbreviations: *Alc* = *Alciphron; Draft* = First Draft of the Introduc-
tion to the *Principles; G* = Essays in the *Guardian; HP* = *Three Dia-
logues Between Hylas and Philonous; PC* = *Philosophical Commentaries;
PO* = *Passive Obedience; Pr* = *Principles of Human Knowledge;
TV* = *Essays Towards a New Theory of Vision; TVV* = *The Theory of
Vision Vindicated*
  References to Berkeley are from *The Works of George Berkeley,* ed.
A. A. Luce and T. E. Jessop (9 vols.; Edinburgh: Thomas Nelson and
Sons, 1948–1957).

2) The natural world is literally a language through which God teaches man, and through which we can infer that God has certain attributes essential for a rational, moral universe.

3) From the natural language, we can learn both prudential and moral rules, the chief one being that it is "the general well-being of all men, of all nations, of all ages of the world, which God designs should be procured by the concurring actions of each individual" (PO 7).

4) For moral purposes, the most important sorts of signs in the natural language are those of pain and pleasure, for when they are properly (rationally) interpreted, they enable us to distinguish different kinds and values of pleasures and short- from long-run consequences of our actions.

5) Our souls are immortal, so long-run consequences are for humans the more important ones.

6) In the natural language, there are two sorts of laws: "a rule or precept for the direction of the voluntary actions of reasonable agents," and "any general rule which we observe to obtain in the works of nature, independent of the wills of men." Only the former imply a moral duty, and there is a further division of this sort into "positive" and "negative" law (PO 33, 26).

7) The third and sixth principles imply two others: a) the moral life is an ordered one, and b) our moral decisions must be free.

The language of the Author of Nature

In section 147 of the *Essay on Vision*, Berkeley coins the phrase "Language of the Author of Nature." In section 252 of *Siris*, he speaks of natural laws as a "grammar" for understanding the "rational discourse" of nature. In between these first and last works, he makes constant use of the "metaphor." For example, he calls God an "author" nine times in the *Principles*, and at least five in *Passive Obedience*. The characterization of nature as a language has an intimate relation to the establishing of his two basic moral principles, for on its literal acceptance rest Berkeley's conclusions about the attributes of God and our ability to learn and apply the rules of morality. The actual proof for God's existence does not depend upon the "natural language" thesis. It is supposed to be "necessary," and it rests upon Berkeley's fundamental analysis of the possible objects of human knowledge. All knowledge can only be about what is given in sensation, or inferences based upon it, or about minds, known directly or by analogy, or about relations. Minds and relations are not possible data of the senses. Of them we have "notions" (*Pr* 1; *PC* 176A; *HP* III 4). What is given in sensation are "ideas." Motion is not given in sensation. Berkeley also assumes a very few axioms of inference: 1) everything has a cause; 2) causes are active; 3) like effects have like causes. We can now complete the proof for God's existence:

1) Everything has a cause.

2) Only causes are active.

3) No ideas are active.

4) Thus, no ideas are causes.

5) Though our minds are active, and hence causes, no human mind can be the cause of all the ideas in the universe.

6) Hence there must be a cosmic mind. One other assumed principle now comes to the fore. It is: from a difference in degree, magnitude, etc. in an effect, we can infer like differences in the cause or causes of effects. Thus:

7) As the effects of the cosmic mind are infinitely greater, etc. than those of human minds, so the cosmic mind, God, is infinitely greater, etc. With this statement, the importance of the Language of Nature begins.

For moral purposes, it is not sufficient that there is a cosmic cause. The cause must be intelligent, good, and provident. How could we show that God has these properties? It is through language that we infer the existence of other minds and their properties. If nature is a language, then we can make the same sorts of inference about its author. But the argument must enable me to infer the nature of God's attributes "as certainly, and with the *same* evidence, at least, as any other signs perceived by sense do suggest to me the existence of your soul, spirit, or thinking principle" (*Alc* IV 2. Cf. IV 4, 5, 21, 22 on arguments from analogy). The first thing to do, then, is to adduce some of the obvious features of language from Berkeley's account (*PC* 221; HP III 9; *Alc* VII 12; *TVV* 39, 40, 42; *TV* 109, 140, 143, 147; *Alc* IV 5, 7, 12; *Draft* 20):

1) Words may suggest absent or present things.

2) As sounds suggest things, so characters suggest sounds.

3) The relation between a heard or written word and what it signifies is not necessary, but is founded simply upon constant conjunction.

4) Words have no meaning until we understand what they signify.

5) The choice of words is arbitrary, in the sense that other vehicles could convey the same meaning.

6) Since words are arbitrary, it is their scope, variety, etc., that is, their use, which constitutes a language.

7) Mistakes about language are in the realm of the understanding, for sense never errs.

8) Inference about the future meanings of language can only be probable, since language is arbitrary.

9) Though arbitrary, language must be consistent to have meaning.

10) Because words are arbitrary, we must learn some of them by ostensive definition.

11) The same word can have different meanings in different contexts.

12) Because we are usually more interested in the meaning than in the word, we often overlook the sign and concentrate on what is signified.

13) Not every word need name or denote something. Some words, for example, are used primarily to cause or inhibit action or emotion.

Does nature have these properties? Berkeley claims that nature is composed of "arbitrary, outward, sensible signs, having no resemblance or necessary connection with the things they stand for and suggest," that these signs "make known an endless variety of things" by which we are "instructed or informed in their different natures . . . taught and admonished what to shun, and what to pursue . . . directed how to regulate our motions, and how to act with respect to things different from us, as well in time as in place" (*Alc* IV 5). He claims that "the connexion of ideas does not imply the relation of cause and effect, but only of a mark or sign with the thing signified. The fire which I see is not the cause of the pain I feel upon my approaching it, but the mark that forewarns me of it," and he believes that the reason "ideas are formed into machines," that is, objects, is identical with the reason we combine letters into words, namely, that "a few original ideas may be made to signify a great number of effects and actions" (*Pr* 65). In order to understand natural signs, we must learn them ostensively (*TV* 147). It is "the articulation, combination, variety, copiousness, extensive and general use and easy application of signs . . . that constitute the true nature of language." These ingredients are to be found in nature, and therefore nature is a language. Asked whether he "really think[s] that God Himself speaks every day and in every place to the eyes of all men," he replies that "you have as much reason to think that the Universal Agent or God speaks to your eyes, as you can have for thinking any particular person speaks to your ears" (*Alc* IV 12). Given this, we can argue from analogy that God is wise, benevolent, provident, and good. He teaches us that we must eat and sleep to be healthy, that there are times to reap and times to sow, that we must act in certain ways to avoid pain and gain pleasure, that to achieve given ends there are certain means, and finally that "all things are made for the supreme good . . . and we may be said to account for a thing when we shew that it is so best" (*Siris* 260).

Pain and pleasure, private and public interest

Pleasure and pain are particular sorts of signs in the language of nature to which no agent is indifferent, and which teach us what is in our own interest. Berkeley thought it impossible to distinguish between interest and profit, and that every agent acts for his own interest (*PC* 541, 542, 569). Pleasure and pain do not depend upon our wills, but upon God's, as known by us through the regular manifestations of what are called the Laws of Nature (*PC* 143, 144, 542). Thus, what is in our own interests is taught to us by God through the laws of pain and pleasure. The study of these laws reveals that there are different kinds and values of pleasures, and it shows us the relation between personal and social well-being. The third principle states that the general well-being is the highest moral rule, and it is through the laws of pain and pleasure that we discover this, ascertain what the general well-being *is,* and learn how to achieve it, that is, what moral rules to follow. Thus, a knowledge of the role of these signs is essential to an understanding of the foundations of Berkeley's moral philosophy.

Some pleasures are valuable as means, and others as ends (*PC* 852). Some are "natural" pleasures and others are "fantastical." Natural pleasures do not depend upon:

. . . the fashion and caprice of any particular age or nation, and are suited to human nature in general, and were intended by Providence as rewards for the using our faculties agreeably to the ends for which they were given us (*G* IV).

Fantastical pleasures "presuppose some particular whim or taste accidentally prevailing in a sect of people, to which it is owing that they please" *(ibid)*. They carry their own penalties with them: they cause a "restlessness of mind," forcing us into the pursuit of "imaginary goods, in which there is nothing can raise desire, but the difficulty of obtaining them. Thus men become contrivers of their own misery, as a punishment on themselves for departing from the measures of nature" *(ibid)*. In the "scale of pleasure":

the lowest are sensual delights . . . succeeded by the more enlarged views and gay portraitures of a lively imagination; and these give way to the sublimer pleasures of reason . . . [which] fill the mind with the contemplation of intellectual beauty, order, and truth (*G* IV, VIII).

Thus there are three sorts of pleasure, each divided into natural and fantastical.

The three sorts of pleasure presuppose three faculties: sense, imagination, and reason. As the faculties are different, so are the "pleasures perfective of [their] acts." As reason is qualitatively superior to sense, so the pleasures perfective of acts of reason are also superior. The happiness of a bat is different from that of an eagle (*Alc* II 14). Some may disagree, but that is no ground in itself for argument. The "vulgar sort of men" might prefer "a sign-post painting to one of Raphael's, or a Grubstreet ballad to an ode of Horace" (*Alc* II 15). It takes "maturity and improvement of understanding" to see the qualitative differences among pleasures, and what they teach about vice and virtue *(ibid)*. To compute our long-run interests on the basis of present sense pleasure alone is simply to be guilty of bad calculating (*Alc* II 18).

With these distinctions in mind, what is it that we learn about the moral end through the language of nature? We learn, for example, that gluttons and drunkards are less healthy than sober and moderate men, and that the lives of the latter are more conducive to the public well-being than those of the former. Experience teaches that neither individuals, nor families, nor societies flourish on immoderate conduct of any sort. The state of happiness for man, therefore:

> . . . consists in having both soul and body sound and in good condition, enjoying those things which their respective natures require and free from those things which are odious or hurtful to them. . . (*Alc* II 9).

Fantastical pleasures will not lead to this state. Money is useless if we do not know the end for which it is good as a means (*Alc* II 10). A wealthy individual, or nation, is not necessarily happy, and happiness is good:

> . . . it is natural for us to regard things as they are fitted to augment or impair our own happiness; and accordingly we denominate them *good* or *evil*. Our judgment is ever employed in distinguishing between these two, and it is the whole business of our lives to endeavour, by a proper application of our faculties, to procure the one and avoid the other (*PO* 5).

Happiness depends, in the case of the body, on the "bodily composition of a man" and its maintenance, and, in the case of mental health, on "right notions," "true judgments," "regular will," and a state such that "the passions and appetites are directed to their proper objects, and confined within due bounds," namely the bounds of reason (*Alc* II 12).

Yet, we cannot consider our personal interests independently from those of our fellows. The language of nature teaches us that cooperation among the members or parts of any species is essential to the well-being of the whole. This is true throughout the entire universe, and so it is true of us. It follows that ". . . a wise man should consider and pursue his private good, with regard to and in conjunction with that of other men" and that consequently the general good must be "the rule or measure of moral truths," truths "which direct or influence the moral actions of men." Thus, the general happiness is "a greater good than the private happiness of one man, or of certain men," and the wisest and most virtuous man will be he who serves this end by the best means (*Alc* I 16).

Passive Obedience

In *Passive Obedience,* the conclusion that the utility principle is the cardinal ethical rule is reached by a different means. There, it is *assumed* that God exists and has certain morally relevant attributes, and then in conjunction with certain other premises, the utility principle is *deduced*. Three methods for discovering moral laws are rejected by Berkeley in favor of deduction, but significantly their discovery through the natural language is not one of them. I say "significantly" because that is obviously the method he uses in his other works. The deduction, made in sections 6 and 7, can be stated briefly:

1) ". . . It is a truth evident by the light of nature, that there is a sovereign omniscient Spirit, who alone can make us for ever happy, . . . or miserable."

2) ". . . A conformity to His will . . . is the sole rule whereby every man who acts up to the principles of reason must govern and square his actions."

3) No man is entitled to more than another from God, except according to the criterion of moral goodness.

4) The criterion of moral goodness presupposes that there was no morally relevant distinction between men prior to God's establishment of the moral end.

5) God is perfect, so (a) whatever end he proposes must be good, and (b) it cannot be his own good, since he needs nothing. Thus, it is the good of his creatures.

6) Four and five imply that the general good of all men, for all times and places, is the moral end.

After this, deductions of subsidiary rules in ethics can be simply performed, and this might be taken as Berkeley's meaning when he says that

> . . . the rational deduction of those laws is founded on the intrinsic tendency they have to promote the well-being of mankind . . . (PO 31),

and,

> . . . whatsoever practical proposition doth to right reason evidently appear to have a necessary connection with the universal well-being included in it is to be looked upon as enjoined by the will of God (PO 11).

An example of a practical proposition is, "Thou shalt not commit adultery," and a simple deduction of this rule would appear as follows:

1) One ought to obey the utility principle.
2) The practice of adultery is an infraction of this principle.
3) Thus, thou shalt not commit adultery.

Certainly, such deductions are actually performed by Berkeley, the most notable examples in *Passive Obedience* being found in section 15. But, at the same time, the discovery *that* the practice of adultery is not conducive to the public well-being is *not* deduced from anything. It is discovered by ". . . an impartial survey of the general frame and circumstances of human nature"

(*PO* 15); it is ". . . collected from observation" (*PO* 14). It is, therefore, no contradiction to hold, on the one hand, that deductions of moral injunctions from rules and descriptions of practices can be performed, and, on the other, that the rules and practices are discoverable from the language of nature. It is, furthermore, no contradiction to hold on the one hand that the utility principle may be discovered from the language of nature, *and* that it is deducible from propositions about God and his attributes. Berkeley makes the former inference in *Alciphron* and the *Three Dialogues,* the latter in *Passive Obedience.* Finally, it is no contradiction to hold both that the existence of God and his attributes are known by "the light of nature," and may be inferred from the sorts of things we find in the world and their natures (minds, bodies, and relations), and from the theory that nature is a language. Berkeley uses both these methods, the analytic and synthetic, the latter being the method of *Passive Obedience.* The advantage of the analytic method is that it provides a study of the *foundations* of his moral principles, and that is one of my aims. Other problems with *Passive Obedience* remain, and I shall discuss some of them in the next section.

The role of rules in normative ethics

There are two kinds of moral laws which we know from the language of nature to serve the universal well-being: positive and negative rules. The difference is this: We can abstain from the performance of any positive action enjoined by a rule, and, thus, given the appropriate circumstances, positive law admits ". . . of suspension, limitation, and diversity of degrees." But negative laws, such as "Thou shalt not commit adultery, "do not depend upon circumstances in any sense in Berkeley's view, and have no exceptions (*PO* 26). *If* we obey these laws, then they will serve the moral end, but God cannot be blamed if the tyrant chooses not to obey them (*PO* 41). Berkeley thinks that we must observe these "determinate, established laws, with an essential fitness" to serve the general happiness, even if undesirable consequences occasionally result, because of circumstances or bad intentions. The reasons the laws are essential are these: 1) the most intelligent of men now and then cannot make an accurate moral decision because of circumstances; 2) it is easier to decide if a given practice is in accordance with a rule than to decide its rightness on the basis of consequences; 3) moral decisions cannot be left merely to individual impulses and consciences because these vary, and are subject to abuse (*PO* 8–12). In short, "our practice must always be shaped immediately by the rule" (*PO* 31). We can conclude that Berkeley thinks an act is right if it falls under a rule when practice in accordance with that rule brings about the greatest happiness.

A further distinction among the sorts of rules relevant to morals is made in reply to an objection considered in *Passive Obedience*. The objection is that political loyalty considered as enjoined by a negative precept would violate a still more fundamental law, that of self-preservation. In reply, Berkeley divides natural law into two sorts: (*a*) "rule[s] or precept[s] for the direction of the voluntary actions of reasonable agents" and (*b*) "any general rule which we observe to obtain in the works of nature, independent of the wills of men." Only type (*a*) imply moral duties, but self-preservation is a type (*b*) law. Were this not so, it would follow that we could do anything to preserve our lives, which Berkeley thought absurd (*PO* 33–35).

Serious problems are raised by assertions such as this in *Passive Obedience:*

> In morality the eternal rules of action have the same immutable universal truth with propositions in geometry. Neither of them

depend upon circumstances or accidents, being at all times, and
in all places, without limitation or exception, true . . . (*PO* 53).

Berkeley goes on to say that the fact that a rule does not "reach
a man's practice" in all cases is no more reason to deny its universality than it would be to deny it for the rule "multiply the
height by half the base" for measuring triangles because the
thing to be measured was not an exact triangle. The difficulties
of interpretation here are compounded by the use of expressions
such as "necessary connection" to describe the relation between
rules and the beneficial effects when followed. I cannot deal
with this subject adequately here, for reasons of space. Many
of the problems involved have in my opinion been solved by G.
P. Conroy's excellent article "George Berkeley on Moral Demonstration."[1]

I shall confine myself to two points, the first being that the
connection between moral laws and our universal well-being,
even if necessary in some sense, cannot be necessary in a *logical*
sense. This is so because otherwise God could not be free. A
necessary condition for occurrence of *any* consequences following upon our action in accordance with a rule is God's concurrence. If it were a contradiction to assert that the law was
obeyed, but the consequence did not follow, God would not be
free to intervene. Of course, consequences do in fact follow; but
so long as God need will no particular thing, the connection between them and the laws under which we act must be contingent. Even in *Passive Obedience*, Berkeley affirms that nature
is nothing but "a series of *free* actions produced by the best and
wisest Agent" (*PO* 14, my italics). If God is free, omniscient,
and all-powerful, as Berkeley thought, then the effects of obedience to moral laws cannot follow logically from them.

[1] G. P. Conroy, "George Berkeley on Moral Demonstration," *Journal of
the History of Ideas,* 22 (April 1961), 205–214.

The second point turns on Berkeley's theory of truth. This, too, is a complex problem that I can discuss only briefly. Whatever else is true, this is: Berkeley's views of the nature of truth were not the traditional ones. Locke and the deists had held that truth was a function of the agreement of ideas. The sentence "Melampus is an animal" would be true for them if the idea denoted by "Melampus" and that denoted by "animal" are related in certain ways. Berkeley rejects this view because he thought that the sentence was an instruction telling us that we could also call Melampus by the name "animal" (*Draft* 19). Further, since we have no ideas of relations, minds, and several other things, propositions about them could not be true or false according to whether ideas denoted by their names stood in appropriate relations (*Pr* 89, 90, 100). In addition, if nature is a language, then in what sense are its rules "true"? The question is absurd if we must pretend that truth in the natural language is a matter of the correspondence of ideas, for even if resemblance among ideas, or class membership, is to be the foundation of the correspondence, resemblance and class inclusion are relations of which we can have no ideas (*Pr* 89, 90), and there are no natural classes for Berkeley. Finally, natural moral laws are "rules directive of our actions" (*PO* 7), and even if Berkeley did accept some sort of correspondence theory in the case of descriptions, which is doubtful (see *Pr* 49), rules would not fall into the same category. He argues that the laws of arithmetic and geometry do not denote abstract general ideas, as the Lockeans had held, and that the universality of geometrical signs, for example, a one-inch line, and thence presumably of the propositions formed from them, consists ". . . only in its signification, whereby it represents innumerable lines greater than itself" (*Pr* 126). Mathematical propositions are concerned directly with signs or symbols and indirectly with particulars; they "direct us how to act with relation to things, and dispose rightly of them" (*Pr* 122). The same themes are found through-out *De Motu* and the *Analyst*. In my view, Berkeley's theory of truth is closely akin to pragmatism or instrumentalism, and, if this is true, then remarks such as those in *Passive Obedience* must be interpreted accordingly.

Free will and immortality

Free will was the second of the two fundamental principles of morality specified by Berkeley. Minds are the opposite of body: They are unextended, independent of natural change though not of God, and active. Minds are known either directly or by analogy, and we have "notions" of them rather than ideas. Volitions, which are mental acts, are distinguishable only by their effects, and understanding and willing are not two differ-ent "things," but two activities of the one mind. Guilt is a func-tion of the will alone, and power or agency implies both volition and its effects (*PC* 669; Letter to Johnson, *Works*, II, 281). Vice and virtue thus consist in the will (*PC* 149, 669). The freedom essential for this position consists in spontaneous acts of will, undetermined by anything (*PC* 156–161). Thus:

> Men impute their actions to themselves because they will'd them, and that not out of ignorance but whereas they knew the consequences of them whether good or bad (*PC* 157).

It is because the mind is not a "thing," not a possible object of perception, that it is not subject to natural law. Its existence consists in perceiving, thinking, and willing rather than in being perceived (*Pr* 139). But decay, degeneration, etc., are events which only occur subject to natural law, and thus it follows that the soul is "naturally immortal" (*Pr* 141). Motion is a relative concept, a function of the measurement of the position of at least two bodies at different points in time (*Pr* 112–116). But since minds have no spatial position they are not moved, and "motion is one thing and volition another." Determinism, the thesis that the mind is causally affected by the natural world, must assume that this is false, thus begging the question (*Alc* VII 16).

There are many Berkeleian arguments against various versions of determinism, most of them in the seventh dialogue of *Alciphron*. The one just mentioned depends upon Berkeley's theory of the natural language and his analysis of the components of reality. Another concerns the determinists' claim that God's foreknowledge is certain, and since what is certain is necessary, his foreknowledge implies determinism. Berkeley's reply is twofold: First, there is a difference between certainty and necessity, the latter implying constraint and the former not; secondly,

> . . . If it is foreseen that such an action shall be done, may it not also be foreseen that it shall be an effect of human choice and liberty? (*Alc* VII 18).

For Berkeley, it all ultimately boils down to this:

> I know I act, and what I act I am accountable for . . . (*Alc* VII 19).

The theological foundations for the definition of "good"

Happiness is good for Berkeley, but that is not its definition, for it still makes sense for him to ask *why* happiness is good. Berkeley's favorite quotation from scripture was Paul's characterization of God as the being in whom "we live, and move, and have our being." For the Bishop of Cloyne, there is nothing without God; no natural world of ideas, no minds, no moral end, no means to fulfilling that end, no rationality in the universe, no answer to injustice, no foundation for morality. In modern philosophy, authoritarian theories about the origin of moral obligations are suspect, because they seem to involve the "factualistic" fallacy. Thus "God wills X" would not, if this objection is true, entail either that "X is right" or that "One ought to do X." Berkeley simply would not have understood this objection, and the reasons why are cryptically stated in this comment:

> God Ought to be worship'd. This Easily demonstrated when once we axcertain the signification of the word God, worship, ought (*PC* 705).

It is for Berkeley impossible to do good and not act in accordance with God's will because good *is* whatever God wills. In *Siris* 320 he says: "Evil, defect, negation, is not the object of God's creative power"; and, as H. W. Orange noted,[2] since there can be no good independent of a mind for Berkeley, to say that good might be something other than it is is simply a violation of the law of identity, for it presumes that what is absent from God's mind, evil, might be present with what is in his mind, good. If I have been correct, "right" is defined in terms of "good" for Berkeley, for what is right is what tends to the general happiness, the good which happens to be present to God's mind. To say that one ought to do actions which tend to the good is, I think, a tautology for Berkeley, though I admit that on this point there is little evidence. "Happiness is good" will be synthetically true, because what is present to God's mind *need* not be any particular thing, given his omnipotence. Thus, Berkeley's definition of good is simply "that which is present to the mind of God." In the end, then, his moral philosophy cannot be divorced from his theology and religion.

[2] H. W. Orange, "Berkeley as a Moral Philosopher," *Mind*, 15 Old Series (1890), 552.

Conclusions

Much remains to be discussed about Berkeley's moral philosophy: the rather startling claim that he may have been a noncognitivist; the different sorts of evidence he adduces for his arguments (there are at least three); his other arguments against determinism; further investigations into his view of mathematical propositions and his comparisons of them with the laws of nature; more detailed studies of the differences in method between *Passive Obedience* and the other works, etc. But enough has been said to prove the three claims I set out to prove, and to warrant a few other general conclusions. Berkeley's theory is largely utilitarian in character, as his arguments about the utility principle show, though there are important differences. There are also elements of the more modern theory of rule-utilitarianism, as his remarks about the relations between moral decisions, rules, and practices show. He believes that good can ultimately be defined, and that the basis of the definition is a theory about God. Theories of this sort are now called "theological definist" theories, though naturally Berkeley would never have heard of any of this terminology.

He reaches his principles analytically, much after the method of Descartes in the *Rules for the Direction of the Mind* and the *Discourse on Method*, and uses synthesis to show how subsidiary rules are derivable from them. His principles are founded in the very fabric of his general philosophy, and to the extent that that is unique, so is his moral philosophy. One might even say, without stretching a point, that he had an ethical theory.

J. D. Mabbott / The place of

God in Berkeley's philosophy

Berkeley is commonly regarded as an idealist whose system is saved from subjectivism only by the advent of a God more violently _ex machina_ than the God of any other philosopher. I hope to show that this accusation rests on a misunderstanding of his central theory, a misunderstanding which gives God a place both inconsistent with his main premises and useless in his system. I hope also to display by quotation the real Berkeley, whose theory of God's place and nature is directly supported by argument and consistent with his premises, and makes (with his account of self) a system which, if it is less than a completely coherent philosophy, is more than an episcopal assumption.

From THE JOURNAL OF PHILOSOPHY (_now_ PHILOSOPHY), VI (_January 1931_), 18–29. _Reprinted by permission of the author and_ PHILOSOPHY.

I shall first show how the usual conception of Berkeley's God arose. Locke had shown that our ideas of colour, taste and other secondary qualities depend on the percipient, but he held that primary qualities (shape, size, solidity, etc.) reside in the object just as we perceive them. Berkeley applied Locke's arguments about colour against shape and size, and showed that our ideas of the latter qualities were also relative to the percipient. Thus all my ideas depend on my perceiving them. This raises the obvious problem. "You ask me whether the books are in the study now, when no one is there to see them?"[1] "Upon shutting my eyes all the furniture in the room is reduced to nothing, and barely upon opening them it is again created."[2] Berkeley first suggests two inadequate solutions. "Whenever they [the books] are mentioned or discours'd of they are imagin'd and thought on. Therefore you can at no time ask me whether they exist or no, but by reason of that very question they must necessarily exist."[3] Not only perception but imagination (or conception) also confers existence, and it is therefore impossible to conceive something existing unconceived. He also suggests that physical objects may have a hypothetical or potential existence, anticipating Mill's view that an object is a permanent possibility of sensation. "The question whether the earth moves or no amounts in reality to no more than this, to wit, whether we have reason to conclude, from what has been observed by astronomers, that if we were placed in such and such circumstances, and such or such a position, and distance both from the earth and sun, we should perceive the former to move among the choir of the planets."[4] Neither of these two solutions confer

---

[1] C. i. 15. All references are to the Oxford Edition of Berkeley's Works (ed. A. Campbell Fraser, 4 vols., 1901). C. = *Commonplace Book*. P. = *Principles*. D. = *Dialogues*.

[2] P. 45, i. 281.

[3] C. i. 15. Cf. P. 23; D. I, i. 411.

[4] P. 58, i. 290.

any real permanence or stability on the world of nature. "The trees are in the park, i.e., whether I will or no, whether I imagine anything about them or no. Let me but go thither and open my eyes by day, and I shall not avoid seeing them."[5] If *esse* is *percipi*, objects when perceived by no finite spirit must be kept in existence by God's perceiving them. "Seeing that they . . . have an existence distinct from being perceived by me, *there must be some other Mind wherein they exist.* As sure, therefore, as the sensible world really exists, so sure is there an infinite, omnipresent Spirit who contains and supports it."[6] This completes the orthodox account of Berkeley's view of the status of physical objects. The *esse* of ideas is *percipi*; the *esse* of spirt is *percipere*. "From what has been said it is evident that there is no other Substance than *Spirit*, or that which perceives."[7] "The question between me and the Materialists is not whether things have a *real* existence out of the mind of this or that person, but whether they have an *absolute* existence, distinct from being perceived by God, and exterior to *all* minds."[8] The *esse* of physical objects is therefore their being perceived by God. It is clear that this theory will save Berkeley from subjectivism, and it is to Divine perception that his editor, in defending him on the subjectivist charge, constantly makes appeal.[9] Yet it is a solution of the problem which excludes much of his most valuable work and raises more difficulties than it solves.

The alternative theory can best be approached through Berkeley's account of power or activity. We usually speak as if conditions of physical objects were due to the activity of other physical objects. But, in reducing physical objects to ideas in the mind, Berkeley saw that this view of cause could not stand. If

5 C. i. 65.
6 D. II, i. 424; Berkeley's italics. Cf. P. 46.
7 P. 7, i. 261.
8 D. III, i. 452.
9 Cf. i. 50, n. 4, 258, n. 3, 259, n. 5 and *passim*.

the *esse* of ideas is *percipi*, "it follows that there is nothing in them but what is perceived; but whoever shall attend to his ideas, whether of sense or of reflexion, will not perceive in them any power or activity." Therefore "the very being of an idea implies passivity or inertness in it:"[10] Sometimes, however, I know that I have created my own ideas. When I imagine a ship, I am aware of the image but also of the activity of my self. Here perception differs from imagination; if I perceive a ship, I have no such awareness of spiritual activity. "It is that passive recognition of my own ideas that denominates the mind perceiving— that being the very essence of perception or that wherein perception consists."[11] Since I am aware that I do not create my own ideas of perception, some other agent must produce them in me. "I find I can excite ideas in my mind at pleasure. . . . This making and unmaking of ideas doth very properly denominate the mind active. . . . But, whatever powers I may have over my own thoughts, I find the ideas actually perceived by Sense have not a like dependence on *my* will."[12] The agent which produces them cannot be matter, for "Doth not *Matter*, in the common current acceptation of the word, signify an extended, solid, moveable, unthinking, inactive substance?"[13] This was indeed the account of matter current in Berkeley's day. Subsequent theories of atoms as centres of force, and the replacement of the Indestructibility of Matter by the Conservation of Energy as the basic principle of physics, left later scientists a way out of Berkeley's dilemma which was closed to his contemporaries. Against them his argument was conclusive. Since the agent affecting me when I perceive cannot be matter, and since spirit can be active, the cause must be spirit. "There is therefore some

[10] P. 25, i. 271.
[11] C. i. 83.
[12] P. 28, 29, i. 272–273.
[13] D. II, i. 429.

other Will or Spirit that produces them."[14] The nature of this Spirit can be deduced from its effects on me, from the character of my ideas of sense. Its power is clear from the fact that, however I try, I cannot perceive things otherwise than as I do. "The ideas of Sense are more strong, lively, and distinct than those of the Imagination; they have likewise a steadiness, order, and coherence, and are not excited at random, as those which are the effects of human wills often are, but in a regular train or series —the admirable connexion whereof sufficiently testifies the wisdom and benevolence of its Author."[15] It may be noted in passing that Berkeley uses no arguments from theology to support his belief in the existence of God, nor does he appeal to religious experience. He holds, indeed, that we have no immediate intuition of God.[16]

From the argument so far several difficulties in the usual account at once emerge. If mind is essentially active and perceiving essentially passive the *esse* of mind cannot be *percipere*. At the one place where in the *Commonplace Book* Berkeley says the *esse* of mind is *percipere* he has added later "or *velle*, i.e., *agere*."[17] I am most myself not in perceiving but in willing or imagining. "This making or unmaking of ideas doth very properly denominate the mind active."[18] God is Spirit, and to suppose that He perceives would be to make Him the passive recipient of ideas impressed on Him by some more powerful agency. Volition and not perception is therefore our clue to the nature of God. "The Spirit—the active thing—that which is soul and God—is the Will alone."[19] "Substance of a spirit is

---

[14] P. 29, i. 273.
[15] P. 30, i. 273.
[16] C. i. 51. Cf. P. 148.
[17] C. i. 10.
[18] P. 28, i. 273.
[19] C. i. 41.

that it acts, causes, wills, operates."[20] Nor can the *esse* of ideas be *percipi*. The *esse* of my own fancies is that they are imagined, created by me; of my sense-data that they are created in me by God. The *esse* of God's ideas (if we find any reason to believe in them, which we shall not) would be that they were imagined by Him, and even this is made difficult by Berkeley's view that imagination presupposes perception. "The having ideas is not the same thing with perception. A man may have ideas when he only imagines. But then this imagination presupposeth perception."[21]

So we are led to a new conception of God, and of His relation to the stable world which our senses reveal. Its stability will now be due to the regularity and orderliness of His activity, and not to His permanently perceiving it. "Nothing without corresponds to our primary ideas but powers. Hence a direct and brief demonstration of an active, powerful Being, distinct from us, on whom we depend."[22] The laws of nature are not modes of relation between God's ideas, but "set rules, or established methods, wherein the Mind we depend on excites in us the ideas of Sense."[23] We learn that certain of our ideas regularly accompany others. This concomitance is due to "the Goodness and Wisdom of that Governing Spirit whose Will constitutes the laws of nature."[24] The situation is like that created by a "good resolution." If I resolve to tidy up my papers regularly on Ember Days, what exists permanently is a disposition of my will. What exists only on Ember Days is the spatial pattern I call "tidy papers." So the trees in the park are permanently represented only by a "resolve" of the will of God such that as

---

[20] C. i. 53.
[21] C. i. 28. Cf. i. 52.
[22] C. i. 60.
[23] P. 30, i. 273.
[24] P. 32, i. 274.

occasion arises a spatial visual pattern (my idea of the trees) appears regularly in my mind. The physical world is thus really a complicated "good resolution" of God's. Two further illustrations may be adduced to show how a spatial datum may be regular and reliable, but not itself permanent. If I run my head into a brick wall, I see stars. The stars are not permanently there; they are the regular product of the meeting of my wayward steps with the permanent wall. So the table I perceive has no permanent shape or size; it is the regular product of the collision of my wayward activity with the permanent volition of God. Again, a magnetic field is force in itself invisible, but such that when iron filings are introduced into it they form regular, visible patterns. The application is obvious. We noticed above that one of Berkeley's inadequate solutions of his main problem was to allow the physical world a hypothetical or potential existence. This solution is now made possible for us by our having some reality from which the possibility is derived—the orderly volitional activity of God. "Bodies, etc., do exist even when not perceived—they being powers in the active being."[25]

This complete and coherent theory is much more entitled to be regarded as Berkeley's main position than that previously sketched. It alone is consistent with his distinction between perception and imagination, with his view that spirit is essentially active, and with his account of the relation between finite spirits and God. There seems, indeed, to be no need whatever in such a system for the realm of God's ideas. Yet Berkeley appears to have believed in them, as several references show, and as one of his special discussions may illustrate. One of the earliest queries in the *Commonplace Book* is, "Qu: Whether succession of ideas in the Divine Intellect?"[26] He later answers

[25] C. i. 61.
[26] C. i. 58, accepting the view of Lorenz that p. 58 is Berkeley's earliest writing.

this query in the negative, and is then faced with the problem of the meaning of the Creation. He solves it by saying that, while God's ideas have existed from eternity, Creation occurred when He made them perceptible to finite spirits. But if "they became perceptible in the same manner and order as is described in Genesis,"[27] a further difficulty appears. The creation of sun and moon could not have meant their becoming perceptible to man, who was created two days later. Berkeley ingeniously introduces the angels, "there being other intelligences before man was created."[28] Berkeley also gives reasons why we cannot dispense with God's ideas. God must be omniscient as well as omnipotent, for "to know everything knowable is certainly a perfection."[29] "There is in the Deity Understanding as well as Will. He is no blind agent, and in truth a blind agent is a contradiction."[30] In the Third Dialogue Hylas suggests that power alone is sufficient to account for our sense-data without God's having ideas. Philonous replies, "A thing which hath no ideas in itself cannot impart them to me."[31] This does not seem obvious, especially when he goes on to allow[32] that God, without having sense-data, can impart sense-data to me, and when we recall that all ideas are sense-data or are derived from them. "Ideas of Sense are the archetypes. Ideas of imagination, dreams, etc., are copies, images, of these."[33] I hope to show that, despite these definite expressions of opinion, Berkeley did not make the Divine Ideas an essential part of his system, and that there is good reason to doubt whether he believed in them at all.

[27] Letter to Percival, i. 353.
[28] C. i. 42. Cf. D. III, i. 472, 473.
[29] D. III, i. 459.
[30] C. i. 51.
[31] D. III, i. 457.
[32] D. III, i. 459.
[33] C. i. 52. Cf. i. 28.

There are many reasons why he should not believe in them. What is to be the relation between my ideas and God's? At this moment I have my idea of the table before me, and God has His. Surely this raises all the difficulties of a correspondence theory against which Berkeley fought so persistently. All that he says against Matter can be applied to attack this new correspondence. "Qu. Did ever any man see any other things besides his own ideas, that he should compare them to these, and make these like unto them?"[34] "Well, say I, Do you apprehend or conceive what you say extension is like unto, or do you not? If the latter, how know you they are alike? How can you compare any things besides your own ideas?"[35] God's ideas are as useless as Matter in Locke's theory. "Ask a man, I mean a philosopher, why he supposes this vast structure, this compages of bodies? he shall be at a stand; he'll not have one word to say."[36] "But then, that they should suppose an innumerable multitude of created beings, which they acknowledge are not capable of producing any one effect in nature, and which therefore are made to no manner of purpose, since God might have done everything as well without them—this, I say, though we should allow it possible, must yet be a very unaccountable and extravagant supposition."[37] "How therefore can you suppose that an All-perfect Spirit, on whose Will all things have an absolute and immediate dependence, should need an instrument in His operations, or, not needing it, make use of it? Thus it seems to me you are obliged to own the use of a lifeless inactive instrument to be incompatible with the infinite perfection of God."[38] "The Will of an Omnipotent Spirit is no sooner exerted than executed,

[34] C. i. 61.
[35] C. i. 82.
[36] C. i. 16.
[37] P. 53, i. 287. Cf. D. II, i. 427.
[38] D. II, i. 432.

without the application of means."[39] In all these passages the objections are as valid against God's ideas—all ideas being inactive—as against Matter.

Again, if the reality our ideas represent is the world of God's ideas, Berkeley's principal claim for his theory must fall —his claim that it is a direct theory of perception. "We must with the mob place certainty in the senses."[40] "There are others who say the wall is not white, the fire is not hot, etc. We Irishmen cannot attain to these truths."[41] "We see the house itself, the church itself; it being an idea and nothing more."[42] What I perceive directly *is* the physical object, and all theories to the contrary are agnostic. "The reverse of the Principle introduced Scepticism."[43] "Colour, figure, motion, extension, and the like, considered only as so many *sensations* in the mind, are perfectly known. . . . But, if they are looked on as notes or images referred to *things* or *archetypes existing without the mind*, then we are involved all in scepticism. We see only the appearances, and not the real qualities of things. . . . All this scepticism follows from our supposing a difference between *things* and *ideas*."[44] It follows no less inevitably from supposing a difference between our ideas and God's.

A further reason why Berkeley might well have dispensed with a belief in Divine Ideas is his reiterated assertion that ideas are inert and passive[45] and the fact that God's ideas would have necessarily to be spatial.[46] " 'Tis nevertheless of great use to

[39] *Ibid.*, 433.
[40] C. i. 44. Cf. D. I, i. 383.
[41] C. i. 91.
[42] C. i. 9. Cf. D. III, i. 463, and especially i. 445. ". . . the real things are those very things I see and feel."
[43] C. i. 83.
[44] P. 87, i. 305–306. Cf. D. I, i. 382, 418.
[45] E.g., i. 10, 13, 37, 41, 271, 429.
[46] This will be defended later. See *Note*, p. 217.

religion to take extension out of our idea of God, and put a power in its place. It seems dangerous to suppose extension, which is manifestly inert, in God."[47] It is equally dangerous to suppose any ideas (for all are inert) in God, who is pure activity. "I do not understand how our ideas, which are things altogether passive and inert, can be the essence, or any part (or like any part) of the essence or substance of God, who is an impassive, indivisible, pure, active being."[48]

It may be suggested that Berkeley can avoid the correspondence difficulty and the scepticism it involves by identifying our ideas with God's. On this view, when we perceive, God reveals His ideas to us. "There is an *omnipresent eternal Mind*, which Knows and comprehends all things, and exhibits them to our view in such a manner . . . as He Himself hath ordained."[49] This view is still open to the objection that things passive and inert can be no part of God, and to the further difficulty that all our sense-data are private, because of our varied view-points, as the *New Theory of Vision* exhaustively proved. An identification of our ideas with God's is also attributed by Berkeley to Malebranche as the view "that we see all things in God," and attacked accordingly. The dualism might also be avoided by holding that, in the act of perceiving, my mind is identified with God's—the theory used by T. H. Green in the case of conceptual relation. But Berkeley was much too vague about the implications of personality, and too stout a spiritual pluralist for moral reasons, to rob the finite self of any independence. If both these theories are rejected, the correspondence with its difficulties must stand.

For the reasons given above, it does not seem likely that Berkeley himself believed in the Divine Ideas, at least as a

47 C. i. 82.
48 D. II, i. 426.
49 D. III, i. 447.

necessary part of his system. It is true that he frequently mentions them, but we shall now show that some of these expressions are suggestively guarded. In one place[50] he discusses the view that "Matter, though it be not perceived by us, is nevertheless perceived by God, to whom it is the occasion of exciting ideas in our minds." He remarks first that this theory gives up the absolute independence of matter, and is therefore "the only intelligible one that I can pick from what is said of unknown occasions," but he adds that "it seems too extravagant to deserve a confutation." Yet this extravaganza is identified by most critics with Berkeleianism. "The upshot of all is, that there are certain *unknown* Ideas in the mind of God." "Whether there are such ideas in the mind of God I shall not dispute."[51] "I shall not dispute"—not only here, but in other places also, this is the best he can say for those Divine Ideas which are supposed to be the keystone of his own theory. Philonous is prepared to "allow" Hylas that there may be certain things perceived by the mind of God, which are to Him the occasion of producing ideas in us.[52] Berkeley is consulted on this very point by Rev. Samuel Johnson, who aims here a more shrewd blow against the Bishop than his notorious namesake. In reply Berkeley says he "has no objection against calling the Ideas in the Mind of God archetypes of ours."[53] He is prepared to "allow" Divine Ideas because they do not offend against his central doctrine that nothing is independent of Mind. But the admission is not readily made, for they are really foreign to his system.

It remains to ask why he should have mentioned them at all. Three reasons can be found. He probably came to them first; the simple symmetry of the crude theory sketched at the

[50] P. 70–75, i. 296 ff.
[51] P. 76, i. 300.
[52] D. II, i. 434.
[53] Letter to Johnson, quoted, ii. 19.

beginning of this paper makes it an obvious first refuge for a sinking subjectivist. If, however, such a development took place, it must have preceded all his published works, for the *Commonplace Book* shows the mature theory complete. The only shred of evidence for this suggestion may perhaps be found in the alteration of *percipere* to *agere* as the *esse* of spirit.[54] Secondly, theological considerations about omniscience would suggest the addition of the Divine Ideas to his completed system. Thirdly, it is much less alarming and revolutionary to think of the trees in the park existing when nobody perceives them, because they, with all their friendly, familiar qualities, are perceived by God, than to think of them as represented in God's mind by powers or volitions quite unlike them in character. Here is the real reason for the appearance of God's ideas in the published works, and especially in the popular *Dialogues*. In the *Commonplace Book*, Berkeley is uncompromising. "Bodies *taken for powers* do exist when not perceived."[55] "*Nothing* without corresponds to our primary ideas but powers."[56] But he resolves "Not to mention the combination of powers, but to say the things—*the effects themselves*—do really exist, even when not actually perceived, but still with relation to perception."[57] And why? " 'Tis prudent to correct men's mistake without altering their language. This makes truth glide into their souls insensibly."[58]

If it is said that Divine perception is after all a possible theory and is quite definitely asserted by Berkeley, a much more striking example of his way of "humouring" his audience "in their own way of talking"[59] can be adduced. In the *New Theory*

---

54 C. i. 10, quoted above.
55 C. i. 82.
56 C. i. 60.
57 C. i. 50. Italics in last three quotations mine.
58 C. i. 71.
59 C. i. 92.

of Vision he writes throughout as if tangible sense-data were independent of the percipient. The *Commonplace Book* shows that he had already decided that all sense-data were mind-dependent, so that this is part of a policy of gradualness. Not until the *Principles* does he attack tangibilia also. There is no question of development. The *Commonplace Book* (1705–08) gives the material for his whole system (except the technical term "notion"—the need of which is noted[60]); and the *New Theory* (1709), the *Principles* (1710), and the *Dialogues* (1713) show differences which are merely strategic. The Divine perception of the physical world is no more part of the system than is the independent reality of tangibilia. Both appear in the published works to mitigate the jar which the undiluted theory would administer to the plain man's system. The only difference between the two cases is that the reality of tangibilia (which is the more bluntly stated of the two) is incompatible with the whole system, while the existence of Divine Ideas conflicts only with parts of it, so that he can continue to treat their existence as an independently possible theological tenet, as the doctrine of the Trinity might be, but with as little connection with his philosophy as it has. "N.B. To use utmost caution not to give the least handle of offense to the Church or Churchmen."[61]

Campbell Fraser raises one point of difficulty for our insistence on the irrelevance of God's Ideas. The theory that our sense-data form a "natural language" continually recurs in Berkeley's works, and his editor explains the conception by saying "Sense-ideas are the letters of the alphabet in that language of natural order which God employs for the expression of *His* Ideas to us."[62] If this is correct, the natural language requires the existence of God's Ideas; otherwise the words of the lan-

[60] i. 21, "improper . . . to make ourselves ideas, or thinking things ideas."
[61] C. i. 41.
[62] i. 309, n. 2.

guage would be meaningless or express nothing. There are certainly difficulties about Berkeley's language theory. In the *New Theory of Vision* the words of the language were visible colours and shapes, and they stood for the real or tangible objects. But when tangibilia are overtly admitted to be mind-dependent a difficulty arises. If we say one type of sense-datum (visible) expresses another (tangible), we lose the distinction of status which we should expect to separate a language from what it means. If, on the other hand, we make the whole world of sense-data the language, and also eliminate God's Ideas as unknown and self-contradictory, what will the language express? Berkeley sometimes answers—the attributes of God. "The steady consistent methods of nature may not unfitly be styled the Language of its Author whereby he discovers his attributes to our view."[63] But in other places he says that sense-data stand for other sense-data: "the proper objects of sight"—light and colours—"do form a language wonderfully adapted to suggest and exhibit to us the distances, figures, situations, and various qualities of tangible objects . . . as words suggest the things signified by them."[64] Perhaps a *modus vivendi* might be arranged by distinguishing what words *express* from what they *evince*. If I say "There is the door," my words express a relation in space, but they evince anger. So God's words—our sense-data —express or suggest other sense-data, but evince His power and good will. Whatever our solution may be, there is never a suggestion in the whole of Berkeley's work that the "natural language" stands for God's ideas. This possibility is definitely rejected in the pamphlet *The Theory of Vision . . . Vindicated and Explained*, which was published in 1732, and which is interesting also as giving one of the clearest statements of the view we have ventured to call "the real Berkeley." "The objects of

63 P. 108, i. 317.
64 *Alciphron* IV, 10, ii. 168.

sense . . . are called ideas. . . . From our ideas of sense, the inference of reason is good to power, cause, agent. But we may not
infer that our ideas are like unto this Power, Cause, or Active
Being. On the contrary, it seems evident that an idea can be only
like another idea, and that in our ideas . . . there is nothing of
power, causality, or agency included. . . . Whenever, therefore,
the appellation of sensible *object* is used in a determined, intelligible sense, it is not applied to signify this absolutely existing
outward cause or power, but the ideas themselves produced
thereby. Ideas which are observed to be connected together are
vulgarly considered under the relation of cause and effect,
whereas, in strict and philosophic truth, they are only related as
sign to the thing signified."[65]

It may also be objected that we have left *Siris* out of
account. The reasons are many. If we exclude *Siris*, Berkeley's
system shows no development except the use of the word
"notion" to cover our knowledge of spirits and some dissatisfaction with his attack on Abstract Ideas. In the *Siris* we find
a new world. Its Platonic mysticism, its toleration of forms and
influences, its reverent agnosticism, its dependence on the
Timæus and Proclus, are poles apart from the Berkeley of the
other works. It is true that Divine Ideas are important in *Siris*,
but they are no more than those "Forms" of Plato which the
misunderstandings of Albinus and his followers (popularized by
the deceptive transliteration of the Greek word "idea") had
transmuted into "Ideas in the Divine Mind." There is nothing
Berkeleian about them. To attempt to unite the hints and grop-
ings of *Siris* into some kind of dusky Christian Platonism,
and then to regard the result as characteristic of Berkeley, would
be like making the Catholic faith the central belief of Voltaire
on the strength of his reputed death-bed conversion. Catholi-

[65] *Op. cit.*, 12, 13, ii. 386.

cism and Voltaire make as strange bed-fellows as *Siris* and Berkeley.

If it is said that God must have some theoretical activity— He cannot be a blind agent—our answer is that this may well be true, but that all Berkeley's main tenets preclude it. His mistake no doubt was to limit theoretical activity to the passive reception of sense-data and their imaginative reproduction, and thereby to make such experience impossible for God. But Berkeley without these limitations is not Berkeley, but Kant or (as in *Siris*) Plato. If he had extended his so-called doctrine of notions from spirits to relations, as he did, and from relations to universals, as he did not, he could have allowed God to have notions. "God knows or has ideas, but his ideas are not conveyed to him by sense as ours are."[66] But the first extension, to relations, is illegitimate, for relations are passive and notions are of the active. Such extensions would take us far beyond Berkeleianism, though they might take us nearer truth. They would recall too much the methods of last century's Hegelians, who, when they had to examine a philosopher, tended inevitably to "elicit" from him the Hegelian position or to "develop" him until it emerged.[67] Berkeley in the history of philosophy must always be the Berkeley of 1705 to 1713, and that means a Berkeley to whom God is essentially Will and not Thought.

Note.—There are certain considerations which suggest that God's ideas, if He has any, must be spatial. We might be tempted to hold that they are "unknown"[68] in character, but represented to us by spatial data, as are Kant's things-in-themselves. In illustration of this we might quote the army system in which disciplinary relationships are represented in most lan-

[66] D. III, i. 458.
[67] Cf. Caird on Kant, or Bosanquet on Plato.
[68] P. 75, quoted, p. 25.

guages by spatial terms. Lance-corporals and bombardiers are "on the same level," and "above them" are corporals. If a savage had this organization described to him, he would naturally suppose that an army meant a large pyramidal pile of men with a Field-Marshal sitting "at the top" and a thick layer of oppressed privates "at the bottom." The growing use of graphs has familiarized most people with this idea of representing a function with two variables (non-spatial in character) by means of a line plotted with the aid of two spatial axes. Why should not God's ideas (themselves non-spatial, like the spiritual relationships which unite an army) be represented to us by spatial sense-data (as we say "transfer, degrade, sous-officier, High Command," etc.)?

The answer is that the two dimensions in an army are not interconvertible. You could explain to a savage movements in each "dimension" taken separately; the ease with which a private could become a corporal compared with the difficulty of his becoming a general marks one "dimension," the simplicity of transferring from one company to another contrasted with the difficulty of the transfer to another regiment giving the other. But you could not combine the two in a single measure; the distance between a Sergeant in the Seaforths and a Private of the Buffs is strictly immeasurable. In a spatial field there is such a "diagonal" distance. If X is three miles north of O and P is four miles west of X, then P is five miles northwest of O, both direction and distance being fully determinable. Space is a continuum whose three dimensions have a common unit of measure, and—here is the crucial point—it is the only continuum of this kind; therefore if God's ideas are to have all the varieties of relation which our ideas manifest, they must have a character which we find exemplified only in space itself. Otherwise the derivative will be richer in relations than that from which it is derived. Thus our illustrations by means of army organization, etc., all break down, and it seems that the reality our spatial ideas represent must itself be spatial. Here also, perhaps, we may find a reason for rejecting Berkeley's theory of the physical world, placing power in God, in favour of the view that places power in spatial centres. But the main aim of this paper was to determine what Berkeley himself believed, and not to find difficulties in his system.

A treatise

concerning

the principles

of human knowledge

Wherein the chief causes of error and difficulty
in the sciences, with the grounds of skepticism,
atheism, and irreligion, are inquired into.

Preface[1]

What I here make public has, after a long and scrupulous inquiry, seemed to me evidently true and not unuseful to be known—particularly to those who are tainted with skepticism or want a demonstration of the existence and immateriality of God or the natural immortality of the soul. Whether it be so or no, I am content the reader should impartially examine, since I do not think myself any further concerned for the success of what I have written than as it is agreeable to truth. But to the end this may not suffer I make it my request that the reader suspend his judgment till he has once at least read the whole through with that degree of attention and thought which the subject matter shall seem to deserve. For as there are some

1 [This Preface was not included in the second edition.]

passages that, taken by themselves, are very liable (nor could it be remedied) to gross misinterpretation, and to be charged with most absurd consequences which, nevertheless, upon an entire perusal will appear not to follow from them, so likewise, though the whole should be read over, yet, if this be done transiently, it is very probable my sense may be mistaken; but to a thinking reader, I flatter myself, it will be throughout clear and obvious. As for the characters of novelty and singularity which some of the following notions may seem to bear, it is, I hope, needless to make any apology on that account. He must surely be either very weak or very little acquainted with the sciences who shall reject a truth that is capable of demonstration for no other reason but because it is newly known and contrary to the prejudices of mankind. Thus much I thought fit to premise in order to prevent, if possible, the hasty censures of a sort of men who are too apt to condemn an opinion before they rightly comprehend it.

Introduction

1. Philosophy being nothing else but the study of wisdom and truth, it may with reason be expected that those who have spent most time and pains in it should enjoy a greater calm and serenity of mind, a greater clearness and evidence of knowledge, and be less disturbed with doubts and difficulties than other men. Yet so it is, we see the illiterate bulk of mankind that walk the high road of plain common sense, and are governed by the dictates of nature, for the most part easy and undisturbed. To them nothing that is familiar appears unaccountable or difficult to comprehend. They complain not of any want of evidence in their senses, and are out of all danger of becoming skeptics. But no sooner do we depart from sense and instinct to follow the light of a superior principle, to reason, meditate, and reflect on the nature of things, but a thousand

scruples spring up in our minds concerning those things which before we seemed fully to comprehend. Prejudices and errors of sense do from all parts discover themselves to our view; and, endeavoring to correct these by reason, we are insensibly drawn into uncouth paradoxes, difficulties, and inconsistencies, which multiply and grow upon us as we advance in speculation, till at length, having wandered through many intricate mazes, we find ourselves just where we were, or, which is worse, sit down in a forlorn skepticism.

2. The cause of this is thought to be the obscurity of things, or the natural weakness and imperfection of our understandings. It is said the faculties we have are few and those designed by nature for the support and comfort of life, and not to penetrate into the inward essence and constitution of things. Besides, the mind of man being finite, when it treats of things which partake of infinity it is not to be wondered at if it run into absurdities and contradictions, out of which it is impossible it should ever extricate itself, it being of the nature of infinite not to be comprehended by that which is finite.

3. But, perhaps, we may be too partial to ourselves in placing the fault originally in our faculties and not rather in the wrong use we make of them. It is a hard thing to suppose that right deductions from true principles should ever end in consequences which cannot be maintained or made consistent. We should believe that God has dealt more bountifully with the sons of men than to give them a strong desire for that knowledge which he had placed quite out of their reach. This were not agreeable to the wonted, indulgent methods of Providence, which, whatever appetites it may have implanted in the creatures, does usually furnish them with such means as, if rightly made use of, will not fail to satisfy them. Upon the whole, I am inclined to think that the far greater part, if not all, of those difficulties which have hitherto amused philosophers and

blocked up the way to knowledge, are entirely owing to ourselves—that we have first raised a dust and then complain we
cannot see.

4. My purpose therefore is to try if I can discover what
those principles are which have introduced all that doubtfulness
and uncertainty, those absurdities and contradictions, into the
several sects of philosophy—insomuch that the wisest men have
thought our ignorance incurable, conceiving it to arise from
the natural dullness and limitation of our faculties. And surely
it is a work well deserving our pains to make a strict inquiry
concerning the first principles of human knowledge, to sift and
examine them on all sides, especially since there may be some
grounds to suspect that those lets and difficulties which stay
and embarrass the mind in its search after truth do not spring
from any darkness and intricacy in the objects or natural defect
in the understanding so much as from false principles which
have been insisted on, and might have been avoided.

5. How difficult and discouraging soever this attempt may
seem when I consider how many great and extraordinary men
have gone before me in the same designs, yet I am not without
some hopes—upon the consideration that the largest views are
not always the clearest, and that he who is shortsighted will be
obliged to draw the object nearer, and may, perhaps, by a close
and narrow survey discern that which had escaped far better
eyes.

6. In order to prepare the mind of the reader for the easier
conceiving what follows, it is proper to premise somewhat, by
way of introduction, concerning the nature and abuse of language. But the unraveling this matter leads me in some measure
to anticipate my design by taking notice of what seems to have
had a chief part in rendering speculation intricate and perplexed
and to have occasioned innumerable errors and difficulties in almost all parts of knowledge. And that is the opinion that the

mind has a power of framing *abstract ideas* or notions of things. He who is not a perfect stranger to the writings and disputes of philosophers must needs acknowledge that no small part of them are spent about abstract ideas. These are in a more especial manner thought to be the object of those sciences which go by the name of logic and metaphysics, and of all that which passes under the notion of the most abstracted and sublime learning, in all which one shall scarce find any question handled in such a manner as does not suppose their existence in the mind, and that it is well acquainted with them.

7. It is agreed on all hands that the qualities or modes of things do never really exist each of them apart by itself and separated from all others, but are mixed, as it were, and blended together, several in the same object. But we are told the mind, being able to consider each quality singly, or abstracted from those other qualities with which it is united, does by that means frame to itself abstract ideas. For example, there is perceived by sight an object extended, colored, and moved: this mixed or compound idea the mind, resolving into its simple, constituent parts and viewing each by itself, exclusive of the rest, does frame the abstract ideas of extension, color, and motion. Not that it is possible for color or motion to exist without extension, but only that the mind can frame to itself by *abstraction* the idea of color exclusive of extension, and of motion exclusive of both color and extension.

8. Again, the mind having observed that in the particular extensions perceived by sense there is something common and alike in all, and some other things peculiar, as this or that figure or magnitude, which distinguish them one from another, it considers apart or singles out by itself that which is common, making thereof a most abstract idea of extension, which is neither line, surface, nor solid, nor has any figure or magnitude, but is an idea entirely prescinded from all these. So likewise the

mind, by leaving out of the particular colors perceived by sense that which distinguishes them one from another, and retaining that only which is common to all, makes an idea of color in abstract, which is neither red, nor blue, nor white, nor any other determinate color. And, in like manner, by considering motion abstractedly not only from the body moved, but likewise from the figure it describes, and all particular directions and velocities, the abstract idea of motion is framed, which equally corresponds to all particular motions whatsoever that may be perceived by sense.

9. And as the mind frames to itself abstract ideas of qualities or modes, so does it, by the same precision or mental separation, attain abstract ideas of the more compounded beings which include several coexistent qualities. For example, the mind, having observed that Peter, James, and John resemble each other in certain common agreements of shape and other qualities, leaves out of the complex or compounded idea it has of Peter, James, and any other particular man that which is peculiar to each, retaining only what is common to all, and so makes an abstract idea wherein all the particulars equally partake— abstracting entirely from and cutting off all those circumstances and differences which might determine it to any particular existence. And after this manner it is said we come by the abstract idea of *man* or, if you please, humanity, or human nature; wherein it is true there is included color, because there is no man but has some color, but then it can be neither white, nor black, nor any particular color, because there is no one particular color wherein all men partake. So likewise there is included stature, but then it is neither tall stature, nor low stature, nor yet middle stature, but something abstracted from all these. And so of the rest. Moreover, there being a great variety of other creatures that partake in some parts, but not all, of the complex idea of man, the mind, leaving out those parts which are peculiar to

men, and retaining those only which are common to all the living creatures, frames the idea of *animal*, which abstracts not only from all particular men, but also all birds, beasts, fishes, and insects. The constituent parts of the abstract idea of animal are body, life, sense, and spontaneous motion. By "body" is meant body without any particular shape or figure, there being no one shape or figure common to all animals, without covering, either of hair, or feathers, or scales, etc., nor yet naked: hair, feathers, scales, and nakedness being the distinguishing properties of particular animals, and for that reason left out of the *abstract idea*. Upon the same account the spontaneous motion must be neither walking, nor flying, nor creeping; it is nevertheless a motion, but what that motion is it is not easy to conceive.

10. Whether others have this wonderful faculty of abstracting their ideas, they best can tell; for myself I find indeed I have a faculty of imagining, or representing to myself, the ideas of those particular things I have perceived, and of variously compounding and dividing them. I can imagine a man with two heads, or the upper parts of a man joined to the body of a horse. I can consider the hand, the eye, the nose, each by itself abstracted or separated from the rest of the body. But then whatever hand or eye I imagine, it must have some particular shape and color. Likewise the idea of man that I frame to myself must be either of a white, or a black, or a tawny, a straight, or a crooked, a tall, or a low, or a middle-sized man. I cannot by any effort of thought conceive the abstract idea above described. And it is equally impossible for me to form the abstract idea of motion distinct from the body moving, and which is neither swift nor slow, curvilinear nor rectilinear; and the like may be said of all other abstract general ideas whatsoever. To be plain, I own myself able to abstract in one sense, as when I consider some particular parts or qualities

separated from others, with which, though they are united in some object, yet it is possible they may really exist without them. But I deny that I can abstract one from another, or conceive separately, those qualities which it is impossible should exist so separated; or that I can frame a general notion by abstracting from particulars in the manner aforesaid—which two last are the two proper acceptations of "abstraction." And there are grounds to think most men will acknowledge themselves to be in my case. The generality of men which are simple and illiterate never pretend to *abstract notions*. It is said they are difficult and not to be attained without pains and study; we may therefore reasonably conclude that, if such there be, they are confined only to the learned.

11. I proceed to examine what can be alleged in defense of the doctrine of abstraction, and try if I can discover what it is that inclines the men of speculation to embrace an opinion so remote from common sense as that seems to be. There has been a late, deservedly esteemed philosopher[2] who, no doubt, has given it very much countenance by seeming to think the having abstract general ideas is what puts the widest difference in point of understanding betwixt man and beast.—

> The having of general ideas (he says) is that which puts a perfect distinction betwixt man and brutes, and is an excellency which the faculties of brutes do by no means attain unto. For, it is evident we observe no footsteps in them of making use of general signs for universal ideas; from which we have reason to imagine that they have not the faculty of abstract-

[2] [John Locke (1632–1794). He published his revolutionary *Essay Concerning Human Understanding* in 1690. This work, which had a profound influence upon the development of Berkeley's philosophy, was available to him when he entered Trinity in 1700. "Locke's *Essay* was on the course there, within two years of its publication, years before it received general recognition in England . . . and was working like leaven." A. A. Luce, *Life of George Berkeley* (Edinburgh: Thomas Nelson, 1949), pp. 31, 39.]

ing, or making general ideas, since they have no use of words or any other general signs.

And a little after:

> Therefore, I think, we may suppose that it is in this that the species of brutes are discriminated from men, and it is that proper difference wherein they are wholly separated, and which at last widens to so wide a distance. For, if they have any ideas at all, and are not bare machines (as some would have them), we cannot deny them to have some reason. It seems as evident to me that they do, some of them, in certain instances reason as that they have sense; but it is only in particular ideas, just as they receive them from their senses. They are the best of them tied up within those narrow bounds, and have not (as I think) the faculty to enlarge them by any kind of abstraction. —*Essay on Human Understanding*, Bk. II, chap. 11, secs. 10 f.

I readily agree with this learned author that the faculties of brutes can by no means attain to abstraction. But then if this be made the distinguishing property of that sort of animals, I fear that many of those that pass for men must be reckoned into their number. The reason that is here assigned why we have no grounds to think brutes have abstract general ideas is that we observe in them no use of words or any other general signs; which is built on this supposition—that the making use of words implies the having general ideas. From which it follows that men who use language are able to abstract or generalize their ideas. That this is the sense and arguing of the author will further appear by his answering the question he in another place puts: "Since all things that exist are only particulars, how come we by general terms?" His answer is: "Words become general by being made the signs of general ideas."—(*Essay on Human Understanding*, Bk. III, chap. 3, sec. 6.) But it seems that a word becomes general by being made the sign, not of an abstract general idea, but of several particular ideas, any one of which it indifferently suggests to the mind. For example, when it is said, "the change of motion is proportional to the impressed force," or that, "whatever has extension is divisible," these propositions are to be understood of motion and extension in general; and nevertheless it will not follow that they suggest to my thoughts an idea of motion without a body moved, or any determinate direction and velocity, or that I must conceive an abstract general idea of extension which is neither line, surface, nor solid, neither great nor small, black, white, nor red, nor of any other determinate color. It is only implied that whatever motion I consider, whether it be swift or slow, perpendicular, horizontal, or oblique, or in whatever object, the axiom concerning it holds equally true. As does the other of every particular extension, it matters not whether line, surface, or solid, whether of this or that magnitude or figure.

12. By observing how ideas become general we may the better judge how words are made so. And here it is to be noted that I do not deny absolutely there are general ideas, but only that there are any *abstract* general ideas; for, in the passages above quoted, wherein there is mention of general ideas, it is always supposed that they are formed by abstraction, after the manner set forth in sections 8 and 9. Now, if we will annex a meaning to our words and speak only of what we can conceive, I believe we shall acknowledge that an idea which, considered in itself, is particular, becomes general by being made to represent or stand for all other particular ideas of the same sort. To make this plain by an example, suppose a geometrician is demonstrating the method of cutting a line in two equal parts. He draws, for instance, a black line of an inch in length: this, which in itself is a particular line, is nevertheless with regard to its signification general, since, as it is there used, it represents all particular lines whatsoever; for that which is demonstrated of

it is demonstrated of all lines or, in other words, of a line in general. And, as that *particular* line becomes general by being made a sign, so the *name* "line," which taken absolutely is particular, by being a sign is made general. And as the former owes its generality not to its being the sign of an abstract or general line, but of all particular right lines that may possibly exist, so the latter must be thought to derive its generality from the same cause, namely, the various particular lines which it indifferently denotes.

13. To give the reader a yet clearer view of the nature of abstract ideas, and the uses they are thought necessary to, I shall add one more passage out of the *Essay on Human Understanding*, which is as follows:

> *Abstract ideas* are not so obvious or easy to children or the yet unexercised mind as particular ones. If they seem so to grown men it is only because by constant and familiar use they are made so. For, when we nicely reflect upon them, we shall find that general ideas are fictions and contrivances of the mind, that carry difficulty with them, and do not so easily offer themselves as we are apt to imagine. For example, does it not require some pains and skill to form the general idea of a triangle (which is yet none of the most abstract, comprehensive, and difficult); for it must be neither oblique nor rectangle, neither equilateral, equicrural, nor scalenon, but *all and none* of these at once? In effect, it is something imperfect that cannot exist, an idea wherein some parts of several different and *inconsistent* ideas are put together. It is true the mind in this imperfect state has need of such ideas and makes all the haste to them it can, for the convenience of communication and enlargement of knowledge to both which it is naturally very much inclined. But yet one has reason to suspect such ideas are marks of our imperfection. At least this is enough to show that the most abstract and general ideas are not those that the mind is first and most easily acquainted with, nor such as its earliest knowledge is conversant about.—Bk. IV, chap. 7, sec. 9.

If any man has the faculty of framing in his mind such an idea of a triangle as is here described, it is in vain to pretend to dispute him out of it, nor would I go about it. All I desire is that the reader would fully and certainly inform himself whether he has such an idea or no. And this, methinks, can be no hard task for anyone to perform. What more easy than for anyone to look a little into his own thoughts, and there try whether he has, or can attain to have, an idea that shall correspond with the description that is here given of the general idea of a triangle, which is "neither oblique nor rectangle, equilateral, equicrural nor scalenon, but all and none of these at once"?

14. Much is here said of the difficulty that abstract ideas carry with them, and the pains and skill requisite to the forming them. And it is on all hands agreed that there is need of great toil and labor of the mind to emancipate our thoughts from particular objects and raise them to those sublime speculations that are conversant about abstract ideas. From all which the natural consequence should seem to be, that so difficult a thing as the forming abstract ideas was not necessary for *communication*, which is so easy and familiar to all sorts of men. But, we are told, if they seem obvious and easy to grown men, "it is only because by constant and familiar use they are made so." Now, I would fain know at what time it is men are employed in surmounting that difficulty and furnishing themselves with those necessary helps for discourse. It cannot be when they are grown up, for then it seems they are not conscious of any such painstaking; it remains, therefore, to be the business of their childhood. And surely the great and multiplied labor of framing abstract notions will be found a hard task for that tender age. Is it not a hard thing to imagine that a couple of children cannot prate together of their sugar plums and rattles and the rest of their little trinkets till they have first tacked together numberless inconsistencies and so framed in their

minds abstract general ideas and annexed them to every common name they make use of?

15. Nor do I think them a whit more needful for the *enlargement of knowledge* than for *communication*. It is, I know, a point much insisted on, that all knowledge and demonstration are about universal notions, to which I fully agree; but then it does not appear to me that those notions are formed by abstraction in the manner premised—*universality*, so far as I can comprehend, not consisting in the absolute, positive nature or conception of any thing, but in the relation it bears to the particulars signified or represented by it; by virtue whereof it is that things, names, or notions, being in their own nature *particular*, are rendered *universal*. Thus, when I demonstrate any proposition concerning triangles, it is to be supposed that I have in view the universal idea of a triangle, which ought not to be understood as if I could frame an idea of a triangle which was neither equilateral, nor scalenon, nor equicrural, but only that the particular triangle I consider, whether of this or that sort it matters not, does equally stand for and represent all rectilinear triangles whatsoever, and is in that sense *universal*. All which seems very plain and not to include any difficulty in it.

16. But here it will be demanded how we can know any proposition to be true of all particular triangles, except we have first seen it demonstrated of the abstract idea of a triangle which equally agrees to all? For, because a property may be demonstrated to agree to some one particular triangle, it will not thence follow that it equally belongs to any other triangle which in all respects is not the same with it. For example, having demonstrated that the three angles of an isosceles rectangular triangle are equal to two right ones, I cannot therefore conclude this affection agrees to all other triangles which have neither a right angle nor two equal sides. It seems therefore that, to be

certain this proposition is universally true, we must either make a particular demonstration for every particular triangle, which is impossible, or once for all demonstrate it of the abstract idea of a triangle in which all the particulars do indifferently partake and by which they are all equally represented. To which I answer that, though the idea I have in view whilst I make the demonstration be, for instance, that of an isosceles rectangular triangle whose sides are of a determinate length, I may nevertheless be certain it extends to all other rectilinear triangles, of what sort or bigness soever. And that because neither the right angle, nor the equality, nor determinate length of the sides are at all concerned in the demonstration. It is true the diagram I have in view includes all these particulars, but then there is not the least mention made of them in the proof of the proposition. It is not said the three angles are equal to two right ones, because one of them is a right angle, or because the sides comprehending it are of the same length. Which sufficiently shows that the right angle might have been oblique, and the sides unequal, and for all that the demonstration have held good. And for this reason it is that I conclude that to be true of any obliquangular or scalenon which I had demonstrated of a particular right-angled equicrural triangle, and not because I demonstrated the proposition of the abstract idea of a triangle. [And here it must be acknowledged that a man may consider a figure merely as triangular, without attending to the particular qualities of the angles or relations of the sides. So far he may abstract, but this will never prove that he can frame an abstract, general, inconsistent idea of a triangle. In like manner we may consider Peter so far forth as man, or so far forth as animal, without framing the forementioned abstract idea either of man or of animal, inasmuch as all that is perceived is not considered.][3]

[3] [This addition in 1734 does not represent a change of doctrine. The same view was presented in the first edition of the *Dialogues*, I, sec. 8.]

17. It were an endless as well as a useless thing to trace the Schoolmen, those great masters of abstraction, through all the manifold, inextricable labyrinths of error and dispute which their doctrine of abstract natures and notions seems to have led them into. What bickerings and controversies, and what a learned dust have been raised about those matters, and what mighty advantage has been from thence derived to mankind, are things at this day too clearly known to need being insisted on. And it had been well if the ill effects of that doctrine were confined to those only who make the most avowed profession of it. When men consider the great pains, industry, and parts that have for so many ages been laid out on the cultivation and advancement of the sciences, and that notwithstanding all this the far greater part of them remains full of darkness and uncertainty, and disputes that are like never to have an end, and even those that are thought to be supported by the most clear and cogent demonstrations, contain in them paradoxes which are perfectly irreconcilable to the understandings of men, and that, taking all together, a small portion of them does supply any real benefit to mankind, otherwise than by being an innocent diversion and amusement—I say the consideration of all this is apt to throw them into a despondency and perfect contempt of all study. But this may, perhaps, cease upon a view of the false principles that have obtained in the world, amongst all which there is none, methinks, has a more wide influence over the thoughts of speculative men than this of *abstract* general ideas.

18. I come now to consider the *source* of this prevailing notion, and that seems to me to be language. And surely nothing of less extent than reason itself could have been the source of an opinion so universally received. The truth of this appears, as from other reasons, so also from the plain confession of the ablest patrons of abstract ideas, who acknowledge that they are made in order to naming; from which it is a clear consequence

that if there had been no such thing as speech or universal signs there never had been any thought of abstraction. See Bk. III, chap. 6, sec. 39, and elsewhere of the *Essay on Human Understanding*. Let us examine the manner wherein words have contributed to the origin of that mistake: First then, it is thought that every name has, or ought to have, one only precise and settled signification, which inclines men to think there are certain abstract, determinate ideas which constitute the true and only immediate signification of each general name; and that it is by the mediation of these abstract ideas that a general name comes to signify any particular thing. Whereas, in truth, there is no such thing as one precise and definite signification annexed to any general name, they all signifying indifferently a great number of particular ideas. All which does evidently follow from what has been already said, and will clearly appear to anyone by a little reflection. To this it will be objected that every name that has a definition is thereby restrained to one certain signification. For example, a "triangle" is defined to be "a plane surface comprehended by three right lines," by which that name is limited to denote one certain idea and no other. To which I answer that in the definition it is not said whether the surface be great or small, black or white, nor whether the sides are long or short, equal or unequal, nor with what angles they are inclined to each other; in all which there may be great variety, and consequently there is no one settled idea which limits the signification of the word "triangle." It is one thing for to keep a name constantly to the same definition, and another to make it stand everywhere for the same idea; the one is necessary, the other useless and impracticable.

19. But, to give a further account of how words came to produce the doctrine of abstract ideas, it must be observed that it is a received opinion that language has no other end but the communicating our ideas, and that every significant name stands

for an idea. This being so, and it being withal certain that names which yet are not thought altogether insignificant do not always mark out particular conceivable ideas, it is straightway concluded that they stand for abstract notions. That there are many names in use amongst speculative men which do not always suggest to others determinate, particular ideas is what nobody will deny. And a little attention will discover that it is not necessary (even in the strictest reasonings) that significant names which stand for ideas should, every time they are used, excite in the understanding the ideas they are made to stand for—in reading and discoursing, names being for the most part used as letters are in algebra, in which, though a particular quantity be marked by each letter, yet to proceed right it is not requisite that in every step each letter suggest to your thoughts that particular quantity it was appointed to stand for.

20. Besides, the communicating of ideas marked by words is not the chief and only end of language, as is commonly supposed. There are other ends, as the raising of some passion, the exciting to or deterring from an action, the putting the mind in some particular disposition—to which the former is in many cases barely subservient, and sometimes entirely omitted, when these can be obtained without it, as I think does not unfrequently happen in the familiar use of language. I entreat the reader to reflect with himself and see if it does not often happen, either in hearing or reading a discourse, that the passions of fear, love, hatred, admiration, disdain, and the like, arise immediately in his mind upon the perception of certain words, without any ideas coming between. At first, indeed, the words might have occasioned ideas that were fit to produce those emotions; but, if I mistake not, it will be found that, when language is once grown familiar, the hearing of the sounds or sight of the characters is oft immediately attended with those passions which at first were wont to be produced by the intervention of ideas that

are now quite omitted. May we not, for example, be affected with the promise of a *good thing*, though we have not an idea of what it is? Or is not the being threatened with danger sufficient to excite a dread, though we think not of any particular evil likely to befall us, nor yet frame to ourselves an idea of danger in abstract? If anyone shall join ever so little reflection of his own to what has been said, I believe that it will evidently appear to him that general names are often used in the propriety of language without the speaker's designing them for marks of ideas in his own, which he would have them raise in the mind of the hearer. Even proper names themselves do not seem always spoken with a design to bring into our view the ideas of those individuals that are supposed to be marked by them. For example, when a Schoolman tells me, "Aristotle has said it," all I conceive he means by it is to dispose me to embrace his opinion with the deference and submission which custom has annexed to that name. And this effect may be so instantly produced in the minds of those who are accustomed to resign their judgment to the authority of that philosopher, as it is impossible any idea either of his person, writings, or reputation should go before. Innumerable examples of this kind may be given, but why should I insist on those things which everyone's experience will, I doubt not, plentifully suggest unto him?

21. We have, I think, shown the impossibility of abstract ideas. We have considered what has been said for them by their ablest patrons, and endeavored to show they are of no use for those ends to which they are thought necessary. And lastly, we have traced them to the source from whence they flow, which appears to be language. It cannot be denied that words are of excellent use, in that by their means all that stock of knowledge which has been purchased by the joint labors of inquisitive men in all ages and nations may be drawn into the view and made the possession of one single person. But at the same time it must be

owned that most parts of knowledge have been strangely perplexed and darkened by the abuse of words, and general ways of speech wherein they are delivered. Since therefore words are so apt to impose on the understanding, whatever ideas I consider, I shall endeavor to take them bare and naked into my view, keeping out of my thoughts so far as I am able those names which long and constant use has so strictly united with them; from which I may expect to derive the following advantages:

22. *First*, I shall be sure to get clear of all controversies purely verbal—the springing up of which weeds in almost all the sciences has been a main hindrance to the growth of true and sound knowledge. *Secondly*, this seems to be a sure way to extricate myself out of that fine and subtle net of *abstract ideas* which has so miserably perplexed and entangled the minds of men; and that with this peculiar circumstance, that by how much the finer and more curious was the wit of any man, by so much the deeper was he likely to be ensnared and faster held therein. *Thirdly*, so long as I confine my thoughts to my own ideas divested of words, I do not see how I can easily be mistaken. The objects I consider I clearly and adequately know. I cannot be deceived in thinking I have an idea which I have not. It is not possible for me to imagine that any of my own ideas are alike or unlike that are not truly so. To discern the agreements or disagreements there are between my ideas, to see what ideas are included in any compound idea and what not, there is nothing more requisite than an attentive perception of what passes in my own understanding.

23. But the attainment of all these advantages does presuppose an entire deliverance from the deception of words, which I dare hardly promise myself—so difficult a thing it is to dissolve a union so early begun and confirmed by so long a habit as that betwixt words and ideas. Which difficulty seems to have

been very much increased by the doctrine of *abstraction*. For so long as men thought abstract ideas were annexed to their words, it does not seem strange that they should use words for ideas— it being found an impracticable thing to lay aside the word and retain the *abstract* idea in the mind, which in itself was perfectly inconceivable. This seems to me the principal cause why those men who have so emphatically recommended to others the laying aside all use of words in their meditations, and contemplating their bare ideas, have yet failed to perform it themselves. Of late many have been very sensible of the absurd opinions and insignificant disputes which grow out of the abuse of words. And, in order to remedy these evils, they advise well that we attend to the ideas signified and draw off our attention from the words which signify them. But, how good soever this advice may be they have given others, it is plain they could not have a due regard to it themselves so long as they thought the only immediate use of words was to signify ideas, and that the immediate signification of every general name was a determinate abstract idea.

24. But, these being known to be mistakes, a man may with greater ease prevent his being imposed on by words. He that knows he has no other than *particular* ideas will not puzzle himself in vain to find out and conceive the *abstract* idea annexed to any name. And he that knows names do not always stand for ideas will spare himself the labor of looking for ideas where there are none to be had. It were, therefore, to be wished that everyone would use his utmost endeavors to obtain a clear view of the ideas he would consider, separating from them all that dress and encumbrance of words which so much contribute to blind the judgment and divide the attention. In vain do we extend our view into the heavens and pry into the entrails of the earth, in vain do we consult the writings of learned men and

trace the dark footsteps of antiquity—we need only draw the curtain of words, to behold the fairest tree of knowledge, whose fruit is excellent and within the reach of our hand.

25. Unless we take care to clear the first principles of knowledge from the embarrassment and delusion of words, we may make infinite reasonings upon them to no purpose; we may draw consequences from consequences, and be never the wiser. The further we go, we shall only lose ourselves the more irrecoverably, and be the deeper entangled in difficulties and mistakes. Whoever, therefore, designs to read the following sheets, I entreat him to make my words the occasion of his own thinking and endeavor to attain the same train of thoughts in reading that I had in writing them. By this means it will be easy for him to discover the truth or falsity of what I say. He will be out of all danger of being deceived by my words, and I do not see how he can be led into an error by considering his own naked, undisguised ideas.

Of the principles

of human knowledge

Part I[4]

It is evident to anyone who takes a survey of the *objects* of
human knowledge that they are either ideas actually imprinted
on the senses, or else such as are perceived by attending to the
passions and operations of the mind, or lastly, ideas formed by
help of memory and imagination—either compounding, dividing, or barely representing those originally perceived in the
aforesaid ways. By sight I have the ideas of light and colors,
with their several degrees and variations. By touch I perceive,
for example, hard and soft, heat and cold, motion and resistance,

[4] ["Part I" was omitted from the title page of the second edition, apparently because Berkeley had given up the plan of publishing Part II. See
Correspondence, Letter II, sec. 6, and *Dialogues*, Preface.]

and of all these more and less either as to quantity or degree. Smelling furnishes me with odors, the palate with tastes, and hearing conveys sounds to the mind in all their variety of tone and composition. And as several of these are observed to accompany each other, they come to be marked by one name, and so to be reputed as one thing. Thus, for example, a certain color, taste, smell, figure, and consistence having been observed to go together, are accounted one distinct thing signified by the name "apple"; other collections of ideas constitute a stone, a tree, a book, and the like sensible things—which as they are pleasing or disagreeable excite the passions of love, hatred, joy, grief, and so forth.

2. But, besides all that endless variety of ideas or objects of knowledge, there is likewise something which knows or perceives them and exercises divers operations, as willing, imagining, remembering, about them. This perceiving, active being is what I call "mind," "spirit," "soul," or "myself." By which words I do not denote any one of my ideas, but a thing entirely distinct from them, wherein they exist or, which is the same thing, whereby they are perceived—for the existence of an idea consists in being perceived.

3. That neither our thoughts, nor passions, nor ideas formed by the imagination exist without the mind is what everybody will allow. And it seems no less evident that the various sensations or ideas imprinted on the sense, however blended or combined together (that is, whatever objects they compose), cannot exist otherwise than in a mind perceiving them.—I think an intuitive knowledge may be obtained of this by anyone that shall attend to what is meant by the term "exist" when applied to sensible things. The table I write on I say exists, that is, I see and feel it; and if I were out of my study I should say it existed —meaning thereby that if I was in my study I might perceive it, or that some other spirit actually does perceive it. There was an

odor, that is, it was smelled; there was a sound, that is to say, it was heard; a color or figure, and it was perceived by sight or touch. This is all that I can understand by these and the like expressions. For as to what is said of the absolute existence of unthinking things without any relation to their being perceived, that seems perfectly unintelligible. Their *esse* is *percipi*, nor is it possible they should have any existence out of the minds or thinking things which perceive them.

4. It is indeed an opinion strangely prevailing amongst men that houses, mountains, rivers, and, in a word, all sensible objects have an existence, natural or real, distinct from their being perceived by the understanding. But with how great an assurance and acquiescence soever this principle may be entertained in the world, yet whoever shall find in his heart to call it in question may, if I mistake not, perceive it to involve a manifest contradiction. For what are the forementioned objects but the things we perceive by sense? And what do we perceive besides our own ideas or sensations? And is it not plainly repugnant that any one of these, or any combination of them, should exist unperceived?

5. If we thoroughly examine this tenet it will, perhaps, be found at bottom to depend on the doctrine of *abstract ideas*. For can there be a nicer strain of abstraction than to distinguish the existence of sensible objects from their being perceived, so as to conceive them existing unperceived? Light and colors, heat and cold, extension and figures—in a word, the things we see and feel—what are they but so many sensations, notions, ideas, or impressions on the sense? And is it possible to separate, even in thought, any of these from perception? For my part, I might as easily divide a thing from itself. I may, indeed, divide in my thoughts, or conceive apart from each other, those things which, perhaps, I never perceived by sense so divided. Thus I imagine the trunk of a human body without the limbs, or conceive the

smell of a rose without thinking on the rose itself. So far, I will not deny, I can abstract—if that may properly be called "abstraction" which extends only to the conceiving separately such objects as it is possible may really exist or be actually perceived asunder. But my conceiving or imagining power does not extend beyond the possibility of real existence or perception. Hence, as it is impossible for me to see or feel anything without an actual sensation of that thing, so it is impossible for me to conceive in my thoughts any sensible thing or object distinct from the sensation or perception of it.

6. Some truths there are so near and obvious to the mind that a man need only open his eyes to see them. Such I take this important one to be, to wit, that all the choir of heaven and furniture of the earth, in a word, all those bodies which compose the mighty frame of the world, have not any subsistence without a mind—that their *being* is to be perceived or known, that, consequently, so long as they are not actually perceived by me or do not exist in my mind or that of any other created spirit, they must either have no existence at all or else subsist in the mind of some eternal spirit—it being perfectly unintelligible, and involving all the absurdity of abstraction, to attribute to any single part of them an existence independent of a spirit. To be convinced of which, the reader need only reflect, and try to separate in his own thoughts, the *being* of a sensible thing from its *being perceived*.

7. From what has been said it follows there is not any other substance than *spirit*, or that which perceives. But, for the fuller proof of this point, let it be considered the sensible qualities are color, figure, motion, smell, taste, and such like—that is, the ideas perceived by sense. Now, for an idea to exist in an unperceiving thing is a manifest contradiction, for to have an idea is all one as to perceive; that, therefore, wherein color, figure, and the like qualities exist must perceive them; hence it

is clear there can be no unthinking substance or *substratum* of those ideas.

8. But, say you, though the ideas themselves do not exist without the mind, yet there may be things like them, whereof they are copies or resemblances, which things exist without the mind in an unthinking substance. I answer, an idea can be like nothing but an idea; a color or figure can be like nothing but another color or figure. If we look but ever so little into our thoughts, we shall find it impossible for us to conceive a likeness except only between our ideas. Again, I ask whether those supposed originals or external things, of which our ideas are the pictures or representations, be themselves perceivable or no? If they are, then they are ideas and we have gained our point; but if you say they are not, I appeal to anyone whether it be sense to assert a color is like something which is invisible; hard or soft, like something which is intangible; and so of the rest.

9. Some there are who make a distinction betwixt *primary* and *secondary* qualities.[5] By the former they mean extension, figure, motion, rest, solidity or impenetrability, and number; by the latter they denote all other sensible qualities, as colors, sounds, tastes, and so forth. The ideas we have of these they acknowledge not to be the resemblances of anything existing without the mind, or unperceived, but they will have our ideas of the primary qualities to be patterns or images of things which exist without the mind, in an unthinking substance which they call "matter." By "matter," therefore, we are to understand an inert, senseless substance, in which extension, figure, and motion do actually subsist. But it is evident from what we have already shown that extension, figure, and motion are only ideas existing in the mind, and that an idea can be like nothing but another idea, and that consequently neither they nor their ar-

[5] [E.g., Locke, *Essay*, Bk. II, chap. 8.]

chetypes can exist in an unperceiving substance. Hence it is plain that the very notion of what is called "matter" or "corporeal substance" involves a contradiction in it.

10. They who assert that figure, motion, and the rest of the primary or original qualities do exist without the mind in unthinking substances do at the same time acknowledge that colors, sounds, heat, cold, and suchlike secondary qualities do not—which they tell us are sensations existing in the mind alone, that depend on and are occasioned by the different size, texture, and motion of the minute particles of matter. This they take for an undoubted truth which they can demonstrate beyond all exception. Now, if it be certain that those original qualities are inseparably united with the other sensible qualities, and not, even in thought, capable of being abstracted from them, it plainly follows that they exist only in the mind. But I desire anyone to reflect and try whether he can, by any abstraction of thought, conceive the extension and motion of a body without all other sensible qualities. For my own part, I see evidently that it is not in my power to frame an idea of a body extended and moved, but I must withal give it some color or other sensible quality which is acknowledged to exist only in the mind. In short, extension, figure, and motion, abstracted from all other qualities, are inconceivable. Where therefore the other sensible qualities are, there must these be also, to wit, in the mind and nowhere else.

11. Again, *great* and *small*, *swift* and *slow* are allowed to exist nowhere without the mind, being entirely relative, and changing as the frame or position of the organs of sense varies. The extension, therefore, which exists without the mind is neither great nor small, the motion neither swift nor slow; that is, they are nothing at all. But, say you, they are extension in general, and motion in general: thus we see how much the tenet of extended movable substances existing without the mind de-

pends on that strange doctrine of *abstract ideas*. And here I cannot but remark how nearly the vague and indeterminate description of matter or corporeal substance, which the modern philosophers are run into by their own principles, resembles that antiquated and so much ridiculed notion of *materia prima*, to be met with in Aristotle and his followers. Without extension, solidity cannot be conceived; since, therefore, it has been shown that extension exists not in an unthinking substance, the same must also be true of solidity.

12. That number is entirely the creature of the mind, even though the other qualities be allowed to exist without, will be evident to whoever considers that the same thing bears a different denomination of number as the mind views it with different respects. Thus the same extension is one, or three, or thirty-six, according as the mind considers it with reference to a yard, a foot, or an inch. Number is so visibly relative and dependent on men's understanding that it is strange to think how anyone should give it an absolute existence without the mind. We say one book, one page, one line; all these are equally units, though some contain several of the others. And in each instance it is plain the unit relates to some particular combination of ideas arbitrarily put together by the mind.

13. Unity I know some will have to be a simple or uncompounded idea accompanying all other ideas into the mind.[6] That I have any such idea answering the word "unity" I do not find; and if I had, methinks I could not miss finding it; on the contrary, it should be the most familiar to my understanding, since it is said to accompany all other ideas and to be perceived by all the ways of sensation and reflection. To say no more, it is an *abstract idea*.

---

[6] [E.g., Locke, *Essay*, Bk. II, chap. 16, sec. 1: "Amongst all the ideas we have, there is none more simple than that of unity."]

14. I shall further add that, after the same manner as modern philosophers prove certain sensible qualities to have no existence in matter, or without the mind, the same thing may be likewise proved of all other sensible qualities whatsoever. Thus, for instance, it is said that heat and cold are affections only of the mind, and not at all patterns of real beings existing in the corporeal substances which excite them, for that the same body which appears cold to one hand seems warm to another. Now, why may we not as well argue that figure and extension are not patterns or resemblances of qualities existing in matter, because to the same eye at different stations, or eyes of a different texture at the same station, they appear various and cannot, therefore, be the images of anything settled and determinate without the mind? Again, it is proved that sweetness is not really in the sapid thing, because, the thing remaining unaltered, the sweetness is changed into bitter, as in case of a fever or otherwise vitiated palate. Is it not as reasonable to say that motion is not without the mind, since if the succession of ideas in the mind become swifter, the motion, it is acknowledged, shall appear slower without any alteration in any external object?

15. In short, let anyone consider those arguments which are thought manifestly to prove that colors and tastes exist only in the mind, and he shall find they may with equal force be brought to prove the same thing of extension, figure, and motion. Though it must be confessed this method of arguing does not so much prove that there is no extension or color in an outward object as that we do not know by sense which is the true extension or color of the object. But the arguments foregoing plainly show it to be impossible that any color or extension at all, or other sensible quality whatsoever, should exist in an unthinking subject without the mind, or, in truth, that there should be any such thing as an outward object.

16. But let us examine a little the received opinion.—It is said extension is a mode or accident of matter, and that matter is the *substratum* that supports it. Now I desire that you would explain what is meant by matter's "supporting" extension. Say you, I have no idea of matter and, therefore, cannot explain it. I answer, though you have no positive, yet, if you have any meaning at all, you must at least have a relative idea of matter; though you know not what it is, yet you must be supposed to know what relation it bears to accidents, and what is meant by its supporting them. It is evident "support" cannot here be taken in its usual or literal sense—as when we say that pillars support a building; in what sense therefore must it be taken?

17. If we inquire into what the most accurate philosophers[7] declare themselves to mean by "material substance," we shall find them acknowledge they have no other meaning annexed to those sounds but the idea of being in general together with the relative notion of its supporting accidents. The general idea of being appears to me the most abstract and incomprehensible of all other; and as for its supporting accidents, this, as we have just now observed, cannot be understood in the common sense of those words; it must, therefore, be taken in some other sense, but what that is they do not explain. So that when I consider the two parts or branches which make the signification of the words "material substance," I am convinced there is no distinct meaning annexed to them. But why should we trouble ourselves any further in discussing this material *substratum* or support of figure and motion and other sensible

---

[7] [E.g., Locke, *Essay*, Bk. II, chap. 23, sec. 2: "If anyone will examine himself concerning his notion of pure substance in general, he will find he has no other idea of it all but only a supposition of he knows not what support of such qualities which are capable of producing simple ideas in us; which qualities are commonly called accidents."]

qualities? Does it not suppose they have an existence without the mind? And is not this a direct repugnancy and altogether inconceivable?

18. But, though it were possible that solid, figured, movable substances may exist without the mind, corresponding to the ideas we have of bodies, yet how is it possible for us to know this? Either we must know it by sense or by reason. As for our senses, by them we have the knowledge only of our sensations, ideas, or those things that are immediately perceived by sense, call them what you will; but they do not inform us that things exist without the mind, or unperceived, like to those which are perceived. This the materialists themselves acknowledge. It remains therefore that if we have any knowledge at all of external things, it must be by reason, inferring their existence from what is immediately perceived by sense. But what reason can induce us to believe the existence of bodies without the mind, from what we perceive, since the very patrons of matter themselves do not pretend there is any necessary connection betwixt them and our ideas? I say it is granted on all hands (and what happens in dreams, frenzies, and the like, puts it beyond dispute) that it is possible we might be affected with all the ideas we have now, though no bodies existed without resembling them. Hence it is evident the supposition of external bodies is not necessary for the producing our ideas; since it is granted they are produced sometimes, and might possibly be produced always in the same order we see them in at present, without their concurrence.

19. But though we might possibly have all our sensations without them, yet perhaps it may be thought easier to conceive and explain the manner of their production by supposing external bodies in their likeness rather than otherwise; and so it might be at least probable there are such things as bodies that excite their ideas in our minds. But neither can this be said, for,

though we give the materialists their external bodies, they by their own confession are never the nearer knowing how our ideas are produced, since they own themselves unable to comprehend in what manner body can act upon spirit, or how it is possible it should imprint any idea in the mind. Hence it is evident the production of ideas or sensations in our minds can be no reason why we should suppose matter or corporeal substances, since that is acknowledged to remain equally inexplicable with or without this supposition. If therefore it were possible for bodies to exist without the mind, yet to hold they do so must needs be a very precarious opinion, since it is to suppose, without any reason at all, that God has created innumerable beings that are entirely useless and serve to no manner of purpose.

20. In short, if there were external bodies, it is impossible we should ever come to know it; and if there were not, we might have the very same reasons to think there were that we have now. Suppose—what no one can deny possible—an intelligence without the help of external bodies, to be affected with the same train of sensations or ideas that you are, imprinted in the same order and with like vividness in his mind. I ask whether that intelligence has not all the reason to believe the existence of corporeal substances, represented by his ideas and exciting them in his mind, that you can possibly have for believing the same thing? Of this there can be no question— which one consideration is enough to make any reasonable person suspect the strength of whatever arguments he may think himself to have for the existence of bodies without the mind.

21. Were it necessary to add any further proof against the existence of matter after what has been said, I could instance several of those errors and difficulties (not to mention impieties) which have sprung from that tenet. It has occasioned number-

less controversies and disputes in philosophy, and not a few of far greater moment in religion. But I shall not enter into the detail of them in this place as well because I think arguments a posteriori are unnecessary for confirming what has been, if I mistake not, sufficiently demonstrated a priori, as because I shall hereafter find occasion to speak somewhat of them.

22. I am afraid I have given cause to think me needlessly prolix in handling this subject. For to what purpose is it to dilate on that which may be demonstrated with the utmost evidence in a line or two to anyone that is capable of the least reflection? It is but looking into your own thoughts, and so trying whether you can conceive it possible for a sound, or figure, or motion, or color to exist without the mind or unperceived. This easy trial may make you see that what you contend for is a downright contradiction. Insomuch that I am content to put the whole upon this issue: if you can but conceive it possible for one extended movable substance, or, in general, for any one idea, or anything like an idea, to exist otherwise than in a mind perceiving it, I shall readily give up the cause. And, as for all that compages of external bodies which you contend for, I shall grant you its existence, though you cannot either give me any reason why you believe it exists, or assign any use to it when it is supposed to exist. I say the bare possibility of your opinion's being true shall pass for an argument that it is so.

23. But, say you, surely there is nothing easier than to imagine trees, for instance, in a park, or books existing in a closet, and nobody by to perceive them. I answer you may so, there is no difficulty in it; but what is all this, I beseech you, more than framing in your mind certain ideas which you call books and trees, and at the same time omitting to frame the idea of anyone that may perceive them? But do not you yourself perceive or think of them all the while? This therefore is nothing to the purpose; it only shows you have the power of imagining

or forming ideas in your mind; but it does not show that you can conceive it possible the objects of your thought may exist without the mind. To make out this, it is necessary that you conceive them existing unconceived or unthought of, which is a manifest repugnancy. When we do our utmost to conceive the existence of external bodies, we are all the while only contemplating our own ideas. But the mind, taking no notice of itself, is deluded to think it can and does conceive bodies existing unthought of or without the mind, though at the same time they are apprehended by or exist in itself. A little attention will discover to anyone the truth and evidence of what is here said, and make it unnecessary to insist on any other proofs against the existence of *material substance*.

24. It is very obvious, upon the least inquiry into our own thoughts, to know whether it be possible for us to understand what is meant by "the absolute existence of sensible objects in themselves, or without the mind." To me it is evident those words mark out either a direct contradiction or else nothing at all. And to convince others of this, I know no readier or fairer way than to entreat they would calmly attend to their own thoughts; and if by this attention the emptiness or repugnancy of those expressions does appear, surely nothing more is requisite for their conviction. It is on this, therefore, that I insist, to wit, that "the absolute existence of unthinking things" are words without a meaning, or which include a contradiction. This is what I repeat and inculcate, and earnestly recommend to the attentive thoughts of the reader.

25. All our ideas, sensations, or the things which we perceive, by whatsoever names they may be distinguished, are visibly inactive—there is nothing of power or agency included in them. So that one idea or object of thought cannot produce or make any alteration in another. To be satisfied of the truth of this, there is nothing else requisite but a bare observation

of our ideas. For since they and every part of them exist only in the mind, it follows that there is nothing in them but what is perceived; but whoever shall attend to his ideas, whether of sense or reflection, will not perceive in them any power or activity; there is, therefore, no such thing contained in them. A little attention will discover to us that the very being of an idea implies passiveness and inertness in it, insomuch that it is impossible for an idea to do anything or, strictly speaking, to be the cause of anything; neither can it be the resemblance or pattern of any active being, as is evident from sec. 8. Whence it plainly follows that extension, figure, and motion cannot be the cause of our sensations. To say, therefore, that these are the effects of powers resulting from the configuration, number, motion, and size of corpuscles must certainly be false.

26. We perceive a continual succession of ideas, some are anew excited, others are changed or totally disappear. There is, therefore, some cause of these ideas, whereon they depend and which produces and changes them. That this cause cannot be any quality or idea or combination of ideas is clear from the preceding section. It must therefore be a substance; but it has been shown that there is no corporeal or material substance: it remains, therefore, that the cause of ideas is an incorporeal, active substance or spirit.

27. A spirit is one simple, undivided, active being—as it perceives ideas it is called "the understanding," and as it produces or otherwise operates about them it is called "the will." Hence there can be no *idea* formed of a soul or spirit; for all ideas whatever, being passive and inert (*vide* sec. 25), they cannot represent unto us, by way of image or likeness, that which acts. A little attention will make it plain to anyone that to have an idea which shall be like that active principle of motion and change of ideas is absolutely impossible. Such is the nature of *spirit*, or that which acts, that it cannot be of itself perceived, but

only by the effects which it produces. If any man shall doubt of the truth of what is here delivered, let him but reflect and try if he can frame the idea of any power or active being, and whether he has ideas of two principal powers marked by the names "will" and "understanding," distinct from each other as well as from a third idea of substance or being in general, with a relative notion of its supporting or being the subject of the aforesaid powers—which is signified by the name "soul" or "spirit." This is what some hold; but, so far as I can see, the words "will," "soul," "spirit" do not stand for different ideas or, in truth, for any idea at all, but for something which is very different from ideas, and which, being an agent, cannot be like unto, or represented by, any idea whatsoever. [Though it must be owned at the same time that we have some notion of soul, spirit, and the operations of the mind, such as willing, loving, hating—in as much as we know or understand the meaning of those words.][8]

28. I find I can excite ideas in my mind at pleasure, and vary and shift the scene as oft as I think fit. It is no more than willing, and straightway this or that idea arises in my fancy; and by the same power it is obliterated and makes way for another. This making and unmaking of ideas does very properly denominate the mind active. Thus much is certain and grounded on experience; but when we talk of unthinking agents or of exciting ideas exclusive of volition, we only amuse ourselves with words.

29. But, whatever power I may have over my own thoughts, I find the ideas actually perceived by sense have not a like dependence on my will. When in broad daylight I open my

---

[8] [This sentence, added to the second edition of 1734, introduces the technical term "notion," but it is doubtful whether it marks a change of doctrine. Similar changes were made in *Principles*, secs. 89, 140, 142; and *Dialogues*, III, sec. 4.]

eyes, it is not in my power to choose whether I shall see or no, or to determine what particular objects shall present themselves to my view; and so likewise as to the hearing and other senses; the ideas imprinted on them are not creatures of my will. There is therefore some *other* will or spirit that produces them.

30. The ideas of sense are more strong, lively, and distinct than those of the imagination; they have likewise a steadiness, order, and coherence, and are not excited at random, as those which are the effects of human wills often are, but in a regular train or series, the admirable connection whereof sufficiently testifies the wisdom and benevolence of its Author. Now the set rules or established methods wherein the mind we depend on excites in us the ideas of sense are called "the laws of nature"; and these we learn by experience, which teaches us that such and such ideas are attended with such and such other ideas in the ordinary course of things.

31. This gives us a sort of foresight which enables us to regulate our actions for the benefit of life. And without this we should be eternally at a loss; we could not know how to act anything that might procure us the least pleasure or remove the least pain of sense. That food nourishes, sleep refreshes, and fire warms us; that to sow in the seedtime is the way to reap in the harvest; and in general that to obtain such or such ends, such or such means are conducive—all this we know, not by discovering any necessary connection between our ideas, but only by the observation of the settled laws of nature, without which we should be all in uncertainty and confusion, and a grown man no more know how to manage himself in the affairs of life than an infant just born.

32. And yet this consistent, uniform working which so evidently displays the goodness and wisdom of that Governing Spirit whose Will constitutes the laws of nature, is so far

from leading our thoughts to Him that it rather sends them awandering after second causes. For when we perceive certain ideas of sense constantly followed by other ideas, and we know this is not of our own doing, we forthwith attribute power and agency to the ideas themselves and make one the cause of another, than which nothing can be more absurd and unintelligible. Thus, for example, having observed that when we perceive by sight a certain round, luminous figure, we at the same time perceive by touch the idea or sensation called "heat," we do from thence conclude the sun to be the cause of heat. And in like manner perceiving the motion and collision of bodies to be attended with sound, we are inclined to think the latter an effect of the former.

33. The ideas imprinted on the senses by the Author of Nature are called "real things"; and those excited in the imagination, being less regular, vivid, and constant, are more properly termed "ideas" or "images of things" which they copy and represent. But then our sensations, be they never so vivid and distinct, are nevertheless ideas, that is, they exist in the mind, or are perceived by it, as truly as the ideas of its own framing. The ideas of sense are allowed to have more reality in them, that is, to be more strong, orderly, and coherent than the creatures of the mind; but this is no argument that they exist without the mind. They are also less dependent on the spirit, or thinking substance which perceives them, in that they are excited by the will of another and more powerful spirit; yet still they are *ideas;* and certainly no idea, whether faint or strong, can exist otherwise than in a mind perceiving it.

34. Before we proceed any further it is necessary to spend some time in answering objections which may probably be made against the principles hitherto laid down. In doing of which, if I seem too prolix to those of quick apprehensions, I

hope it may be pardoned, since all men do not equally apprehend things of this nature, and I am willing to be understood by everyone.

First, then, it will be objected that by the foregoing principles all that is real and substantial in nature is banished out of the world, and instead thereof a chimerical scheme of *ideas* takes place. All things that exist, exist only in the mind, that is, they are purely notional. What therefore becomes of the sun, moon, and stars? What must we think of houses, rivers, mountains, trees, stones, nay, even of our own bodies? Are all these but so many chimeras and illusions on the fancy? To all which, and whatever else of the same sort may be objected, I answer that by the principles premised we are not deprived of any one thing in nature. Whatever we see, feel, hear, or anywise conceive or understand remains as secure as ever, and is as real as ever. There is a *rerum natura,* and the distinction between realities and chimeras retains its full force. This is evident from secs. 29, 30, and 33, where we have shown what is meant by "real things" in opposition to "chimeras" or ideas of our own framing; but then they both equally exist in the mind, and in that sense they are alike *ideas*.

35. I do not argue against the existence of any one thing that we can apprehend either by sense or reflection. That the things I see with my eyes and touch with my hands do exist, really exist, I make not the least question. The only thing whose existence we deny is that which philosophers call matter or corporeal substance. And in doing of this there is no damage done to the rest of mankind, who, I dare say, will never miss it. The atheist indeed will want the color of an empty name to support his impiety; and the philosophers may possibly find they have lost a great handle for trifling and disputation.

36. If any man thinks this detracts from the existence or

reality of things, he is very far from understanding what has been premised in the plainest terms I could think of. Take here an abstract of what has been said: there are spiritual substances, minds, or human souls, which will or excite ideas in themselves at pleasure, but these are faint, weak, and unsteady in respect of others they perceive by sense—which, being impressed upon them according to certain rules or laws of nature, speak themselves the effects of a mind more powerful and wise than human spirits. These latter are said to have more *reality* in them than the former—by which is meant that they are more affecting, orderly, and distinct, and that they are not fictions of the mind perceiving them. And in this sense the sun that I see by day is the real sun, and that which I imagine by night is the idea of the former. In the sense here given of "reality" it is evident that every vegetable, star, mineral, and in general each part of the mundane system, is as much a *real being* by our principles as by any other. Whether others mean anything by the term "reality" different from what I do, I entreat them to look into their own thoughts and see.

37. It will be urged that thus much at least is true, to wit, that we take away all corporeal substances. To this my answer is that if the word "substance" be taken in the vulgar sense— for a combination of sensible qualities, such as extension, solidity, weight, and the like—this we cannot be accused of taking away; but if it be taken in a philosophic sense—for the support of accidents or qualities without the mind—then indeed I acknowledge that we take it away, if one may be said to take away that which never had any existence, not even in the imagination.

38. But, say you, it sounds very harsh to say we eat and drink ideas, and are clothed with ideas. I acknowledge it does so—the word "idea" not being used in common discourse to

signify the several combinations of sensible qualities which are called "things"; and it is certain that any expression which varies from the familiar use of language will seem harsh and ridiculous. But this does not concern the truth of the proposition which, in other words, is no more than to say we are fed and clothed with those things which we perceive immediately by our senses. The hardness or softness, the color, taste, warmth, figure, and suchlike qualities, which combined together constitute the several sorts of victuals and apparel, have been shown to exist only in the mind that perceives them; and this is all that is meant by calling them "ideas," which word if it was as ordinarily used as "thing," would sound no harsher nor more ridiculous than it. I am not for disputing about the propriety, but the truth of the expression. If therefore you agree with me that we eat and drink and are clad with the immediate objects of sense, which cannot exist unperceived or without the mind, I shall readily grant it is more proper or conformable to custom that they should be called "things" rather than "ideas."

39. If it be demanded why I make use of the word "idea," and do not rather in compliance with custom call them "things," I answer I do it for two reasons; first, because the term "thing" in contradistinction to "idea" is generally supposed to denote somewhat existing without the mind; secondly, because "thing" has a more comprehensive signification than "idea," including spirits or thinking things as well as ideas. Since therefore the objects of sense exist only in the mind and are withal thoughtless and inactive, I chose to mark them by the word "idea," which implies those properties.

40. But, say what we can, someone perhaps may be apt to reply he will still believe his senses, and never suffer any arguments, how plausible soever, to prevail over the certainty of them. Be it so; assert the evidence of sense as high as you please, we are willing to do the same. That what I see, hear, and feel

does exist—that is to say, is perceived by me—I no more doubt than I do of my own being. But I do not see how the testimony of sense can be alleged as a proof for the existence of anything which is not perceived by sense. We are not for having any man turn skeptic and disbelieve his senses; on the contrary, we give them all the stress and assurance imaginable; nor are there any principles more opposite to skepticism than those we have laid down, as shall be hereafter clearly shown.

41. *Secondly,* it will be objected that there is a great difference betwixt real fire, for instance, and the idea of fire, betwixt dreaming or imagining oneself burned, and actually being so. This and the like may be urged in opposition to our tenets. To all which the answer is evident from what has been already said; and I shall only add in this place that if real fire be very different from the idea of fire, so also is the real pain that it occasions very different from the idea of the same pain, and yet nobody will pretend that real pain either is, or can possibly be, in an unperceiving thing, or without the mind, any more than its idea.

42. *Thirdly,* it will be objected that we see things actually without or at a distance from us, and which, consequently, do not exist in the mind, it being absurd that those things which are seen at the distance of several miles should be as near to us as our own thoughts. In answer to this I desire it may be considered that in a dream we do oft perceive things as existing at a great distance off, and yet for all that those things are acknowledged to have their existence only in the mind.

43. But for the fuller clearing of this point it may be worth while to consider how it is that we perceive distance and things placed at a distance by sight. For that we should in truth see external space, and bodies actually existing in it, some nearer, others farther off, seems to carry with it some opposition to what has been said of their existing nowhere without the mind.

The consideration of this difficulty it was that gave birth to my *Essay Towards a New Theory of Vision*,[9] which was published not long since, wherein it is shown that distance or outness is neither immediately of itself perceived by sight, nor yet apprehended or judged of by lines and angles, or anything that has a necessary connection with it; but that it is only suggested to our thoughts by certain visible ideas and sensations attending vision, which in their own nature have no manner of similitude or relation either with distance or things placed at a distance; but by a connection taught us by experience they come to signify and suggest them to us after the same manner that words of any language suggest the ideas they are made to stand for; insomuch that a man born blind and afterwards made to see would not, at first sight, think the things he saw to be without his mind or at any distance from him. See sec. 41 of the forementioned treatise.

44. The ideas of sight and touch make two species entirely distinct and heterogeneous. The former are marks and prognostics of the latter. That the proper objects of sight neither exist without mind, nor are the images of external things, was shown even in that treatise. Though throughout the same the contrary be supposed true of tangible objects—not that to suppose that vulgar error was necessary for establishing the notion therein laid down, but because it was beside my purpose to examine and refute it in a discourse concerning *vision*. So that in strict truth the ideas of sight, when we apprehend by them distance and things placed at a distance, do not suggest or mark out to us things actually existing at a distance, but only admonish us what ideas of touch will be imprinted in our minds

[9] [See the *Essay* (1709), *The Theory of Vision, or Visual Language Vindicated and Explained* (1733), and *Alciphron* (1732), excerpts from Dialogue IV, in Berkeley, *Works on Vision*, "Library of Liberal Arts," No. 83 (Indianapolis and New York: The Bobbs-Merrill Company, Inc., 1963).]

at such and such distances of time, and in consequence of such and such actions. It is, I say, evident from what has been said in the foregoing parts of this treatise, and in sec. 147 and elsewhere of the *Essay Concerning Vision,* that visible ideas are the language whereby the Governing Spirit on whom we depend informs us what tangible ideas he is about to imprint upon us in case we excite this or that motion in our own bodies. But for a fuller information in this point I refer to the *Essay* itself.

45. *Fourthly,* it will be objected that from the foregoing principles it follows things are every moment annihilated and created anew. The objects of sense exist only when they are perceived; the trees, therefore, are in the garden, or the chairs in the parlor, no longer than while there is somebody by to perceive them. Upon shutting my eyes all the furniture in the room is reduced to nothing, and barely upon opening them it is again created. In answer to all which I refer the reader to what has been said in secs. 3, 4, etc., and desire he will consider whether he means anything by the actual existence of an idea distinct from its being perceived. For my part, after the nicest inquiry I could make, I am not able to discover that anything else is meant by those words; and I once more entreat the reader to sound his own thoughts and not suffer himself to be imposed on by words. If he can conceive it possible either for his ideas or their archetypes to exist without being perceived, then I give up the cause; but if he cannot, he will acknowledge it is unreasonable for him to stand up in defense of he knows not what and pretend to charge on me as an absurdity the not assenting to those propositions which at bottom have no meaning in them.

46. It will not be amiss to observe how far the received principles of philosophy are themselves chargeable with those pretended absurdities. It is thought strangely absurd that upon closing my eyelids all the visible objects around me should be

reduced to nothing; and yet is not this what philosophers commonly acknowledge when they agree on all hands that light and colors, which alone are the proper and immediate objects of sight, are mere sensations that exist no longer than they are perceived? Again, it may to some, perhaps, seem very incredible that things should be every moment creating, yet this very notion is commonly taught in the Schools. For the Schoolmen, though they acknowledge the existence of matter, and that the whole mundane fabric is framed out of it, are nevertheless of opinion that it cannot subsist without the divine conservation, which by them is expounded to be a continual creation.

47. Further, a little thought will discover to us that though we allow the existence of matter or corporeal substance, yet it will unavoidably follow, from the principles which are now generally admitted, that the particular bodies of what kind soever do none of them exist whilst they are not perceived. For it is evident from sec. 11 and the following sections that the matter philosophers contend for is an incomprehensible somewhat, which has none of those particular qualities whereby the bodies falling under our senses are distinguished one from another. But, to make this more plain, it must be remarked that the infinite divisibility of matter is now universally allowed, at least by the most approved and considerable philosophers, who on the received principles demonstrate it beyond all exception. Hence it follows that there is an infinite number of parts in each particle of matter which are not perceived by sense. The reason, therefore, that any particular body seems to be of a finite magnitude, or exhibits only a finite number of parts to sense, is not because it contains no more, since in itself it contains an infinite number of parts, but because the sense is not acute enough to discern them. In proportion, therefore, as the sense is rendered more acute, it perceives a greater number of parts in the object; that is, the object appears greater, and its figure varies, those

parts in its extremities which were before unperceivable appearing now to bound it in very different lines and angles from those perceived by an obtuser sense. And at length, after various changes of size and shape, when the sense becomes infinitely acute, the body shall seem infinite. During all which there is no alteration in the body, but only in the sense. Each body, therefore, considered in itself, is infinitely extended, and consequently void of all shape or figure. From which it follows that, though we should grant the existence of matter to be ever so certain, yet it is withal as certain—the materialists themselves are by their own principles forced to acknowledge—that neither the particular bodies perceived by sense, nor anything like them, exist without the mind. Matter, I say, and each particle thereof, is according to them infinite and shapeless, and it is the mind that frames all that variety of bodies which compose the visible world, any one whereof does not exist longer than it is perceived.

48. If we consider it, the objection proposed in sec. 45 will not be found reasonably charged on the principles we have premised, so as in truth to make any objection at all against our notions. For though we hold indeed the objects of sense to be nothing else but ideas which cannot exist unperceived, yet we may not hence conclude they have no existence except only while they are perceived by us, since there may be some other spirit that perceives them, though we do not. Wherever bodies are said to have no existence without the mind, I would not be understood to mean this or that particular mind, but all minds whatsoever. It does not therefore follow from the foregoing principles that bodies are annihilated and created every moment or exist not at all during the intervals between our perception of them.

49. *Fifthly*, it may perhaps be objected that if extension and figure exist only in the mind, it follows that the mind is

extended and figured, since extension is a mode or attribute which (to speak with the Schools) is predicated of the subject in which it exists. I answer, those qualities are in the mind only as they are perceived by it—that is, not by way of *mode* or *attribute*, but only by way of *idea*; and it no more follows that the soul or mind is extended, because extension exists in it alone, than it does that it is red or blue, because those colors are on all hands acknowledged to exist in it, and nowhere else. As to what philosophers say of subject and mode, that seems very groundless and unintelligible. For instance, in this proposition "a die is hard, extended, and square," they will have it that the word "die" denotes a subject or substance distinct from hardness, extension, and figure which are predicated of it, and in which they exist. This I cannot comprehend; to me a die seems to be nothing distinct from those things which are termed its modes or accidents. And to say a die is hard, extended, and square is not to attribute those qualities to a subject distinct from and supporting them, but only an explication of the meaning of the word "die."

50. *Sixthly*, you will say there have been a great many things explained by matter and motion; take away these and you destroy the whole corpuscular philosophy and undermine those mechanical principles which have been applied with so much success to account for the phenomena. In short, whatever advances have been made, either by ancient or modern philosophers, in the study of nature do all proceed on the supposition that corporeal substance or matter does really exist. To this I answer that there is not any one phenomenon explained on that supposition which may not as well be explained without it, as might easily be made appear by an induction of particulars. To explain the phenomena is all one as to show why, upon such and such occasions, we are affected with such and such ideas. But how matter should operate on a spirit, or produce any idea in it,

is what no philosopher will pretend to explain; it is therefore evident there can be no use of matter in natural philosophy. Besides, they who attempt to account for things do it not by corporeal substance, but by figure, motion, and other qualities, which are in truth no more than mere ideas and, therefore, cannot be the cause of anything, as has been already shown. See sec. 25.

51. *Seventhly*, it will upon this be demanded whether it does not seem absurd to take away natural causes and ascribe everything to the immediate operation of spirits? We must no longer say, upon these principles, that fire heats, or water cools, but that a spirit heats, and so forth. Would not a man be deservedly laughed at who should talk after this manner? I answer, he would so; in such things we ought to "think with the learned and speak with the vulgar."[10] They who by demonstration are convinced of the truth of the Copernican system do nevertheless say, "the sun rises," "the sun sets," or "comes to the meridian"; and if they affected a contrary style in common talk it would without doubt appear very ridiculous. A little reflection on what is here said will make it manifest that the common use of language would receive no manner of alteration or disturbance from the admission of our tenets.

52. In the ordinary affairs of life, any phrases may be retained so long as they excite in us proper sentiments or dispositions to act in such a manner as is necessary for our well-being, how false soever they may be if taken in a strict and speculative sense. Nay, this is unavoidable, since, propriety

10 [Perhaps Berkeley found this epigram in Francis Bacon, *De Augmentis Scientiarium* (London, 1623), Bk. V, chap. 4: "Loquendum esse ut vulgus, sentiendum ut sapientes." A similar version was given in the sixteenth century by Augustine Niphus in his *Comm. in Aristotelem de Gen. et Corr.*, Bk. I, folio 29. G: "Loquendum enim est ut plures, sentiendum ut pauci." See *The Works of Francis Bacon*, ed. James Spedding (Boston: Brown and Taggard, 1861), II, 403.]

being regulated by custom, language is suited to the received opinions, which are not always the truest. Hence it is impossible, even in the most rigid, philosophic reasonings, so far to alter the bent and genius of the tongue we speak, as never to give a handle for cavilers to pretend difficulties and inconsistencies. But a fair and ingenuous reader will collect the sense from the scope and tenor and connection of a discourse, making allowances for those inaccurate modes of speech which use has made inevitable.

53. As to the opinion that there are no corporeal causes, this has been heretofore maintained by some of the Schoolmen, as it is of late by others among the modern philosophers[11] who, though they allow matter to exist, yet will have God alone to be the immediate efficient cause of all things. These men saw that amongst all the objects of sense there was none which had any power or activity included in it, and that by consequence this was likewise true of whatever bodies they supposed to exist without the mind, like unto the immediate objects of sense. But then, that they should suppose an innumerable multitude of created beings which they acknowledge are not capable of producing any one effect in nature, and which therefore are made to no manner of purpose, since God might have done everything as well without them—this I say, though we should allow it possible, must yet be a very unaccountable and extravagant supposition.

54. In the *eighth* place, the universal concurrent assent of mankind may be thought by some an invincible argument in behalf of matter, or the existence of external things. Must we suppose the whole world to be mistaken? And if so, what cause can be assigned of so widespread and predominant an error? I answer, first, that, upon a narrow inquiry, it will not perhaps

[11] [E.g., by the occasionalists. See below, note 13, pp. 281–282.]

be found so many as is imagined do really believe the existence of matter or things without the mind. Strictly speaking, to believe that which involves a contradiction, or has no meaning in it, is impossible; and whether the foregoing expressions are not of that sort, I refer it to the impartial examination of the reader. In one sense, indeed, men may be said to believe that matter exists, that is, they act as if the immediate cause of their sensations, which affects them every moment and is so nearly present to them, were some senseless unthinking being. But that they should clearly apprehend any meaning marked by those words, and form thereof a settled speculative opinion, is what I am not able to conceive. This is not the only instance wherein men impose upon themselves, by imagining they believe those propositions they have often heard, though at bottom they have no meaning in them.

55. But secondly, though we should grant a notion to be ever so universally and steadfastly adhered to, yet this is but a weak argument of its truth to whoever considers what a vast number of prejudices and false opinions are everywhere embraced with the utmost tenaciousness by the unreflecting (which are the far greater) part of mankind. There was a time when the antipodes and motion of the earth were looked upon as monstrous absurdities even by men of learning; and if it be considered what a small proportion they bear to the rest of mankind, we shall find that at this day those notions have gained but a very inconsiderable footing in the world.

56. But it is demanded that we assign a cause of this prejudice and account for its obtaining in the world. To this I answer that men, knowing they perceived several ideas whereof they themselves were not the authors—as not being excited from within nor depending on the operation of their wills—this made them maintain those ideas, or objects of perception, had an existence independent of and without the mind, without ever

dreaming that a contradiction was involved in those words. But philosophers having plainly seen that the immediate objects of perception do not exist without the mind, they in some degree corrected the mistake of the vulgar, but at the same time run into another which seems no less absurd, to wit, that there are certain objects really existing without the mind or having a subsistence distinct from being perceived, of which our ideas are only images or resemblances, imprinted by those objects on the mind. And this notion of the philosophers owes its origin to the same cause with the former, namely, their being conscious that they were not the authors of their own sensations, which they evidently knew were imprinted from without, and which therefore must have some cause distinct from the minds on which they are imprinted.

57. But why they should suppose the ideas of sense to be excited in us by things in their likeness, and not rather have recourse to *spirit* which alone can act, may be accounted for, first because they were not aware of the repugnancy there is, as well in supposing things like unto our ideas existing without, as in attributing to them power or activity. Secondly, because the supreme spirit which excites those ideas in our minds is not marked out and limited to our view by any particular finite collection of sensible ideas, as human agents are by their size, complexion, limbs, and motions. And thirdly, because His operations are regular and uniform. Whenever the course of nature is interrupted by a miracle, men are ready to own the presence of a superior agent. But when we see things go on in the ordinary course, they do not excite in us any reflection; their order and concatenation, though it be an argument of the greatest wisdom, power, and goodness in their Creator, is yet so constant and familiar to us that we do not think them the immediate effects of a *free spirit*, especially since inconstancy and mutability in acting, though it be an imperfection, is looked on as a mark of *freedom*.

58. *Tenthly,* it will be objected that the notions we advance are inconsistent with several sound truths in philosophy and mathematics. For example, the motion of the earth is now universally admitted by astronomers as a truth grounded on the clearest and most convincing reasons. But on the foregoing principles there can be no such thing. For, motion being only an idea, it follows that if it be not perceived it exists not; but the motion of the earth is not perceived by sense. I answer, that tenet, if rightly understood, will be found to agree with the principles we have premised, for the question whether the earth moves or no amounts in reality to no more than this, to wit, whether we have reason to conclude, from what has been observed by astronomers, that if we were placed in such and such circumstances, and such or such a position and distance both from the earth and sun, we should perceive the former to move among the choir of the planets, and appearing in all respects like one of them; and this, by the established rules of nature which we have no reason to mistrust, is reasonably collected from the phenomena.

59. We may, from the experience we have had of the train and succession of ideas in our minds, often make, I will not say uncertain conjectures, but sure and well-grounded predictions concerning the ideas we shall be affected with pursuant to a great train of actions, and be enabled to pass a right judgment of what would have appeared to us in case we were placed in circumstances very different from those we are in at present. Herein consists the knowledge of nature, which may preserve its use and certainty very consistently with what has been said. It will be easy to apply this to whatever objections of the like sort may be drawn from the magnitude of the stars or any other discoveries in astronomy or nature.

60. In the *eleventh* place, it will be demanded to what purpose serves that curious organization of plants and the admirable mechanism on the parts of animals; might not vegetables

grow and shoot forth leaves and blossoms, and animals perform all their motions as well without as with all that variety of internal parts so elegantly contrived and put together; which, being ideas, have nothing powerful or operative in them, nor have any necessary connection with the effects ascribed to them? If it be a spirit that immediately produces every effect by a fiat or act of his will, we must think all that is fine and artificial in the works, whether of man or nature, to be made in vain. By this doctrine, though an artist has made the spring and wheels, and every movement of a watch, and adjusted them in such a manner as he knew would produce the motions he designed, yet he must think all this done to no purpose, and that it is an Intelligence which directs the index and points to the hour of the day. If so, why may not the Intelligence do it, without his being at the pains of making the movements and putting them together? Why does not an empty case serve as well as another? And how comes it to pass that whenever there is any fault in the going of a watch, there is some corresponding disorder to be found in the movements, which being mended by a skillful hand all is right again? The like may be said of all the clockwork of nature, great part whereof is so wonderfully fine and subtle as scarce to be discerned by the best microscope. In short, it will be asked how, upon our principles, any tolerable account can be given, or any final cause assigned, of an innumerable multitude of bodies and machines, framed with the most exquisite art, which in the common philosophy have very apposite uses assigned them and serve to explain abundance of phenomena?

61. To all which I answer, first, that though there were some difficulties relating to the administration of Providence, and the uses by it assigned to the several parts of nature which I could not solve by the foregoing principles, yet this objection could be of small weight against the truth and certainty of those things which may be proved a priori with the utmost evidence.

Secondly, but neither are the received principles free from the like difficulties, for it may still be demanded to what end God should take those roundabout methods of effecting things by instruments and machines which no one can deny might have been effected by the mere command of His will without all that apparatus; nay, if we narrowly consider it, we shall find the objection may be retorted with greater force on those who hold the existence of those machines without the mind, for it has been made evident that solidity, bulk, figure, motion, and the like have no *activity* or *efficacy* in them so as to be capable of producing any one effect in nature. See sec. 25. Whoever, therefore, supposes them to exist (allowing the supposition possible) when they are not perceived does it manifestly to no purpose, since the only use that is assigned to them, as they exist unperceived, is that they produce those perceivable effects which in truth cannot be ascribed to anything but spirit.

62. But, to come nearer the difficulty, it must be observed that though the fabrication of all those parts and organs be not absolutely necessary to the producing any effect, yet it is necessary to the producing of things in a constant regular way according to the laws of nature. There are certain general laws that run through the whole chain of natural effects; these are learned by the observation and study of nature and are by men applied as well to the framing artificial things for the use and ornament of life as to the explaining the various phenomena —which explication consists only in showing the conformity any particular phenomenon has to the general laws of nature or, which is the same thing, in discovering the *uniformity* there is in the production of natural effects, as will be evident to whoever shall attend to the several instances wherein philosophers pretend to account for appearances. That there is a great and conspicuous use in these regular, constant methods of working observed by the Supreme Agent has been shown in sec. 31. And

it is no less visible that a particular size, figure, motion, and disposition of parts are necessary, though not absolutely, to the producing any effect, yet to the producing it according to the standing mechanical laws of nature. Thus, for instance, it cannot be denied that God, or the Intelligence which sustains and rules the ordinary course of things, might, if He were minded to produce a miracle, cause all the motions on the dial-plate of a watch, though nobody has ever made the movements and put them in it; but yet, if He will act agreeably to the rules of mechanism by Him for wise ends established and maintained in the Creation, it is necessary that those actions of the watchmaker, whereby he makes the movements and rightly adjusts them, precede the production of the aforesaid motions, as also that any disorder in them be attended with the perception of some corresponding disorder in the movements, which, being once corrected, all is right again.

63. It may indeed on some occasions be necessary that the Author of Nature display His overruling power in producing some appearance out of the ordinary series of things. Such exceptions from the general rules of nature are proper to surprise and awe men into an acknowledgement of the Divine Being; but then they are to be used but seldom, otherwise there is a plain reason why they should fail of that effect. Besides, God seems to choose the convincing our reason of His attributes by the works of nature, which discover so much harmony and contrivance in their make and are such plain indications of wisdom and beneficence in their Author rather than to astonish us into a belief of His being by anomalous and surprising events.

64. To set this matter in a yet clearer light, I shall observe that what has been objected in sec. 60 amounts in reality to no more than this: ideas are not anyhow and at random produced, there being a certain order and connection between them, like to that of cause and effect; there are also several

combinations of them made in a very regular and artificial manner, which seem like so many instruments in the hand of nature that, being hidden, as it were, behind the scenes, have a secret operation in producing those appearances which are seen on the theater of the world, being themselves discernible only to the curious eye of the philosopher. But, since one idea cannot be the cause of another, to what purpose is that connection? And, since those instruments, being barely *inefficacious perceptions* in the mind, are not subservient to the production of natural effects, it is demanded why they are made, or, in other words, what reason can be assigned why God should make us, upon a close inspection into His works, behold so great variety of ideas so artfully laid together, and so much according to rule, it not being credible that He would be at the expense (if one may so speak) of all that art and regularity to no purpose.

65. To all which my answer is, first, that the connection of ideas does not imply the relation of *cause* and *effect*, but only of a mark or *sign* with the thing *signified*. The fire which I see is not the cause of the pain I suffer upon my approaching it, but the mark that forewarns me of it. In like manner, the noise that I hear is not the effect of this or that motion or collision of the ambient bodies, but the sign thereof. Secondly, the reason why ideas are formed into machines, that is, artificial and regular combinations, is the same with that for combining letters into words. That a few original ideas may be made to signify a great number of effects and actions, it is necessary they be variously combined together. And, to the end their use be permanent and universal, these combinations must be made by *rule* and with *wise contrivance*. By this means abundance of information is conveyed unto us concerning what we are to expect from such and such actions and what methods are proper to be taken for the exciting such and such ideas, which in effect is all

that I conceive to be distinctly meant when it is said that, by discerning the figure, texture, and mechanism of the inward parts of bodies, whether natural or artificial, we may attain to know the several uses and properties depending thereon, or the nature of the thing.

66. Hence it is evident that those things which, under the notion of a cause cooperating or concurring to the production of effects, are altogether inexplicable and run us into great absurdities may be very naturally explained and have a proper and obvious use assigned to them when they are considered only as marks or signs for our information. And it is the searching after and endeavoring to understand [those signs instituted by][12] the Author of Nature that ought to be the employment of the natural philosopher, and not the pretending to explain things by corporeal causes, which doctrine seems to have too much estranged the minds of men from that active principle, that supreme and wise Spirit "in whom we live, move, and have our being."

67. In the *twelfth* place, it may perhaps be objected that— though it be clear from what has been said that there can be no such thing as an inert, senseless, extended, solid, figured, movable substance existing without the mind, such as philos- ophers describe matter—yet, if any man shall leave out of his idea of *matter* the positive ideas of extension, figure, solidity, and motion and say that he means only by that word an inert, senseless substance that exists without the mind or unperceived, which is the occasion of our ideas, or at the presence whereof God is pleased to excite ideas in us—it does not appear but that matter taken in this sense may possibly exist. In answer to which I say, first, that it seems no less absurd to suppose a sub- stance without accidents than it is to suppose accidents without

---

[12] [The first edition reads: "this language (if I may so call it) of."]

a substance. But secondly, though we should grant this unknown substance may possibly exist, yet where can it be supposed to be? That it exists not in the mind is agreed; and that it exists not in place is no less certain—since all extension exists only in the mind, as has been already proved. It remains therefore that it exists nowhere at all.

68. Let us examine a little the description that is here given us of *matter*. It neither acts, nor perceives, nor is perceived, for this is all that is meant by saying it is an inert, senseless, unknown substance; which is a definition entirely made up of negatives, excepting only the relative notion of its standing under or supporting. But then it must be observed that it supports nothing at all, and how nearly this comes to the description of a *nonentity* I desire may be considered. But, say you, it is the *unknown occasion*[13] at the presence of which

[13] [Occasionalism was a development from Cartesian dualism. If mind and body are separate substances that cannot act upon one another, how do physical and mental events occur? A modified occasionalism was developed by Arnold Geulincx of Antwerp (1625–1669), author of *Metaphysica vera* (1691), while a more extreme view was elaborated by Nicolas Malebranche (1638–1715), author of *De la recherche de la vérité* (Paris, 1674). According to both views an event in one realm is merely an occasion on which God causes an event in that realm or the other. On the former view, we cause our own volitions; on the latter, these too are the effects of divine volition. Berkeley was partly occasionalist, "allowing occasional causes (which are in truth but signs)" (*Correspondence*, Letter II, sec. 2), partly not: "We move our legs our selves, 'tis we that will their movement. Herein I differ from Malbranch" (*Philosophical Commentaries*, Entry 548). In some points the similarity between the two philosophers is close, although Berkeley strongly denied any coincidence. Berkeley's friend and patron, Sir John Percival (1683–1748), reported to Berkeley on October 30, 1710, that Dr. Samuel Clarke (1675–1729), author of *On the Being and Attributes of God* (1705), having read the recently published *Principles*, had ranked Berkeley with Malebranche and John Norris (1657–1711), author of *An Essay Towards the Theory of an Ideal and Intelligible World* (1701–1704). Berkeley replied to Percival from Ireland on November 27, 1710: "I think the notions I embrace

ideas are excited in us by the will of God. Now I would fain
know how anything can be present to us which is neither
perceivable by sense nor reflection, nor capable of producing
any idea in our minds, nor is at all extended, nor has any
form, nor exists in any place. The words "to be present,"
when thus applied, must needs be taken in some abstract and
strange meaning, and which I am not able to comprehend.

69. Again, let us examine what is meant by "occasion." So
far as I can gather from the common use of language, that
word signifies either the agent which produces any effect or
else something that is observed to accompany or go before it in
the ordinary course of things. But when it is applied to matter
as above described, it can be taken in neither of those senses, for
matter is said to be passive and inert, and so cannot be an agent
or efficient cause. It is also unperceivable, as being devoid of all
sensible qualities, and so cannot be the occasion of our percep-

---

are not in the least coincident with, or agreeing with theirs, but indeed
plainly inconsistent with them in the main points." See also *Dialogues*,
II, secs. 4 and 7. It is probable that Berkeley and Malebranche met
during Berkeley's first visit to Paris. In a letter to Percival from Paris
dated November 24, 1713, Berkeley wrote: "Today he [l'abbé d'Aubigne]
is to introduce me to Father Malebranche," and next day he wrote to
Thomas Prior (1679–1751), Berkeley's closest friend: "Tomorrow I intend
to visit Father Malebranche and discourse him on certain points." Joseph
Stock, in his "Life of the Author," added to *Works* (London, 1837; first
published 1784), p. iii, reported a meeting during Berkeley's second visit
to Paris: "But the issue of this debate proved tragical to poor Malebranche. In the heat of disputation he raised his voice so high, and
gave way so freely to the natural impetuosity of a man of parts and a
Frenchman, that he brought on himself a violent increase of his disorder,
which carried him off a few days after." Malebranche died on October 13,
1715, when, it seems, Berkeley was in England. The story that arose that
Berkeley was the *occasional* cause of the death of Malebranche was developed further by Thomas de Quincey (1785–1859) in his "On Murder
as One of the Fine Arts," *Blackwood's Magazine* (Edinburgh, 1827). See
Letters, in *Works*, Vol. VIII (ed. Luce, 1956).]

tions in the latter sense, as when the burning my finger is said to be the occasion of the pain that attends it. What therefore can be meant by calling matter an "occasion"? This term is either used in no sense at all or else in some sense very distant from its received signification.

70. You will perhaps say that matter, though it be not perceived by us, is nevertheless perceived by God, to whom it is the occasion of exciting ideas in our minds. For, say you, since we observe our sensations to be imprinted in an orderly and constant manner, it is but reasonable to suppose there are certain constant and regular occasions of their being produced. That is to say, that there are certain permanent and distinct parcels of matter, corresponding to our ideas, which, though they do not excite them in our minds or anyways immediately affect us, as being altogether passive and unperceivable to us, they are nevertheless to God, by whom they are perceived, as it were, so many occasions to remind Him when and what ideas to imprint on our minds that so things may go on in a constant uniform manner.

71. In answer to this I observe that, as the notion of matter is here stated, the question is no longer concerning the existence of a thing distinct from *spirit* and *idea*, from perceiving and being perceived, but whether there are not certain ideas of I know not what sort in the mind of God which are so many marks or notes that direct Him how to produce sensations in our minds in a constant and regular method—much after the same manner as a musician is directed by the notes of music to produce that harmonious train and composition of sound which is called a "tune," though they who hear the music do not perceive the notes and may be entirely ignorant of them. But this notion of matter seems too extravagant to deserve a confutation. Besides, it is in effect no objection against what we have advanced, to wit, that there is no senseless, unperceived substance.

72. If we follow the light of reason we shall, from the constant uniform method of our sensations, collect the goodness and wisdom of the spirit who excites them in our minds; but this is all that I can see reasonably concluded from thence. To me, I say, it is evident that the being of a spirit infinitely wise, good, and powerful is abundantly sufficient to explain all the appearances of nature. But, as for *inert, senseless matter*, nothing that I perceive has any the least connection with it or leads to the thoughts of it. And I would fain see anyone explain any the meanest phenomenon in nature by it or show any manner of reason, though in the lowest rank of probability, that he can have for its existence, or even make any tolerable sense or meaning of that supposition. For as to its being an occasion we have, I think, evidently shown that with regard to us it is no occasion. It remains therefore that it must be, if at all, the occasion to God of exciting ideas in us, and what this amounts to we have just now seen.

73. It is worth while to reflect a little on the motives which induced men to suppose the existence of *material substance;* that so having observed the gradual ceasing and expiration of those motives or reasons, we may proportionably withdraw the assent that was grounded on them. First, therefore, it was thought that color, figure, motion, and the rest of the sensible qualities or accidents did really exist without the mind; and for this reason it seemed needful to suppose some unthinking *substratum* or substance wherein they did exist, since they could not be conceived to exist by themselves. Afterwards, in process of time, men being convinced that colors, sounds, and the rest of the sensible, secondary qualities had no existence without the mind, they stripped this *substratum* or material substance of those qualities, leaving only the primary ones, figure, motion, and suchlike, which they still conceived to exist without the mind, and consequently to stand in need of a material support.

But it having been shown that none even of these can possibly exist otherwise than in a spirit or mind which perceives them, it follows that we have no longer any reason to suppose the being of matter; nay, that it is utterly impossible there should be any such thing so long as that word is taken to denote an *unthinking substratum* of qualities or accidents wherein they exist without the mind.

74. But though it be allowed by the materialists themselves that matter was thought of only for the sake of supporting accidents, and, the reason entirely ceasing, one might expect the mind should naturally, and without any reluctance at all, quit the belief of what was solely grounded thereon, yet the prejudice is riveted so deeply in our thoughts that we can scarce tell how to part with it, and are therefore inclined, since the *thing* itself is indefensible, at least to retain the *name*, which we apply to I know not what abstracted and indefinite notions of being, or occasion, though without any show of reason, at least so far as I can see. For what is there on our part, or what do we perceive among all the ideas, sensations, notions which are imprinted on our minds, either by sense or reflection, from whence may be inferred the existence of an inert, thoughtless, unperceived occasion? And, on the other hand, on the part of an all-sufficient Spirit, what can there be that should make us believe or even suspect He is directed by an inert occasion to excite ideas in our minds?

75. It is a very extraordinary instance of the force of prejudice, and much to be lamented, that the mind of man retains so great a fondness, against all the evidence of reason, for a stupid, thoughtless *somewhat*, by the interposition whereof it would as it were screen itself from the Providence of God and remove him farther off from the affairs of the world. But though we do the utmost we can to secure the belief of matter, though, when reason forsakes us, we endeavor to support our

opinion on the bare possibility of the thing, and though we indulge ourselves in the full scope of an imagination not regulated by reason to make out that poor possibility, yet the upshot of all is that there are certain *unknown ideas* in the mind of God; for this, if anything, is all that I conceive to be meant by "occasion" with regard to God. And this at the bottom is no longer contending for the thing, but for the name.

76. Whether, therefore, there are such ideas in the mind of God, and whether they may be called by the name "matter," I shall not dispute. But if you stick to the notion of an unthinking substance or support of extension, motion, and other sensible qualities, then to me it is most evidently impossible there should be any such thing, since it is a plain repugnancy that those qualities should exist in or be supported by an unperceiving substance.

77. But, say you, though it be granted that there is no thoughtless support of extension and the other qualities or accidents which we perceive, yet there may, perhaps, be some inert, unperceiving substance or *substratum* of some other qualities, as incomprehensible to us as colors are to a man born blind, because we have not a sense adapted to them. But if we had a new sense, we should possibly no more doubt of their existence than a blind man made to see does of the existence of light and colors. I answer, first, if what you mean by the word "matter" be only the unknown support of unknown qualities, it is no matter whether there is such a thing or no, since it no way concerns us; and I do not see the advantage there is in disputing about we know not *what*, and we know not *why*.

78. But, secondly, if we had a new sense, it could only furnish us with new ideas or sensations; and then we should have the same reason against their existing in an unperceiving substance that has been already offered with relation to figure, motion, color, and the like. Qualities, as has been shown, are

nothing else but *sensations* or *ideas,* which exist only in a *mind* perceiving them; and this is true not only of the ideas we are acquainted with at present, but likewise of all possible ideas whatsoever.

79. But, you will insist, what if I have no reason to believe the existence of matter? What if I cannot assign any use to it or explain anything by it, or even conceive what is meant by that word? Yet still it is no contradiction to say that matter exists, and that this matter is in general a *substance,* or *occasion of ideas,* though, indeed, to go about to unfold the meaning or adhere to any particular explication of those words may be attended with great difficulties. I answer, when words are used without a meaning, you may put them together as you please without danger of running into a contradiction. You may say, for example, that twice two is equal to seven, so long as you declare you do not take the words of that proposition in their usual acceptation but for marks of you know not what. And, by the same reason, you may say there is an inert, thoughtless substance without accidents which is the occasion of our ideas. And we shall understand just as much by one proposition as the other.

80. In the *last* place, you will say, What if we give up the cause of material substance and assert that matter is an unknown *somewhat*—neither substance nor accident, spirit nor idea, inert, thoughtless, indivisible, immovable, unextended, existing in no place? For, say you, whatever may be urged against *substance* or *occasion,* or any other positive or relative notion of matter, has no place at all so long as this *negative* definition of matter is adhered to. I answer, You may, if so it shall seem good, use the word "matter" in the same sense as other men use "nothing," and so make those terms convertible in your style. For, after all, this is what appears to me to be the result of that definition, the parts whereof, when I consider

with attention, either collectively or separate from each other, I do not find that there is any kind of effect or impression made on my mind different from what is excited by the term "nothing."

81. You will reply, perhaps, that in the foresaid definition is included what does sufficiently distinguish it from nothing—the positive, abstract idea of *quiddity, entity,* or *existence.* I own, indeed, that those who pretend to the faculty of framing abstract general ideas do talk as if they had such an idea, which is, say they, the most abstract and general notion of all; that is, to me, the most incomprehensible of all others. That there are a great variety of spirits of different orders and capacities whose faculties both in number and extent are far exceeding those the Author of my being has bestowed on me, I see no reason to deny. And for me to pretend to determine by my own few, stinted, narrow inlets of perception what ideas the inexhaustible power of the Supreme Spirit may imprint upon them were certainly the utmost folly and presumption—since there may be, for aught that I know, innumerable sorts of ideas or sensations, as different from one another, and from all that I have perceived, as colors are from sounds. But how ready soever I may be to acknowledge the scantiness of my comprehension with regard to the endless variety of spirits and ideas that might possibly exist, yet for anyone to pretend to a notion of entity or existence, *abstracted* from *spirit* and *idea,* from perceiving and being perceived is, I suspect, a downright repugnancy and trifling with words.—It remains that we consider the objections which may possibly be made on the part of religion.

82. Some there are who think that, though the arguments for the real existence of bodies which are drawn from reason be allowed not to amount to demonstration, yet the Holy Scriptures are so clear in the point as will sufficiently convince every good Christian that bodies do really exist, and are some-

thing more than mere ideas, there being in Holy Writ innumerable facts related which evidently suppose the reality of timber
and stone, mountains and rivers, and cities, and human bodies.
To which I answer that no sort of writings whatever, sacred or
profane, which use those and the like words in the vulgar acceptation, or so as to have a meaning in them, are in danger of
having their truth called in question by our doctrine. That all
those things do really exist, that there are bodies, even corporeal
substances, when taken in the vulgar sense, has been shown to
be agreeable to our principles; and the difference betwixt *things*
and *ideas, realities* and *chimeras* has been distinctly explained.
See secs. 29, 30, 33, 36, etc. And I do not think that either what
philosophers call "matter," or the existence of objects without
the mind, is anywhere mentioned in Scripture.

83. Again, whether there be or be not external things, it is
agreed on all hands that the proper use of words is the marking
out conceptions, or things only as they are known and perceived
by us; whence it plainly follows that in the tenets we have laid
down there is nothing inconsistent with the right use and significance of *language,* and that discourse, of what kind soever, so
far as it is intelligible, remains undisturbed. But all this seems
so very manifest, from what has been set forth in the premises,
that it is needless to insist any further on it.

84. But it will be urged that miracles do, at least, lose much
of their stress and import by our principles. What must we
think of Moses' rod? Was it not *really* turned into a serpent, or
was there only a change of *ideas* in the minds of the spectators?
And can it be supposed that our Saviour did no more at the
marriage-feast in Cana than impose on the sight and smell and
taste of the guests, so as to create in them the appearance or
idea only of wine? The same may be said of all other miracles,
which, in consequence of the foregoing principles, must be
looked upon only as so many cheats or illusions of fancy. To

this I reply that the rod was changed into a real serpent, and the water into real wine. That this does not in the least contradict what I have elsewhere said will be evident from secs. 34 and 35. But this business of *real* and *imaginary* has been already so plainly and fully explained, and so often referred to, and the difficulties about it are so easily answered from what has gone before, that it were an affront to the reader's understanding to resume the explication of it in this place. I shall only observe that if at table all who were present should see, and smell, and taste, and drink wine, and find the effects of it, with me there could be no doubt of its reality, so that at bottom the scruple concerning real miracles has no place at all on ours, but only on the received principles, and consequently makes rather for than against what has been said.

85. Having done with the objections, which I endeavored to propose in the clearest light, and gave them all the force and weight I could, we proceed in the next place to take a view of our tenets in their consequences. Some of these appear at first sight—as that several difficult and obscure questions, on which abundance of speculation has been thrown away, are entirely banished from philosophy: whether corporeal substance can think; whether matter be infinitely divisible; and how it operates on spirit—these and the like inquiries have given infinite amusement to philosophers in all ages, but, depending on the existence of matter, they have no longer any place on our principles. Many other advantages there are, as well with regard to religion as the sciences, which it is easy for anyone to deduce from what has been premised; but this will appear more plainly in the sequel.

86. From the principles we have laid down it follows human knowledge may naturally be reduced to two heads—that of *ideas* and that of *spirits*. Of each of these I shall treat in order.

And, *first*, as to ideas or unthinking things. Our knowledge of these has been very much obscured and confounded, and we have been led into very dangerous errors, by supposing a two-fold existence of the objects of sense—the one *intelligible* or in the mind, the other *real* and without the mind, whereby unthinking things are thought to have a natural subsistence of their own distinct from being perceived by spirits. This, which, if I mistake not, has been shown to be a most groundless and absurd notion, is the very root of skepticism, for so long as men thought that real things subsisted without the mind, and that their knowledge was only so far forth *real* as it was conformable to *real things*, it follows they could not be certain they had any real knowledge at all. For how can it be known that the things which are perceived are conformable to those which are not perceived or exist without the mind?

87. Color, figure, motion, extension, and the like, considered only as so many *sensations* in the mind, are perfectly known, there being nothing in them which is not perceived. But if they are looked on as notes or images, referred to *things* or *archetypes* existing without the mind, then are we involved all in skepticism. We see only the appearances, and not the real qualities of things. What may be the extension, figure, or motion of anything really and absolutely, or in itself, it is impossible for us to know, but only the proportion or the relation they bear to our senses. Things remaining the same, our ideas vary, and which of them, or even whether any of them at all, represent the true quality really existing in the thing, it is out of our reach to determine. So that, for aught we know, all we see, hear, and feel may be only phantom and vain chimera, and not at all agree with the real things existing in *rerum natura*. All this skepticism follows from our supposing a difference between *things* and *ideas*, and that the former have a subsistence without

the mind or unperceived. It were easy to dilate on this subject and show how the arguments urged by skeptics in all ages depend on the supposition of external objects.

88. So long as we attribute a real existence to unthinking things, distinct from their being perceived, it is not only impossible for us to know with evidence the nature of any real unthinking being, but even that it exists. Hence it is that we see philosophers distrust their senses and doubt of the existence of heaven and earth, of everything they see or feel, even of their own bodies. And after all their labor and struggle of thought, they are forced to own we cannot attain to any self-evident or demonstrative knowledge of the existence of sensible things. But all this doubtfulness which so bewilders and confounds the mind and makes philosophy ridiculous in the eyes of the world vanishes if we annex a meaning to our words and do not amuse ourselves with the terms "absolute," "external," "exist," and suchlike, signifying we know not what. I can as well doubt of my own being as of the being of those things which I actually perceive by sense; it being a manifest contradiction that any sensible object should be immediately perceived by sight or touch and at the same time have no existence in nature, since the very *existence* of an unthinking being consists in *being perceived*.

89. Nothing seems of more importance toward erecting a firm system of sound and real knowledge, which may be proof against the assaults of skepticism, than to lay the beginning in a distinct explication of what is meant by "thing," "reality," "existence"; for in vain shall we dispute concerning the real existence of things or pretend to any knowledge thereof, so long as we have not fixed the meaning of those words. "Thing," or "being" is the most general name of all; it comprehends under it two kinds entirely distinct and heterogeneous, and which

have nothing common but the name, to wit, *spirits* and *ideas*. The former are active, indivisible substances; the latter are inert, fleeting, dependent beings which subsist not by themselves, but are supported by or exist in minds or spiritual substances. [We comprehend our own existence by inward feeling or reflection, and that of other spirits by reason. We may be said to have some knowledge or notion of our own minds, of spirits and active beings, whereof in a strict sense we have not ideas. In like manner, we know and have a notion of relations between things or ideas—which relations are distinct from the ideas or things related, in as much as the latter may be perceived by us without our perceiving the former. To me it seems that *ideas, spirits,* and *relations* are all in their respective kinds the object of human knowledge and subject of discourse, and that the term "idea" would be improperly extended to signify everything we know or have any notion of.]

90. Ideas imprinted on the senses are real things, or do really exist—this we do not deny, but we deny they can subsist without the minds which perceive them, or that they are resemblances of any archetypes existing without the mind, since the very being of a sensation or idea consists in being perceived, and an idea can be like nothing but an idea. Again, the things perceived by sense may be termed "external" with regard to their origin—in that they are not generated from within by the mind itself, but imprinted by a spirit distinct from that which perceives them. Sensible objects may likewise be said to be "without the mind" in another sense, namely, when they exist in some other mind; thus, when I shut my eyes, the things I saw may still exist, but it must be in another mind.

91. It were a mistake to think that what is here said derogates in the least from the reality of things. It is acknowledged, on the received principles, that extension, motion, and, in a

word, all sensible qualities have need of a support, as not being able to subsist by themselves. But the objects perceived by sense are allowed to be nothing but combinations of those qualities, and consequently cannot subsist by themselves. Thus far it is agreed on all hands. So that in denying the things perceived by sense an existence independent of a substance or support wherein they may exist, we detract nothing from the received opinion of their *reality*, and are guilty of no innovation in that respect. All the difference is that, according to us, the unthinking beings perceived by sense have no existence distinct from being perceived, and cannot therefore exist in any other substances than those unextended indivisible substances or *spirits* which act and think and perceive them; whereas philosophers vulgarly hold that the sensible qualities exist in an inert, extended, unperceiving substance which they call "matter," to which they attribute a natural subsistence, exterior to all thinking beings, or distinct from being perceived by any mind whatsoever, even the eternal mind of the Creator, wherein they suppose only ideas of the corporeal substances created by him, if indeed they allow them to be at all created.

92. For as we have shown the doctrine of matter or corporeal substance to have been the main pillar and support of skepticism, so likewise, upon the same foundation, have been raised all the impious schemes of atheism and irreligion. Nay, so great a difficulty has it been thought to conceive matter produced out of nothing that the most celebrated among the ancient philosophers, even of these who maintained the being of a God, have thought matter to be uncreated and coeternal with Him. How great a friend *material substance* has been to atheists in all ages were needless to relate. All their monstrous systems have so visible and necessary a dependence on it that, when this cornerstone is once removed, the whole fabric cannot choose but fall to the ground, insomuch that it is no longer

worth while to bestow a particular consideration on the absurdities of every wretched sect of atheists.

93. That impious and profane persons should readily fall in with those systems which favor their inclinations by deriding immaterial substance and supposing the soul to be divisible and subject to corruption as the body, which exclude all freedom, intelligence, and design from the formation of things, and instead thereof make a self-existent, stupid, unthinking substance the root and origin of all beings; that they should hearken to those who deny a Providence, or inspection of a Superior Mind over the affairs of the world, attributing the whole series of events either to blind chance or fatal necessity arising from the impulse of one body or another—all this is very natural. And, on the other hand, when men of better principles observe the enemies of religion lay so great a stress on *unthinking matter*, and all of them use so much industry and artifice to reduce everything to it, methinks they should rejoice to see them deprived of their grand support and driven from that only fortress without which your Epicureans, Hobbists, and the like, have not even the shadow of a pretense, but become the most cheap and easy triumph in the world.

94. The existence of matter, or bodies unperceived, has not only been the main support of atheists and fatalists, but on the same principle does idolatry likewise in all its various forms depend. Did men but consider that the sun, moon, and stars, and every other object of the senses are only so many sensations in their minds, which have no other existence but barely being perceived, doubtless they would never fall down and worship their own *ideas*, but rather address their homage to that Eternal Invisible Mind which produces and sustains all things.

95. The same absurd principle, by mingling itself with the articles of our faith, has occasioned no small difficulties to Christians. For example, about the resurrection, how many

scruples and objections have been raised by Socinians[14] and others? But do not the most plausible of them depend on the supposition that a body is denominated "the same," with regard not to the form or that which is perceived by sense, but the material substance, which remains the same under several forms? Take away this *material substance*, about the identity whereof all the dispute is, and mean by "body" what every plain, ordinary person means by that word, to wit, that which is immediately seen and felt, which is only a combination of sensible qualities or ideas, and then their most unanswerable objections come to nothing.

96. Matter being once expelled out of nature drags with it so many skeptical and impious notions, such an incredible number of disputes and puzzling questions, which have been thorns in the sides of divines as well as philosophers and made so much fruitless work for mankind, that if the arguments we have produced against it are not found equal to demonstration (as to me they evidently seem), yet I am sure all friends to knowledge, peace, and religion have reason to wish they were.

97. Beside the external existence of the objects of perception, another great source of errors and difficulties with regard to ideal knowledge is the doctrine of *abstract ideas*, such as it has been set forth in the Introduction. The plainest things in the world, those we are most intimately acquainted with and perfectly know, when they are considered in an abstract way, appear strangely difficult and incomprehensible. Time, place, and motion, taken in particular or concrete, are what everybody knows, but, having passed through the hands of a metaphysi-

---

[14] [Followers of Sozinus, i.e., Lelio Francesco Maria Sozini (1525–1562), or Socinus, i.e., Fausto Paolo Sozzini (1539–1604), both of Siena, Italy. Sozinus raised difficulties in regard to the resurrection, salvation, etc., in *De sacramentis dissertatio* and *De resurrectione*, first printed in *F. et L. Socini, item E. Soneri tractatus* (Amsterdam, 1654).]

cian, they become too abstract and fine to be apprehended by men of ordinary sense. Bid your servant meet you at such a *time* in such a *place*, and he shall never stay to deliberate on the meaning of those words; in conceiving that particular time and place, or the motion by which he is to get thither, he finds not the least difficulty. But if *time* be taken exclusive of all those particular actions and ideas that diversify the day, merely for the continuation of existence or duration in abstract, then it will perhaps gravel even a philosopher to comprehend it.

98. Whenever I attempt to frame a simple idea of *time*, abstracted from the succession of ideas in my mind, which flows uniformly and is participated by all beings, I am lost and embrangled in inextricable difficulties. I have no notion of it at all, only I hear others say it is infinitely divisible, and speak of it in such a manner as leads me to entertain odd thoughts of my existence; since that doctrine lays one under an absolute necessity of thinking, either that he passes away innumerable ages without a thought or else that he is annihilated every moment of his life, both which seem equally absurd. Time therefore being nothing, abstracted from the succession of ideas in our minds, it follows that the duration of any finite spirit must be estimated by the number of ideas or actions succeeding each other in that same spirit or mind. Hence, it is a plain consequence that the soul always thinks; and in truth whoever shall go about to divide in his thoughts or abstract the *existence* of a spirit from its *cogitation* will, I believe, find it no easy task.[15]

15 [The manuscript continued the section as follows: "Sure I am that should any one tell me there is a time wherein a spirit actually exists without perceiving, or an idea without being perceived, or that there is a third sort of being which exists though it neither wills nor perceives nor is perceived, his words would have no other effect on my mind than if he talked in an unknown language. It is indeed an easy matter for a man to say, 'the mind exists without thinking,' but to conceive a meaning that may correspond to those sounds, or to frame a notion of a spirit's

99. So likewise when we attempt to abstract extension and motion from all other qualities, and consider them by themselves, we presently lose sight of them, and run into great extravagances. All which depend on a twofold abstraction; first, it is supposed that extension, for example, may be abstracted from all other sensible qualities; and secondly, that the entity of extension may be abstracted from its being perceived. But whoever shall reflect, and take care to understand what he says, will, if I mistake not, acknowledge that all sensible qualities are alike *sensations* and alike *real*; that where the extension is, there is the color, too, to wit, in his mind, and that their archetypes can exist only in some other *mind*; and that the objects of sense are nothing but those sensations combined, blended, or (if one may so speak) concreted together; none of all which can be supposed to exist unperceived.

100. What it is for a man to be happy, or an object good, everyone may think he knows. But to frame an abstract idea of happiness, prescinded from all particular pleasure, or of goodness from everything that is good, this is what few can pretend to. So likewise a man may be just and virtuous without having precise ideas of justice and virtue. The opinion that those and the like words stand for general notions, abstracted from all particular persons and actions, seems to have rendered morality difficult, and the study thereof of less use to mankind. And in effect the doctrine of *abstraction* has not a little contributed toward spoiling the most useful parts of knowledge.

101. The two great provinces of speculative science con-

---

existence abstracted from thinking, this seems to me impossible, and I suspect that even they who are the stiffest abettors of that tenet might abate somewhat of their firmness would they but lay aside the words and, calmly attending to their own thoughts, examine what they meant by them." This passage is from a manuscript of part of the *Principles*, now in the British Museum. Cf. *Works*, II (ed. Jessop, 1949), 84.]

versant about ideas received from sense and their relations are natural philosophy and mathematics; with regard to each of these I shall make some observations. And first I shall say somewhat of natural philosophy.[16] On this subject it is that the skeptics triumph. All that stock of arguments they produce to depreciate our faculties and make mankind appear ignorant and low are drawn principally from this head, to wit, that we are under an invincible blindness as to the *true* and *real* nature of things. This they exaggerate, and love to enlarge on. We are miserably bantered, say they, by our senses, and amused only with the outside and show of things. The real essence, the internal qualities and constitution of every the meanest object, is hidden from our view; something there is in every drop of water, every grain of sand, which it is beyond the power of human understanding to fathom or comprehend. But it is evident from what has been shown that all this complaint is groundless, and that we are influenced by false principles to that degree as to mistrust our senses and think we know nothing of those things which we perfectly comprehend.

102. One great inducement to our pronouncing ourselves ignorant of the nature of things is the current opinion that everything includes within itself the cause of its properties; or that there is in each object an inward essence which is the source whence its discernible qualities flow, and whereon they depend. Some have pretended to account for appearances by occult qualities, but of late they are mostly resolved into mechanical causes, to wit, the figure, motion, weight, and suchlike qualities of insensible particles; whereas, in truth, there is no other agent or efficient cause than *spirit*, it being evident that motion, as well as all other *ideas*, is perfectly inert. See sec. 25. Hence, to endeavor to explain the production of colors or sounds by figure,

[16] [See also *De Motu* (1721); *Alciphron*, Dialogue VII; *Siris* (1774), secs. 220–254.]

motion, magnitude, and the like, must needs be labor in vain. And accordingly we see the attempts of that kind are not at all satisfactory. Which may be said in general of those instances wherein one idea or quality is assigned for the cause of another. I need not say how many hypotheses and speculations are left out, and how much the study of nature is abridged by this doctrine.

103. The great mechanical principle now in vogue is *attraction*. That a stone falls to the earth, or the sea swells toward the moon, may to some appear sufficiently explained thereby. But how are we enlightened by being told this is done by attraction? Is it that that word signifies the manner of the tendency, and that it is by the mutual drawing of bodies instead of their being impelled or protruded toward each other? But nothing is determined of the manner or action, and it may as truly (for aught we know) be termed "impulse," or "protrusion," as "attraction." Again, the parts of steel we see cohere firmly together, and this also is accounted for by attraction; but, in this as in the other instances, I do not perceive that anything is signified besides the effect itself; for as to the manner of the action whereby it is produced, or the cause which produces it, these are not so much as aimed at.

104. Indeed, if we take a view of the several phenomena and compare them together, we may observe some likeness and conformity between them. For example, in the falling of a stone to the ground, in the rising of the sea toward the moon, in cohesion and crystallization, there is something alike, namely, a union or mutual approach of bodies. So that any one of these or the like phenomena may not seem strange or surprising to a man who has nicely observed and compared the effects of nature. For that only is thought so which is uncommon, or a thing by itself, and out of the ordinary course of our observation. That bodies should tend toward the center of the earth is not

thought strange, because it is what we perceive every moment of our lives. But, that they should have a like gravitation toward the center of the moon may seem odd and unaccountable to most men, because it is discerned only in the tides. But a philosopher, whose thoughts take in a larger compass of nature, having observed a certain similitude of appearances, as well in the heavens as the earth, that argue innumerable bodies to have a mutual tendency toward each other, which he denotes by the general name "attraction," whatever can be reduced to that he thinks justly accounted for. Thus he explains the tides by the attraction of the terraqueous globe toward the moon, which to him does not appear odd or anomalous, but only a particular example of a general rule or law of nature.

105. If therefore we consider the difference there is betwixt natural philosophers and other men with regard to their knowledge of the phenomena, we shall find it consists not in an exacter knowledge of the efficient cause that produces them— for that can be no other than the *will of a spirit*—but only in a greater largeness of comprehension, whereby analogies, harmonies, and agreements are discovered in the works of nature, and the particular effects explained, that is, reduced to general rules, see sec. 62, which rules, grounded on the analogy and uniformness observed in the production of natural effects, are most agreeable and sought after by the mind; for that they extend our prospect beyond what is present and near to us, and enable us to make very probable conjectures touching things that may have happened at very great distances of time and place, as well as to predict things to come; which sort of endeavor toward omniscience is much affected by the mind.

106. But we should proceed warily in such things, for we are apt to lay too great a stress on analogies, and, to the prejudice of truth, humor that eagerness of the mind whereby it is carried to extend its knowledge into general theorems. For

example, gravitation or mutual attraction, because it appears in many instances, some are straightway for pronouncing "universal"; and that to attract and be attracted by every other body is an essential quality inherent in all bodies whatsoever. Whereas it appears the fixed stars have no such tendency toward each other; and so far is that gravitation from being *essential* to bodies that in some instances a quite contrary principle seems to show itself; as in the perpendicular growth of plants, and the elasticity of the air. There is nothing necessary or essential in the case, but it depends entirely on the will of the governing spirit, who causes certain bodies to cleave together or tend toward each other according to various laws, whilst he keeps others at a fixed distance; and to some he gives a quite contrary tendency to fly asunder just as he sees convenient.

107. After what has been premised, I think we may lay down the following conclusions. First, it is plain philosophers amuse themselves in vain when they inquire for any natural efficient cause distinct from a *mind* or *spirit*. Secondly, considering the whole creation is the workmanship of a *wise and good agent*, it should seem to become philosophers to employ their thoughts (contrary to what some hold) about the final causes of things; and I must confess I see no reason why pointing out the various ends to which natural things are adapted, and for which they were originally with unspeakable wisdom contrived, should not be thought one good way of accounting for them, and altogether worthy a philosopher. Thirdly, from what has been premised no reason can be drawn why the history of nature should not still be studied, and observations and experiments made; which, that they are of use to mankind, and enable us to draw any general conclusions, is not the result of any immutable habitudes or relations between things themselves, but only of God's goodness and kindness to men in the administration of the world. See secs. 30 and 31. Fourthly, by a diligent observa-

tion of the phenomena within our view, we may discover the general laws of nature, and from them deduce the other phenomena; I do not say "demonstrate," for all deductions of that kind depend on a supposition that the Author of Nature always operates uniformly and in a constant observance of those rules we take for principles, which we cannot evidently know.

108. [Those men who frame general rules from the phenomena and afterwards derive the phenomena from those rules seem to consider signs rather than causes. A man may well understand natural signs without knowing their analogy,][17] or being able to say by what rule a thing is so or so. And, as it is very possible to write improperly, through too strict an observance of general grammar rules; so, in arguing from general rules of nature, it is not impossible we may extend the analogy too far, and by that means run into mistakes.

109. As, in reading other books, a wise man will choose to fix his thoughts on the sense and apply it to use, rather than lay them out in grammatical remarks on the language, so, in perusing the volume of nature, it seems beneath the dignity of the mind to affect an exactness in reducing each particular phenomenon to general rules, or showing how it follows from them. We should propose to ourselves nobler views, such as to recreate and exalt the mind with a prospect of the beauty, order, extent, and variety of natural things: hence, by proper infer-

---

[17] [Section 108 in the first edition began as follows: "It appears from secs. 66, etc., that the steady consistent methods of nature may not unfitly be styled the 'language' of its 'Author,' whereby He discovers His attributes to our view and directs us how to act for the convenience and felicity of life. And to me, those men who frame general rules from the phenomena, and afterwards derive the phenomena from those rules seem to be grammarians, and their art the grammar of nature. Two ways there are of learning a language, either by rule or by practice: a man may be well read in the language of nature without understanding the grammar of it. . . ."]

ences, to enlarge our notions of the grandeur, wisdom, and beneficence of the Creator; and lastly, to make the several parts of the Creation, so far as in us lies, subservient to the ends they were designed for—God's glory and the sustentation and comfort of ourselves and fellow creatures.

110. [The best key for the aforesaid analogy or natural science will be easily acknowledged to be a certain celebrated treatise of *mechanics*.][18] In the entrance of which justly admired treatise, time, space, and motion are distinguished into *absolute* and *relative, true* and *apparent, mathematical* and *vulgar;* which distinction, as it is at large explained by the author, does suppose these quantities to have an existence without the mind; and that they are ordinarily conceived with relation to sensible things, to which nevertheless in their own nature they bear no relation at all.

111. As for "time," as it is there taken in an absolute or abstracted sense, for the duration or perseverance of the existence of things, I have nothing more to add concerning it after what has been already said on that subject. Secs. 97 and 98. For the rest, this celebrated author holds there is an *absolute space,* which, being unperceivable to sense, remains in itself similar and immovable; and relative space to be the measure thereof, which, being movable and defined by its situation in respect of

[18] [Section 110 in the first edition began as follows: "The best grammar of the kind we are speaking of will be easily acknowledged to be a treatise of mechanics, demonstrated and applied to nature by a philosopher of a neighboring nation whom all the world admire. I shall not take upon me to make remarks on the performance of that extraordinary person: only some things he has advanced so directly opposite to the doctrine we have hitherto laid down, that we should be wanting in the regard due to the authority of so great a man did we not take some notice of them." The first edition appeared in Ireland; hence, Newton is spoken of as belonging to a "neighboring nation." The treatise referred to is Sir Isaac Newton's *Philosophiae Naturalis Principia Mathematica* (London, 1687).]

sensible bodies, is vulgarly taken for immovable space. "Place" he defines to be that part of space which is occupied by any body; and according as the space is absolute or relative, so also is the place. "Absolute motion" is said to be the translation of a body from absolute place to absolute place, as relative motion is from one relative place to another. And, because the parts of absolute space do not fall under our senses, instead of them we are obliged to use their sensible measures, and so define both place and motion with respect to bodies which we regard as immovable. But it is said in philosophical matters we must abstract from our senses, since it may be that none of those bodies which seem to be quiescent are truly so, and the same thing which is moved relatively may be really at rest; as likewise one and the same body may be in relative rest and motion, or even moved with contrary relative motions at the same time, according as its place is variously defined. All which ambiguity is to be found in the apparent motions, but not at all in the true or absolute, which should therefore be alone regarded in philosophy. And the true we are told are distinguished from apparent or relative motions by the following properties.—First, in true or absolute motion all parts which preserve the same position with respect to the whole partake of the motions of the whole. Secondly, the place being moved, that which is placed therein is also moved; so that a body moving in a place which is in motion does participate in the motion of its place. Thirdly, true motion is never generated or changed otherwise than by force impressed on the body itself. Fourthly, true motion is always changed by force impressed on the body moved. Fifthly, in circular motion, barely relative, there is no centrifugal force which, nevertheless, in that which is true or absolute, is proportional to the quantity of motion.

112. But, notwithstanding what has been said, it does not appear to me that there can be any motion other than *relative;*

so that to conceive motion there must be at least conceived two bodies, whereof the distance or position in regard to each other is varied. Hence, if there was one only body in being it could not possibly be moved. This seems evident, in that the idea I have of motion does necessarily include relation.

113. But, though in every motion it be necessary to conceive more bodies than one, yet it may be that one only is moved, namely, that on which the force causing the change of distance is impressed, or, in other words, that to which the action is applied. For, however some may define relative motion, so as to term that body "moved" which changes its distance from some other body, whether the force or action causing that change were applied to it or no, yet as relative motion is that which is perceived by sense, and regarded in the ordinary affairs of life, it should seem that every man of common sense knows what it is as well as the best philosopher. Now I ask anyone whether, in his sense of motion as he walks along the streets, the stones he passes over may be said to *move*, because they change distance with his feet? To me it seems that though motion includes a relation of one thing to another, yet it is not necessary that each term of the relation be denominated from it. As a man may think of somewhat which does not think, so a body may be moved to or from another body which is not therefore itself in motion.

114. As the place happens to be variously defined, the motion which is related to it varies. A man in a ship may be said to be quiescent with relation to the sides of the vessel, and yet move with relation to the land. Or he may move eastward in respect of the one, and westward in respect of the other. In the common affairs of life, men never go beyond the earth to define the place of any body; and what is quiescent in respect of that is accounted *absolutely* to be so. But philosophers, who have a greater extent of thought, and juster notions of the system of

things, discover even the earth itself to be moved. In order therefore to fix their notions, they seem to conceive the corporeal world as finite, and the utmost unmoved walls or shell thereof to be the place whereby they estimate true motions. If we sound our own conceptions, I believe we may find all the absolute motion we can frame an idea of to be at bottom no other than relative motion thus defined. For, as has been already observed, absolute motion, exclusive of all external relation, is incomprehensible; and to this kind of relative motion all the above-mentioned properties, causes, and effects ascribed to absolute motion will, if I mistake not, be found to agree. As to what is said of the centrifugal force, that it does not at all belong to circular relative motion, I do not see how this follows from the experiment which is brought to prove it. See *Philosophiae Naturalis Principia Mathematica, in Schol. Def. VIII.* For the water in the vessel at that time wherein it is said to have the greatest relative circular motion, has, I think, no motion at all; as is plain from the foregoing section.

115. For, to denominate a body "moved" it is requisite, first, that it change its distance or situation with regard to some other body; and secondly, that the force or action occasioning that change be applied to it. If either of these be wanting, I do not think that, agreeably to the sense of mankind, or the propriety of language, a body can be said to be in motion. I grant indeed that it is possible for us to think a body which we see change its distance from some other to be moved, though it have no force applied to it (in which sense there may be apparent motion), but then it is because the force causing the change of distance is imagined by us to be applied or impressed on that body thought to move; which indeed shows we are capable of mistaking a thing to be in motion which is not, and that is all.

116. From what has been said, it follows that the philosophic consideration of motion does not imply the being of an

absolute space, distinct from that which is perceived by sense and related to bodies; which that it cannot exist without the mind is clear upon the same principles that demonstrate the like of all other objects of sense. And perhaps, if we inquire narrowly, we shall find we cannot even frame an idea of *pure space* exclusive of all body. This I must confess seems impossible, as being a most abstract idea. When I excite a motion in some part of my body, if it be free or without resistance, I say there is *space;* but if I find a resistance, then I say there is *body;* and in proportion as the resistance to motion is lesser or greater, I say the space is more or less *pure.* So that when I speak of pure or empty space, it is not to be supposed that the word "space" stands for an idea distinct from or conceivable without body and motion—though indeed we are apt to think every noun substantive stands for a distinct idea that may be separated from all others; which has occasioned infinite mistakes. When, therefore, supposing all the world to be annihilated besides my own body, I say there still remains *pure space,* thereby nothing else is meant but only that I conceive it possible for the limbs of my body to be moved on all sides without the least resistance; but if that, too, were annihilated, then there could be no motion, and consequently no space. Some, perhaps, may think the sense of seeing does furnish them with the idea of pure space; but it is plain from what we have elsewhere shown, that the ideas of space and distance are not obtained by that sense. See the *Essay Concerning Vision.*

117. What is here laid down seems to put an end to all those disputes and difficulties that have sprung up amongst the learned concerning the nature of *pure space.* But the chief advantage arising from it is that we are freed from that dangerous dilemma to which several who have employed their thoughts on this subject imagine themselves reduced, to wit, of thinking either that real space is God, or else that there is something

besides God which is eternal, uncreated, infinite, indivisible, immutable. Both which may justly be thought pernicious and absurd notions. It is certain that not a few divines, as well as philosophers of great note, have, from the difficulty they found in conceiving either limits or annihilation of space, concluded it must be divine. And some of late have set themselves particularly to show that the incommunicable attributes of God agree to it. Which doctrine, how unworthy soever it may seem of the Divine Nature, yet I do not see how we can get clear of it so long as we adhere to the received opinions.

118. Hitherto of natural philosophy: we come now to make some inquiry concerning the other great branch of speculative knowledge, to wit, mathematics.[19] These, how celebrated soever they may be for their clearness and certainty of demonstration, which is hardly anywhere else to be found, cannot nevertheless be supposed altogether free from mistakes, if in their principles there lurks some secret error which is common to the professors of those sciences with the rest of mankind. Mathematicians, though they deduce their theorems from a great height of evidence, yet their first principles are limited by the consideration of quantity; and they do not ascend into any inquiry concerning those transcendental maxims which influence all the particular sciences, each part whereof, mathematics not excepted, does consequently participate of the errors involved in them. That the principles laid down by mathematicians are true, and their way of deduction from those principles clear and incontestable, we do not deny; but we hold there may be certain erroneous maxims of greater extent than the object of mathematics, and for that reason not expressly mentioned, though tacitly supposed throughout the whole progress of that science; and that the ill effects of those secret, unexamined

---

[19] [See also *The Analyst* (1734).]

errors are diffused through all the branches thereof. To be plain, we suspect the mathematicians are as well as other men concerned in the errors arising from the doctrine of abstract general ideas and the existence of objects without the mind.

119. Arithmetic has been thought to have for its object abstract ideas of *number*, of which to understand the properties and mutual habitudes is supposed no mean part of speculative knowledge. The opinion of the pure and intellectual nature of numbers in abstract has made them in esteem with those philosophers who seem to have affected an uncommon fineness and elevation of thought. It has set a price on the most trifling numerical speculations which in practice are of no use but serve only for amusement, and has therefore so far infected the minds of some that they have dreamed of mighty mysteries involved in numbers and attempted the explication of natural things by them. But, if we inquire into our own thoughts and consider what has been premised, we may perhaps entertain a low opinion of those high flights and abstractions, and look on all inquiries about numbers only as so many *difficiles nugae*, so far as they are not subservient to practice and promote the benefit of life.

120. Unity in abstract we have before considered in sec. 13, from which and what has been said in the Introduction, it plainly follows there is not any such idea. But, number being defined a "collection of units," we may conclude that, if there be no such thing as unity or unit in abstract, there are no ideas of number in abstract denoted by the numerical names and figures. The theories therefore in arithmetic, if they are abstracted from the names and figures, as likewise from all use and practice, as well as from the particular things numbered, can be supposed to have nothing at all for their object; hence we may see how entirely the science of numbers is subordinate to practice, and how jejune and trifling it becomes when considered as a matter of mere speculation.

121. However, since there may be some who, deluded by the specious show of discovering abstracted verities, waste their time in arithmetical theorems and problems which have not any use, it will not be amiss if we more fully consider and expose the vanity of that pretense; and this will plainly appear by taking a view of arithmetic in its infancy, and observing what it was that originally put men on the study of that science, and to what scope they directed it. It is natural to think that at first, men, for ease of memory and help of computation, made use of counters, or in writing of single strokes, points, or the like, each whereof was made to signify a unit, that is, some one thing of whatever kind they had occasion to reckon. Afterwards they found out the more compendious ways of making one character stand in place of several strokes or points. And, lastly, the notation of the Arabians or Indians came into use, wherein, by the repetition of a few characters or figures, and varying the signification of each figure according to the place it obtains, all numbers may be most aptly expressed; which seems to have been done in imitation of language, so that an exact analogy is observed betwixt the notation by figures and names, the nine simple figures answering the nine first numeral names and places in the former, corresponding to denominations in the latter. And agreeably to those conditions of the simple and local value of figures were contrived methods of finding, from the given figures or marks of the parts, what figures and how placed are proper to denote the whole, or vice versa. And having found the sought figures, the same rule or analogy being observed throughout, it is easy to read them into words; and so the number becomes perfectly known. For then the number of any particular things is said to be known, when we know the name or figures (with their due arrangement) that according to the standing analogy belong to them. For, these signs being known, we can by the operations of arithmetic know the signs of any part of the particular sums signified by them; and, thus computing

in signs (because of the connection established betwixt them and the distinct multitudes of things whereof one is taken for a unit), we may be able rightly to sum up, divide, and proportion the things themselves that we intend to number.

122. In arithmetic, therefore, we regard not the *things*, but the *signs*, which nevertheless are not regarded for their own sake, but because they direct us how to act with relation to things, and dispose rightly of them. Now, agreeable to what we have before observed of words in general (sec. 19, Introd.) it happens here likewise that abstract ideas are thought to be signified by numeral names or characters, while they do not suggest ideas of particular things to our minds. I shall not at present enter into a more particular dissertation on this subject, but only observe that it is evident from what has been said, those things which pass for abstract truths and theorems concerning numbers are in reality conversant about no object distinct from particular numerable things, except only names and characters which originally came to be considered on no other account but their being signs, or capable to represent aptly whatever particular things men had need to compute. Whence it follows that to study them for their own sake would be just as wise, and to as good purpose as if a man, neglecting the true use or original intention and subservience of language, should spend his time in impertinent criticisms upon words, or reasonings and controversies purely verbal.

123. From numbers we proceed to speak of *extension*, which, considered as relative, is the object of geometry. The *infinite* divisibility of *finite* extension, though it is not expressly laid down either as an axiom or theorem in the elements of that science, yet is throughout the same everywhere supposed and thought to have so inseparable and essential a connection with the principles and demonstrations in geometry that mathematicians never admit it into doubt, or make the least question of

it. And, as this notion is the source from whence do spring all those amusing geometrical paradoxes which have such a direct repugnancy to the plain common sense of mankind, and are admitted with so much reluctance into a mind not yet debauched by learning; so is it the principal occasion of all that nice and extreme subtlety which renders the study of mathematics so difficult and tedious. Hence, if we can make it appear that no finite extension contains innumerable parts, or is infinitely divisible, it follows that we shall at once clear the science of geometry from a great number of difficulties and contradictions which have ever been esteemed a reproach to human reason, and withal make the attainment thereof a business of much less time and pains than it hitherto has been.

124. Every particular finite extension which may possibly be the object of our thought is an *idea* existing only in the mind, and consequently each part thereof must be perceived. If, therefore, I cannot perceive innumerable parts in any finite extension that I consider, it is certain they are not contained in it; but it is evident that I cannot distinguish innumerable parts in any particular line, surface, or solid, which I either perceive by sense, or figure to myself in my mind: wherefore I conclude they are not contained in it. Nothing can be plainer to me than that the extensions I have in view are no other than my own ideas; and it is no less plain that I cannot resolve any one of my ideas into an infinite number of other ideas, that is, that they are not infinitely divisible. If by "finite extension" be meant something distinct from a finite idea, I declare I do not know what that is, and so cannot affirm or deny anything of it. But if the terms "extension," "parts," and the like, are taken in any sense conceivable, that is, for ideas, then to say a finite quantity or extension consists of parts infinite in number is so manifest a contradiction that everyone at first sight acknowledges it to be so; and it is impossible it should ever gain the assent of any reasonable

creature who is not brought to it by gentle and slow degrees, as a converted gentile to the belief of transubstantiation. Ancient and rooted prejudices do often pass into principles; and those propositions which once obtain the force and credit of a *principle* are not only themselves, but likewise whatever is deducible from them, thought privileged from all examination. And there is no absurdity so gross which, by this means, the mind of man may not be prepared to swallow.

125. He whose understanding is prepossessed with the doctrine of abstract general ideas may be persuaded that (whatever be thought of the ideas of sense) extension in *abstract* is infinitely divisible. And one who thinks the objects of sense exist without the mind will perhaps in virtue thereof be brought to admit that a line but an inch long may contain innumerable parts—really existing, though too small to be discerned. These errors are grafted as well in the minds of geometricians as of other men, and have a like influence on their reasonings; and it were no difficult thing to show how the arguments from geometry made use of to support the infinite divisibility of extension are bottomed on them. At present we shall only observe in general whence it is that the mathematicians are all so fond and tenacious of this doctrine.

126. It has been observed in another place that the theorems and demonstrations in geometry are conversant about universal ideas (sec. 15, Introd.); where it is explained in what sense this ought to be understood, to wit, that the particular lines and figures included in the diagram are supposed to stand for innumerable others of different sizes; or, in other words, the geometer considers them abstracting from their magnitude—which does not imply that he forms an abstract idea, but only that he cares not what the particular magnitude is, whether great or small, but looks on that as a thing indifferent to the demonstration. Hence it follows that a line in the scheme but an inch long must be spoken of as though it contained ten thou-

sand parts, since it is regarded not in itself, but as it is universal; and it is universal only in its signification, whereby it represents innumerable lines greater than itself, in which may be distinguished ten thousand parts or more, though there may not be above an inch in it. After this manner, the properties of the lines signified are (by a very usual figure) transferred to the sign, and thence, through mistake, thought to appertain to it considered in its own nature.

127. Because there is no number of parts so great but it is possible there may be a line containing more, the inch-line is said to contain parts more than any assignable number; which is true, not of the inch taken absolutely, but only for the things signified by it. But men, not retaining that distinction in their thoughts, slide into a belief that the small particular line described on paper contains in itself parts innumerable. There is no such thing as the ten thousandth part of an inch; but there is of a mile or diameter of the earth, which may be signified by that inch. When therefore I delineate a triangle on paper, and take one side not above an inch, for example, in length to be the radius, this I consider as divided into ten thousand or one hundred thousand parts or more; for, though the ten thousandth part of that line considered in itself is nothing at all, and consequently may be neglected without any error or inconvenience, yet these described lines, being only marks standing for greater quantities, whereof it may be the ten thousandth part is very considerable, it follows that, to prevent notable errors in practice, the radius must be taken of ten thousand parts or more.

128. From what has been said the reason is plain why, to the end any theorem may become universal in its use, it is necessary we speak of the lines described on paper as though they contained parts which really they do not. In doing of which, if we examine the matter thoroughly, we shall perhaps discover that we cannot conceive an inch itself as consisting of,

or being divisible into, a thousand parts, but only some other line which is far greater than an inch, and represented by it; and that when we say a line is "infinitely divisible" we must mean a line which is infinitely great. What we have here observed seems to be the chief cause why to suppose the infinite divisibility of finite extension has been thought necessary in geometry.

129. The several absurdities and contradictions which flowed from this false principle might, one would think, have been esteemed so many demonstrations against it. But, by I know not what logic, it is held that proofs a posteriori are not to be admitted against propositions relating to infinity, as though it were not impossible even for an infinite mind to reconcile contradictions; or as if anything absurd and repugnant could have a necessary connection with truth or flow from it. But whoever considers the weakness of this pretense will think it was contrived on purpose to humor the laziness of the mind which had rather acquiesce in an indolent skepticism than be at the pains to go through with a severe examination of those principles it has ever embraced for true.

130. Of late the speculations about infinites have run so high, and grown to such strange notions, as have occasioned no small scruples and disputes among the geometers of the present age. Some there are of great note who, not content with holding that finite lines may be divided into an infinite number of parts, do yet further maintain that each of those infinitesimals is itself subdivisible into an infinity of other parts or infinitesimals of a second order, and so on ad infinitum. These, I say, assert there are infinitesimals of infinitesimals of infinitesimals, without ever coming to an end: so that according to them an inch does not barely contain an infinite number of parts, but an infinity of an infinity of an infinity ad infinitum of parts. Others there be who hold all orders of infinitesimals below the first to be nothing at

all; thinking it with good reason absurd to imagine there is any positive quantity or part of extension which, though multiplied infinitely, can ever equal the smallest given extension. And yet on the other hand it seems no less absurd to think the square, cube, or other power of a positive real root should itself be nothing at all; which they who hold infinitesimals of the first order, denying all of the subsequent orders, are obliged to maintain.

131. Have we not therefore reason to conclude that they are *both* in the wrong, and that there is in effect no such thing as parts infinitely small, or an infinite number of parts contained in any finite quantity? But you will say that if this doctrine obtains it will follow the very foundations of geometry are destroyed, and those great men who have raised that science to so astonishing a height have been all the while building a castle in the air. To this it may be replied that whatever is useful in geometry and promotes the benefit of human life does still remain firm and unshaken on our principles; that science considered as practical will rather receive advantage than any prejudice from what has been said. But to set this in a due light may be the subject of a distinct inquiry. For the rest, though it should follow that some of the more intricate and subtle parts of speculative mathematics may be pared off without any prejudice to truth, yet I do not see what damage will be thence derived to mankind. On the contrary, it were highly to be wished that men of great abilities and obstinate application would draw off their thoughts from those amusements, and employ them in the study of such things as lie nearer the concerns of life, or have a more direct influence on the manners.

132. If it be said that several theorems undoubtedly true are discovered by methods in which infinitesimals are made use of, which could never have been if their existence included a contradiction in it, I answer that upon a thorough examination

it will not be found that in any instance it is necessary to make use of or conceive infinitesimal parts of finite lines, or even quantities less than the *minimum sensibile;* nay, it will be evident this is never done, it being impossible.

133. By what we have premised it is plain that very numerous and important errors have taken their rise from those false principles which were impugned in the foregoing parts of this treatise; and the opposites of those erroneous tenets at the same time appear to be most fruitful principles, from whence do flow innumerable consequences highly advantageous to true philosophy, as well as to religion. Particularly *matter,* or *the absolute existence of corporeal objects,* has been shown to be that wherein the most avowed and pernicious enemies of all knowledge, whether human or divine, have ever placed their chief strength and confidence. And surely, if by distinguishing the real existence of unthinking things from their being perceived, and allowing them a subsistence of their own out of the minds of spirits, no one thing is explained in nature, but, on the contrary, a great many inexplicable difficulties arise; if the supposition of matter is barely precarious, as not being grounded on so much as one single reason; if its consequences cannot endure the light of examination and free inquiry, but screen themselves under the dark and general pretense of "infinites being incomprehensible"; if withal the removal of this *matter* be not attended with the least evil consequence; if it be not even missed in the world, but everything as well, nay, much easier conceived without it; if, lastly, both skeptics and atheists are forever silenced upon supposing only spirits and ideas, and this scheme of things is perfectly agreeable both to reason and religion: methinks we may expect it should be admitted and firmly embraced, though it were proposed only as a *hypothesis,* and the existence of matter had been allowed possible, which yet I think we have evidently demonstrated that it is not.

134. True it is that, in consequence of the foregoing principles, several disputes and speculations which are esteemed no mean parts of learning are rejected as useless. But, how great a prejudice soever against our notions this may give to those who have already been deeply engaged and made large advances in studies of that nature, yet by others we hope it will not be thought any just ground of dislike to the principles and tenets herein laid down that they abridge the labor of study, and make human sciences more clear, compendious, and attainable than they were before.

135. Having dispatched what we intended to say concerning the knowledge of *ideas*, the method we proposed leads us in the next place to treat of *spirits*—with regard to which, perhaps human knowledge is not so deficient as is vulgarly imagined. The great reason that is assigned for our being thought ignorant of the nature of spirits is our not having an *idea* of it. But surely it ought not to be looked on as a defect in a human understanding that it does not perceive the idea of spirit if it is manifestly impossible there should be any such idea. And this, if I mistake not, has been demonstrated in section 27; to which I shall here add that a spirit has been shown to be the only substance or support wherein the unthinking beings or ideas can exist; but that this *substance* which supports or perceives ideas should itself be an idea or like an idea is evidently absurd.

136. It will perhaps be said that we want a sense (as some have imagined) proper to know substances withal, which, if we had, we might know our own soul as we do a triangle. To this I answer, that, in case we had a new sense bestowed upon us, we could only receive thereby some new sensations or ideas of sense. But I believe nobody will say that what he means by the terms "soul" and "substance" is only some particular sort of idea or sensation. We may therefore infer, that

all things duly considered, it is not more reasonable to think our faculties defective in that they do not furnish us with an idea of spirit or active thinking substance than it would be if we should blame them for not being able to comprehend a *round square*.

137. From the opinion that spirits are to be known after the manner of an idea or sensation have risen many absurd and heterodox tenets, and much skepticism about the nature of the soul. It is even probable that this opinion may have produced a doubt in some whether they had any soul at all distinct from their body, since upon inquiry they could not find they had an idea of it. That an *idea* which is inactive, and the existence whereof consists in being perceived, should be the image or likeness of an agent subsisting by itself seems to need no other refutation than barely attending to what is meant by those words. But perhaps you will say that though an idea cannot resemble a spirit in its thinking, acting, or subsisting by itself, yet it may in some other respects; and it is not necessary that an idea or image be in all respects like the original.

138. I answer, if it does not in those mentioned, it is impossible it should represent it in any other thing. Do but leave out the power of willing, thinking, and perceiving ideas, and there remains nothing else wherein the idea can be like a spirit. For by the word "spirit" we mean only that which thinks, wills, and perceives; this, and this alone, constitutes the signification of that term. If therefore it is impossible that any degree of those powers should be represented in an idea, it is evident there can be no idea of a spirit.

139. But it will be objected that, if there is no idea signified by the terms "soul," "spirit," and "substance," they are wholly insignificant or have no meaning in them. I answer, those words do mean or signify a real thing, which is neither

an idea nor like an idea, but that which perceives ideas, and wills, and reasons about them. What I am myself, that which I denote by the term "I," is the same with what is meant by "soul," or "spiritual substance." If it be said that this is only quarreling at a word, and that, since the immediate significations of other names are by common consent called "ideas," no reason can be assigned why that which is signified by the name "spirit" or "soul" may not partake in the same appellation. I answer, all the unthinking objects of the mind agree in that they are entirely passive, and their existence consists only in being perceived; whereas a soul or spirit is an active being whose existence consists, not in being perceived, but in perceiving ideas and thinking. It is therefore necessary, in order to prevent equivocation and confounding natures perfectly disagreeing and unlike, that we distinguish between *spirit* and *idea*. See sec. 27.

140. In a large sense, indeed, we may be said to have an idea [or rather a notion] of *spirit*; that is, we understand the meaning of the word, otherwise we could not affirm or deny anything of it. Moreover, as we conceive the ideas that are in the minds of other spirits by means of our own, which we suppose to be resemblances of them, so we know other spirits by means of our own soul—which in that sense is the image or idea of them; it having a like respect to other spirits that blueness or heat by me perceived has to those ideas perceived by another.

141. It must not be supposed that they who assert the natural immortality of the soul are of opinion that it is absolutely incapable of annihilation even by the infinite power of the Creator who first gave it being, but only that it is not liable to be broken or dissolved by the ordinary laws of nature or motion. They indeed who hold the soul of man to be only a thin vital flame, or system of animal spirits, make it perishing

and corruptible as the body; since there is nothing more easily dissipated than such a being, which it is naturally impossible should survive the ruin of the tabernacle wherein it is enclosed. And this notion has been greedily embraced and cherished by the worst part of mankind, as the most effectual antidote against all impressions of virtue and religion. But it has been made evident that bodies, of what frame or texture soever, are barely passive ideas in the mind, which is more distant and heterogeneous from them than light is from darkness. We have shown that the soul is indivisible, incorporeal, unextended, and it is consequently incorruptible. Nothing can be plainer than that the motions, changes, decays, and dissolutions which we hourly see befall natural bodies (and which is what we mean by "the course of nature") cannot possibly affect an active, simple, uncompounded substance; such a being is therefore indissoluble by the force of nature; that is to say, the soul of man is naturally immortal.

142. After what has been said, it is, I suppose, plain that our souls are not to be known in the same manner as senseless, inactive objects, or by way of *idea*. *Spirits* and *ideas* are things so wholly different that when we say "they exist," "they are known," or the like, these words must not be thought to signify anything common to both natures. There is nothing alike or common in them: and to expect that by any multiplication or enlargement of our faculties we may be enabled to know a spirit as we do a triangle seems as absurd as if we should hope to see a sound. This is inculcated because I imagine it may be of moment toward clearing several important questions and preventing some very dangerous errors concerning the nature of the soul. [We may not, I think, strictly be said to have an *idea* of an active being, or of an action, although we may be said to have a *notion* of them. I have some knowledge or notion of my mind, and its acts about ideas, inasmuch as I know or under-

stand what is meant by those words. What I know, that I have some notion of. I will not say that the terms "idea" and "notion" may not be used convertibly, if the world will have it so; but yet it conduces to clearness and propriety that we distinguish things very different by different names. It is also to be remarked that, all relations including an act of the mind, we cannot so properly be said to have an idea, but rather a notion of the relations or habitudes between things. But if, in the modern way, the word "idea" is extended to spirits, and relations, and acts, this is, after all, an affair of verbal concern.]

143. It will not be amiss to add that the doctrine of *abstract ideas* has had no small share in rendering those sciences intricate and obscure which are particularly conversant about spiritual things. Men have imagined they could frame abstract notions of the powers and acts of the mind and consider them prescinded as well from the mind or spirit itself as from their respective objects and effects. Hence a great number of dark and ambiguous terms, presumed to stand for abstract notions, have been introduced into metaphysics and morality, and from these have grown infinite distractions and disputes amongst the learned.

144. But nothing seems more to have contributed toward engaging men in controversies and mistakes with regard to the nature and operations of the mind than the being used to speak of those things in terms borrowed from sensible ideas. For example, the will is termed "the motion of the soul": this infuses a belief that the mind of man is as a ball in motion, impelled and determined by the objects of sense, as necessarily as that is by the stroke of a racket. Hence arise endless scruples and errors of dangerous consequence in morality. All which, I doubt not, may be cleared, and truth appear plain, uniform, and consistent, could but philosophers be prevailed on to retire into themselves, and attentively consider their own meaning.

145. From what has been said it is plain that we cannot know the existence of other spirits otherwise than by their operations, or the ideas by them excited in us. I perceive several motions, changes, and combinations of ideas that inform me there are certain particular agents, like myself, which accompany them and concur in their production. Hence, the knowledge I have of other spirits is not immediate, as is the knowledge of my ideas, but depending on the intervention of ideas, by me referred to agents or spirits distinct from myself, as effects or concomitant signs.[20]

146. But though there be some things which convince us human agents are concerned in producing them, yet it is evident to everyone that those things which are called "the works of nature," that is, the far greater part of the ideas or sensations perceived by us, are not produced by, or dependent on, the wills of men. There is therefore some other spirit that causes them; since it is repugnant that they should subsist by themselves. See sec. 29. But, if we attentively consider the constant regularity, order, and concatenation of natural things, the surprising magnificence, beauty, and perfection of the larger, and the exquisite contrivance of the smaller parts of the creation, together with the exact harmony and correspondence of the whole, but above all the never-enough-admired laws of pain and pleasure, and the instincts or natural inclinations, appetites, and passions of animals; I say if we consider all these things, and at the same time attend to the meaning and import of the attributes: one, eternal, infinitely wise, good, and perfect, we shall clearly perceive that they belong to the aforesaid spirit, "who works all in all," and "by whom all things consist."

147. Hence it is evident that God is known as certainly and immediately as any other mind or spirit whatsoever dis-

---

[20] [See also *Alciphron*, Dialogue IV.]

tinct from ourselves. We may even assert that the existence of God is far more evidently perceived than the existence of men; because the effects of nature are infinitely more numerous and considerable than those ascribed to human agents. There is not any one mark that denotes a man, or effect produced by him, which does not more strongly evince the being of that spirit who is the Author of Nature. For it is evident that in affecting other persons the will of man has no other object than barely the motion of the limbs of his body; but that such a motion should be attended by, or excite any idea in the mind of another, depends wholly on the will of the Creator. He alone it is who, "upholding all things by the word of his power," maintains that intercourse between spirits whereby they are able to perceive the existence of each other. And yet this pure and clear light which enlightens everyone is itself invisible.

148. It seems to be a general pretense of the unthinking herd that they cannot *see* God. Could we but see him, say they, as we see a man, we should believe that he is, and, believing, obey his commands. But alas, we need only open our eyes to see the sovereign Lord of all things, with a more full and clear view than we do any one of our fellow creatures. Not that I imagine we see God (as some will have it) by a direct and immediate view; or see corporeal things, not by themselves, but by seeing that which represents them in the essence[21] of God, which doctrine is, I must confess, to me incomprehensible. But I shall explain my meaning: a human spirit or person is not perceived by sense, as not being an idea; when therefore we see the color, size, figure, and motions of a man, we perceive only certain sensations or ideas excited in our own minds; and these being exhibited to our view in

21 [The reference is to Malebranche's view that we directly know the Ideas of all things in God. See note 13, pp. 281–282, and *Dialogues*, II, sec. 4.]

sundry distinct collections, serve to mark out unto us the existence of finite and created spirits like ourselves. Hence it is plain we do not see a man—if by "man" is meant that which lives, moves, perceives, and thinks as we do—but only such a certain collection of ideas as directs us to think there is a distinct principle of thought and motion, like to ourselves, accompanying and represented by it. And after the same manner we see God; all the difference is that, whereas some one finite and narrow assemblage of ideas denotes a particular human mind, whithersoever we direct our view, we do at all times and in all places perceive manifest tokens of the divinity: everything we see, hear, feel, or anywise perceive by sense, being a sign or effect of the power of God; as is our perception of those very motions which are produced by men.

149. It is therefore plain that nothing can be more evident to anyone that is capable of the least reflection than the existence of God, or a spirit who is intimately present to our minds, producing in them all that variety of ideas or sensations which continually affect us, on whom we have an absolute and entire dependence, in short "in whom we live, and move, and have our being." That the discovery of this great truth, which lies so near and obvious to the mind, should be attained to by the reason of so very few, is a sad instance of the stupidity and inattention of men who, though they are surrounded with such clear manifestations of the Deity, are yet so little affected by them that they seem, as it were, blinded with excess of light.

150. But you will say, has nature no share in the production of natural things, and must they be all ascribed to the immediate and sole operation of God? I answer, if by "nature" is meant only the visible *series* of effects or sensations imprinted on our minds, according to certain fixed and general laws, then it is plain that nature, taken in this sense, cannot pro-

duce anything at all. But, if by "nature" is meant some being distinct from God, as well as from the laws of nature, and things perceived by sense, I must confess that word is to me an empty sound without any intelligible meaning annexed to it. Nature, in this acceptation, is a vain chimera, introduced by those heathens who had not just notions of the omnipresence and infinite perfection of God. But it is more unaccountable that it should be received among Christians, professing belief in the Holy Scriptures, which constantly ascribe those effects to the immediate hand of God that heathen philosophers are wont to impute to nature. "The Lord he causeth the vapours to ascend; he maketh lightnings with rain; he bringeth forth the wind out of his treasures." Jerem. 10:13. "He turneth the shadow of death into the morning, and maketh the day dark with night." Amos 5:8. "He visiteth the earth, and maketh it soft with showers: He blesseth the springing thereof, and crowneth the year with his goodness; so that the pastures are clothed with flocks, and the valleys are covered over with corn." See Psalm 65. But notwithstanding that this is the constant language of Scripture, yet we have I know not what aversion from believing that God concerns himself so nearly in our affairs. Fain would we suppose him at a great distance off, and substitute some blind, unthinking deputy in his stead, though (if we may believe Saint Paul) "he be not far from every one of us."

151. It will, I doubt not, be objected that the slow and gradual methods observed in the production of natural things do not seem to have for their cause the immediate hand of an Almighty Agent. Besides, monsters, untimely births, fruits blasted in the blossom, rains failing in desert places, miseries incident to human life, and the like, are so many arguments that the whole frame of nature is not immediately actuated and superintended by a spirit of infinite wisdom and good-

ness. But the answer to this objection is in a good measure plain from sec. 62; it being visible that the aforesaid methods of nature are absolutely necessary, in order to working by the most simple and general rules, and after a steady and consistent manner; which argues both the wisdom and goodness of God. Such is the artificial contrivance of this mighty machine of nature that, whilst its motions and various phenomena strike on our senses, the hand which actuates the whole is itself unperceivable to men of flesh and blood. "Verily" (says the prophet) "thou art a God that hidest thyself." Isaiah 45:15. But, though God conceal himself from the eyes of the sensual and lazy, who will not be at the least expense of thought, yet to an unbiased and attentive mind nothing can be more plainly legible than the intimate presence of an all-wise Spirit, who fashions, regulates, and sustains the whole system of being. It is clear, from what we have elsewhere observed, that the operating according to general and stated laws is so necessary for our guidance in the affairs of life, and letting us into the secret of nature, that without it all reach and compass of thought, all human sagacity and design, could serve to no manner of purpose; it were even impossible there should be any such faculties or powers in the mind. See sec. 31. Which one consideration abundantly outbalances whatever particular inconveniences may thence arise.

152. We should further consider that the very blemishes and defects of nature are not without their use, in that they make an agreeable sort of variety and augment the beauty of the rest of the creation, as shades in a picture serve to set off the brighter and more enlightened parts. We would likewise do well to examine whether our taxing the waste of seeds and embryos, and accidental destruction of plants and animals, before they come to full maturity, as an imprudence in the Author of Nature, be not the effect of prejudice contracted by our familiarity with impotent and saving mortals.

In man indeed a thrifty management of those things which he cannot procure without much pains and industry may be esteemed wisdom. But we must not imagine that the inexplicably fine machine of an animal or vegetable costs the great Creator any more pains or trouble in its production than a pebble does; nothing being more evident than that an omnipotent spirit can indifferently produce everything by a mere fiat or act of his will. Hence, it is plain that the splendid profusion of natural things should not be interpreted weakness or prodigality in the agent who produces them, but rather be looked on as an argument of the riches of his power.

153. As for the mixture of pain or uneasiness which is in the world, pursuant to the general laws of nature, and the actions of finite, imperfect spirits, this, in the state we are in at present, is indispensably necessary to our well-being. But our prospects are too narrow. We take, for instance, the idea of some one particular pain into our thoughts, and account it *evil*; whereas, if we enlarge our view, so as to comprehend the various ends, connections, and dependencies of things, on what occasions and in what proportions we are affected with pain and pleasure, the nature of human freedom, and the design with which we are put into the world; we shall be forced to acknowledge that those particular things which, considered in themselves, appear to be evil, have the nature of good, when considered as linked with the whole system of beings.

154. From what has been said, it will be manifest to any considering person, that it is merely for want of attention and comprehensiveness of mind that there are any favorers of atheism or the Manichaean heresy[22] to be found. Little and

---

[22] [Manichaeism became one of the great religions. Founded by Mani of Persia in the third century, it spread rapidly in the Roman Empire and retained its vigor well into the Middle Ages. It had a wide and deep influence on Christianity. St. Augustine was a follower in his youth

unreflecting souls may indeed burlesque the works of Providence the beauty and order whereof they have not capacity, or will not be at the pains to comprehend; but those who are masters of any justness and extent of thought, and are withal used to reflect, can never sufficiently admire the divine traces of wisdom and goodness that shine throughout the economy of nature. But what truth is there which shines so strongly on the mind that by an aversion of thought, a willful shutting of the eyes, we may not escape seeing it? Is it therefore to be wondered at if the generality of men, who are ever intent on business or pleasure, and little used to fix or open the eye of their mind, should not have all that conviction and evidence of the being of God which might be expected in reasonable creatures?

155. We should rather wonder that men can be found so stupid as to neglect, than that neglecting they should be unconvinced of such an evident and momentous truth. And yet it is to be feared that too many of parts and leisure, who live in Christian countries, are, merely through a supine and dreadful negligence, sunk into a sort of atheism. Since it is downright impossible that a soul pierced and enlightened with a thorough sense of the omnipresence, holiness, and justice of that Almighty Spirit should persist in a remorseless violation of his laws. We ought, therefore, earnestly to meditate and dwell on those important points; that so we may attain conviction without all scruple "that the eyes of the Lord are in every place beholding the evil and the good;

---

but later opposed it. The Albigenses in southern France, who were persecuted in 1207 by Innocent III, shared its views. A fusion of many religions, its central teaching is that the universe is controlled by two antagonistic powers, light or goodness (God's kingdom) and darkness or evil. Evil is thus an ultimate and ineradicable fact. Satan, the prince of darkness, is coeternal with God.]

that he is with us and keepeth us in all places whither we go, and giveth us bread to eat and raiment to put on"; that he is present and conscious to our innermost thoughts; and that we have a most absolute and immediate dependence on him. A clear view of which great truths cannot choose but fill our hearts with an awful circumspection and holy fear, which is the strongest incentive to *virtue* and the best guard against *vice*.

156. For, after all, what deserves the first place in our studies is the consideration of God and our duty; which to promote, as it was the main drift and design of my labors, so shall I esteem them altogether useless and ineffectual if, by what I have said, I cannot inspire my readers with a pious sense of the presence of God; and, having shown the falseness or vanity of those barren speculations which make the chief employment of learned men, the better dispose them to reverence and embrace the salutary truths of the Gospel, which to know and to practice is the highest perfection of human nature.

Index